ANCIENT EGYPTIAN ART

THE CULTS OF OSIRIS AND AMON

ANCIENT EGYPTIAN ART

THE CULTS OF OSIRIS AND AMON

Text by EBERHARD OTTO

Photographs by MAX HIRMER

HARRY N. ABRAMS, INC. *Publishers* New York

TRANSLATED BY KATE BOSSE GRIFFITHS
Library of Congress Catalog Card Number: 67–26469
All rights reserved
No part of the contents of this book may be reproduced
without the written permission of the publishers
HARRY N. ABRAMS, INCORPORATED, NEW YORK
Illustrations printed in West Germany
Text printed in Holland, Bound in Holland

FOR
ERIKA AND WOLFGANG HELCK
WITH FRIENDSHIP AND APPRECIATION

TABLE OF CONTENTS

INTRODUCTION

It is natural for man to try to understand and define those powers or gods who, as he thinks, order, threaten, and regulate the life of the world as well as his own life. For the immaterial is terrifying; further, it is inaccessible to man. But when the divine appears as a mountain or a constellation, as a tree or an animal, as a man or a spirit of the dead, it enters in each case the world of the humanly comprehensible. It moves from the transcendental sphere of power and miracle into a region where man is at home and where relations can be established between the divine and the human. This may be the reason why all ancient higher civilizations, in varying degrees, tend to endow their gods with human qualities by conceiving them either in human form, or else in nonhuman or half-human guise, but regarding them as able to think and act like human beings.

Gerhardus van der Leeuw, the great Dutch authority on the history of religion, says very aptly *(Religion in Essence and Manifestation,* 2nd ed., London, 1964, §19, 4): "It is precisely those attributes of the god which raise him highest above men, that cannot be expressed other than in human analogies: strength of will, spirituality of outlook, certainty in fixing a goal. Physical anthropomorphism, then, can be overcome, even though it is never conquered completely; but psychical anthropomorphism emerges at the same time as human ideas and thoughts.... For all speech is human and creates human forms; and even if animals and fetishes do seem to endow the Wholly Other with peculiarly adequate form, still this is only because animals and things themselves are observed by man."

This is especially true of Egypt. The countless forms of the Egyptian gods may be confusing; they were a cause of derision or a mystery to ancient writers and a stumbling block to the Christian patristic writers. Yet behind the wealth of forms lies hidden a very human conception of God, namely, the idea of divine powers whose actions are directed toward a human world and who in return expect certain acts and attitudes from man. Amon may be carried as a cult image in a procession, or he may appear in the shape of a ram or a goose, or even as the breath of life which is inherent in everything; but in each form he directly intervenes in the life of the state and of the individual, and in differing modes of appearance he is approachable by all. Human destiny and human thought were the material that molded the god of vegetation, Osiris, and from the fate of the god man could draw consolation and strength because he recognized himself in the god.

In order to receive worship, the divine needs not only a form but also a place where man can meet it and offer his adoration. Places of this kind may originally have been natural meeting places of god and man: a mountain, a spring, a desert valley, places which by their very nature seem to be fitting for such an encounter. Such places are known to all civilizations, and certainly to that of Egypt: a river torrent where the power of the spirits of the water reveals itself; a sacred mountain top in Thebes with its sanctuary of the snake goddess "who loves silence"; and many others. In Egypt these more or less natural meeting places have in the course of a long history been submerged and transformed. Only occasionally are we able to recognize vaguely here and there the origin of such a sanctuary.

A place may also become sacred through the memory of something that happened there in ancient times, or was supposed to have happened, and that had far-reaching consequences afterward. In Egypt this is especially the case with Abydos. The fact that the first historic kings were buried here has truly sanctified this site. It attracted from outside new ideas about gods and cults; it was here that Osiris had his most important cult center, but apart from that the original ceremonial of the funerary rites enacted for the ancient kings lived on and continued to form the framework for ritual when the royal burial—its original reason for existence—was no longer performed here. Here, too, we find an impressive example of the intermingling of rites, religious ideas, and myths, with the creation, as a result, of new forms.

But it is not only sacred ritual that can sanctify the place of its occurrence. Political and historical events can give a special sanctity to the region where they happened or originated. This is certainly possible in civilizations and societies that have not yet achieved a separation of profane and religious activities; in which all events and institutions—for example, kingship—possess a secular and a religious side. In Egypt this coincidence of historical events and religious aftermath is valid in a number of towns, especially in "hundred-gates Thebes." Here we can recognize fairly clearly the origin and the sequel, because everything happened in the bright light of history and is attested by contemporary evidence. Here we see how a sacred place is, as it were, created and how the advantage of a historic situation elevates an area which has hitherto been of doubtful importance. We see, too, how different cult centers, certain ideas about divine kingship, and contemporary piety combine in a religious unity and create a center of worship which spreads its influence and experiences its own history.

We shall encounter much that seems distant and strange. Egyptian thought and expression will not reveal themselves easily to us, but the inquisitive mind can always contemplate with profit what mankind has once experienced, thought, and collated, for a whole range of spiritual evolution is thus revealed.

Our attention here will be focused on two Egyptian cult centers, Abydos and Thebes, and on their gods, Osiris and Amon.

PART ONE

OSIRIS

MARGINAL NUMBERS refer to illustrations: Roman numbers to colorplates, Arabic numbers to black-and-white plates, and Fig. numbers to line drawings in the text.

I. ABYDOS IN THE EARLY DYNASTIC PERIOD

For almost three millenniums the town of Abydos was recognized as a holy place, and it was deemed a special privilege to be buried here in the main cult center of the god Osiris. As late as the second century A.D. the Greek writer Plutarch noted that Egyptian noblemen still considered it an honor to share their last resting place with the god.

Nevertheless, the historical and political significance of the town during that period was quite negligible. Abydos was not the capital, nor did it gain temporal importance as the focus of a political complex. Rather, its importance was the product of two separate causes: the continued funerary cult of the earlier Egyptian kings and the worship of the god Osiris.

Egyptian kings were buried here as early as the end of the fourth and the beginning of the third millennium. The Osiris cult was introduced later, and in the course of time the god came to be regarded as the eternal equal and counterpart of the sun-god. Both cults were then linked and in the process transformed each other.

In order to understand this phenomenon properly, one must, as far as possible, examine its initial components separately. One must remove many layers of development and go back to that period when, as far as we know, the area possessed, at least for a brief spell, historical importance. On this historical substratum crystallized new forms of belief and traditions of worship, and in consequence the site did not lose its unique importance, but remained permanently a lively and potent center of religious life.

A glance at the map of Egypt reveals that the land—apart from the expanse of the Delta—is only a narrow strip through which the Nile flows like a main artery, while more or less mountainous deserts border it on either side. On further examination one easily discovers that in a region somewhat to the south of the central area between Cairo and the first cataract, near where the Nile makes a big bend first to the northeast and then to the west, the strictly north-south orientation of the country is relaxed. To the east open up the broad mouths of several big wadies, the most important of which is the Wadi Hammamat, the ancient line of communication with the eastern mountain range and the Red Sea. Several caravan routes lead toward the west and to the complex of western oases, especially to El Kharga, the ancient Oasis Magna. In this region, about twelve miles north of Abydos, even today the railway line to El Kharga leaves the main line through the Nile valley at Oasis Junction. We can think of the area between Quft (Coptos) and Abydos as the intersection of two lines: the north-south line formed by the Nile valley and the east-west line of the desert road. In fact, it seems likely that geography created the historical importance of the region in the early period when the country experienced the transition from prehistory to history and the distinctive civilization of Egypt emerged.

The beginning of the historical period in Egypt was a gradual process resulting from the interchanges between the inhabitants of the Nile valley and the mainly nomadic inhabitants of the adjacent wide steppe and mountainous land. Both groups of people helped to create the historic Egyptian civilization; and elements of both still persist in it. But the emergence of Egypt proper meant a division between the inhabitants of the Nile valley and the inhabitants of the steppe. Some contact between the two, of course, always remained through a pressure of immigrants into the Nile valley and a continuous defense by its inhabitants against the invaders. During that phase of development the most eventful regions were those in which the communication between the two groups was liveliest; and because of its geographical position, the region around Abydos was one of them. Apparently it was from here that the first kings ruled the country, which, perhaps, had not yet reached its later extent. It was probably here that the plan was conceived to create a spacious kingdom including the whole of the Nile valley, a thought fitting for chieftains of a group that was still linked to the patriarchal, tribal way of life with its hankering after sovereignty over a wide area. It is possible that people like these transferred their political organization to the genuinely peasant population, which for its part contributed more or less the substance and abundance of the later Egyptian civilization.

Archaeological discoveries and historical tradition admittedly yield only an indistinct picture of the early history of Abydos and its surroundings. The Egyptian historian Manetho, who lived under Ptolemy I, reports that the Kings of the First and Second Dynasties, the earliest rulers mentioned in the lists, came from the town of This. This (or Thinis) was in historical times the capital of the eighth Upper Egyptian nome, on the western border of which lay the town of Abydos. The city of This was doubtless situated in the cultivated zone, but so far it has not been possible to locate it or to identify it with any modern place. Nothing remains either of the town of Abydos itself. But of greater importance is its necropolis at the edge of the desert near the present-day village of El Arabat El Madfuuna.[1] In this area existed a complete prehistoric cemetery (the so-called Naqada I level).[2] This could be traced again in the so-called Naqada II level, which itself leads on into the historic period. Therefore on a site later sacred to Osiris, a direct line can be traced from the preparatory centuries of the late prehistoric period (probably the last centuries of the fourth millennium B.C.) into the decisively formative epoch at the beginning of the early dynastic period.

The eighth Upper Egyptian nome to which both Abydos and This belonged was called "the oldest land." We do not know the original size of the area thus named. Nor can we be certain of the meaning of the name. In Egypt the concept of an oldest land is usually connected with the picture of a primeval hill, which was supposed to have emerged from the primeval ocean at the beginning of the creation of the world. This picture of the creation of the world in fact materialized every year with the recession of the Nile inundation. Primeval hills of this kind are known in several places, for example, at Heliopolis, Memphis, Hermopolis, and Thebes, and the primeval hill of Abydos may be just one among others. The designation "the oldest land" may, of course, also have a narrower, factual meaning, as describing that region which was supposed to have been the germinating cell and birthplace of the historical kingdom of Egypt.

THE ROYAL TOMBS AND THEIR CULTS DURING THE EARLY DYNASTIC PERIOD

The tombs of the Thinite kings lie on the edge of the western desert. If they disappoint our idea of a model Egyptian royal tomb, the fault lies partly with their own setup and partly with the practices of the early excavators.

What the original superstructure was like is uncertain, and a row of shallow raked-up pits in the stony desert ground is all that remains today of the subterranean buildings. A map made during Flinders Petrie's excavations provides a fairly clear picture of their original layout.

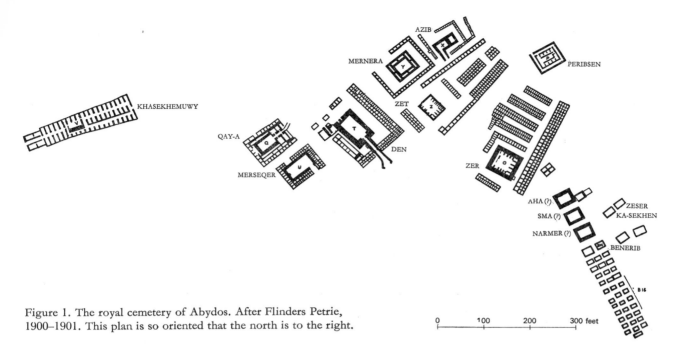

Figure 1. The royal cemetery of Abydos. After Flinders Petrie, 1900–1901. This plan is so oriented that the north is to the right.

All the tombs had been pillaged in antiquity, and their attribution to various kings was possible only through the inscriptions on the funerary equipment, especially sealings with royal names and small tablets with records of annals. In a few cases tombstones were found, for example, the famous stela of "King Snake" in the Louvre). As a result, it proved impossible to identify all the tombs with certainty, and particularly with the most ancient tombs much remains unexplained. It is evident, however, that the occupation of the necropolis developed in a kind of sequence from northeast to southwest.

According to the tradition of the Egyptian royal lists, King Menes was considered the real founder of the kingdom. For the early historic period, however, the lists record only the birth name of the kings, while the contemporary monuments give the Horus name, that is, the name assigned to the rulers when they were identified with the falcon-god Horus. It is therefore not always possible to reconcile beyond doubt the names on the lists with those on the monuments. Nevertheless, it seems to be correct to identify the King Menes of the lists with the king who bears on the monuments the name of Horus Aha, or Horus the Fighter. This king was buried in tomb B 19, which is contemporary with several tombs of the eastern site. From monuments at Abydos as well as at other places, at least three more kings are known who must have ruled before Horus Aha and who were thus more or less prehistoric kings. Unfortunately, their names cannot be read with certainty. The oldest of them may be King Ka-Sekhen,[3] and tomb B 7 is attributed to him. Then followed "King Scorpion," whose name is written with the picture of a scorpion. None of the tombs at Abydos can be attributed to him with certainty. The third and immediate predecessor of Menes was King Narmer, possibly the owner of tomb B 10. We can infer from their monuments, from their royal titles, and from the titles of their officials that these three kings reigned over the whole of Egypt prior to Menes. It is evident, therefore, that the Egyptian tradition ascribing the "union of the two countries" (that is, Upper and Lower Egypt) and the foundation of the kingdom to Menes alone turns out to be a historical legend. For a historic

15

process which undoubtedly extended over a long space of time is here attributed to one king and one single act.

It may be added that apparently already at the time of King Ka-Sekhen the country's center of administration was not (or no longer) at or near Abydos but in the north, at first perhaps near Tarkhan, at the mouth of the Fayum, and then, from the time of Horus Aha, probably near Memphis. It seems that the royal burial place was not chosen because of its relation to the political capital[4] but because of a personal cultural tradition that connected the king with Abydos.

Apart from the royal necropolis at Abydos and the administrative center in the north, we know of yet a third place which must have played a decisive role during the early period: it is the town of Hierakonpolis-Nekhen, between Esna and Edfu, which was also connected with the early kingship and contained, above all, the main temple of the royal god Horus.

From northeast to southwest at Abydos are ranged in sequence the large tombs of King Zer, the Seizer,[5] King Serpent, and King Den, or Dewen. Then came a queen (Den's widow?), Merit-Neith, "beloved by [the goddess] Neith," then their son, Anadj-ib, and finally, at the southernmost end of the site, the tombs of the kings Semerkhet and Qaa.

There is less certainty about the burial places of the first kings of the Second Dynasty. Apparently their graves followed the administrative center to the north and were perhaps at Saqqarah. Then, after the middle of the Second Dynasty, two kings, Peribsen and Khasekhemuwy, returned again to Abydos. This change of burial place was hardly caused by a mere royal whim or by such a practical consideration as nearness to the center of administration. Peribsen also changed his name during his reign and adopted the dual title of Horus and Seth instead of the mere Horus name, and the name Khasekhemuwy means "the two powers appear," apparently a programmatic declaration of the fact that a dual power is revealed in him.

It has been suggested above that Abydos gained its importance as a place of contact between the nomads and the peasant population and that the ruling dynasty had its roots in a nomadic tribal order. If this is true, the return of the two Second Dynasty kings to the home of kingship may signify a return to older religious concepts that had developed here in royal funerary customs. The new importance given to the god Seth may express the same attitude, for he was worshiped mainly as a god of the oasis and the desert.

In the Third Dynasty King Zoser finally transferred the center of administration to the north. This is the beginning of the epoch which we call the Old Kingdom, the time of the pyramid builders and of rigid centralization. On the other hand, the royal tombs, the royal ritual sites, and the community of gods at Abydos before this time reveal something of the double-faced character of the period of transition from the prehistoric struggles for union to the civilized world of historic Egypt.

When the royal tombs of Abydos were discovered, they were already mostly destroyed. Although the interpretation of purely archaeological material is always very difficult, it can teach us some fundamental facts about the ideas of kingship prevalent in the early period. The most ancient of these tombs—the tombs of the predynastic rulers—consist essentially of a rectangular pit lined with mud bricks. The pit itself was not the tomb chamber but only a casing or support for the tomb structure proper, which was apparently a wooden imitation of the royal tent in which the deceased was laid to rest. Above this subterranean part rose a vaulted sand hill facing southeast, thus toward the land of the living. In the middle of the east side was an area for sacrifices, and to the right and left of this area stood a stela carrying the name of the ruler concerned. Near these most ancient tombs, up to and including that of Horus Aha, were a small number of tombs of

16

domestics (although this cannot be proved in every single case), probably some intimate members of the royal household.

From King Zer onward, the orientation of the tomb veers by ninety degrees; now it faces southwest. At the same time the tomb is much larger and its architectural features are more progressive. The posts of the tent are connected by cross walls with the surrounding brick walls. The wooden floor also rested on a layer

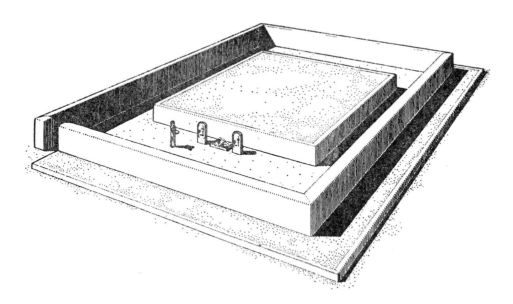

Figure 2. Reconstruction of a royal tomb of the First Dynasty at Abydos. After H. Ricke, 1950.

of bricks, itself separated from the ground by a layer of sand. This separation of a ritual building from its surroundings by means of "clean sand" is a magical rather than an architectural feature: it prevents the influences and powers of the surrounding ground from impinging upon the sacred precinct. From now until the end of the dynasty the number of minor tombs and chambers around the tomb is really remarkable. Their number and arrangement vary with individual cases, but as a rule the western side is sparsely equipped and the southwest corner remains vacant. From the finds recovered, some of the chambers can be identified as storage rooms, while others are burial places of members of the court. The tomb of Zer, for example, contains 318 chambers. Ninety-seven stelae were found, of which seventy-six belonged to women, eleven to men, and two to dwarfs, while eight could not be identified. In the course of time the number of the tombs of the followers decreased. A further innovation took place under King Den: the tomb chamber was made accessible by means of a long passage, which was later filled in, or by a staircase.

It seems that the secondary burials were completed at the same time as the royal tomb to which they belonged. This assumption was prompted by finds made during the excavation of the tomb of King Qaa, and it is also supported by other observations (see below). We must infer that the persons buried here were killed immediately after the death of their king and buried with him.

It is virtually impossible for us to understand the mental attitude that lies behind such a custom: we do it justice neither by speaking romantically about the loyalty which is faithful unto death nor by condemning it as cruel and inhuman. In any case, it presupposes a conception of personality utterly strange to us and an equally strange valuation of kingship. In later times, the beginning of a reign was celebrated in Egypt as a new beginning of the world order and of the state; and so, without its being expressly declared, the end of a reign was compared with the end of the world. In its late form this conception was merely a poetic idea in a literary and mythological vein. In the early period, however, it was taken quite literally. The Egyptians believed, one might suggest, that the king's followers received their own breath of life from the king's existence and that this breath was withdrawn from them with his death. The followers were somehow only a part of the personality of the king, and so receded with him into the subterranean existence. This idea lived on in an attenuated form in later times, when the tombs of the dead were provided not only with the equipment and tools of daily life but also with figures of servants, workers, women, and so on. We may note, too, that—in a different form—the co-burial of women, servants, and animals also occurs in the royal tombs of Ur (Sumer).

The dead king's tomb, where he rested in his tent surrounded by members of his court, was situated away in the desert. It seems to have formed a closed other world without direct communication with the world of the living. But the power of the dead ruler lived on in another form nearer to the living. On the edge of the fertile land the king possessed another cult center, a "house," in which he continued to live in the form of a statue. During the First Dynasty these buildings were apparently constructed of wood and mats only, and as a result there is nothing left of them today. It is possible that Queen Merit-Neith and after her the kings of the Second Dynasty, Peribsen and Khasekhemuwy, built such houses of bricks or else surrounded them with a brick wall. These sites have been erroneously called forts; that of Khasekhemuwy carries today the name of Shunet-ez-Zebib. Rows of tombs were found near these houses; indeed, for the most ancient sites such tombs are the only indication of the existence of houses that once stood in their midst but that have since vanished. Here, too, the number of graves decreases with the progress of time. The identity of the buried persons is uncertain, but an examination of the skeletons proved almost beyond doubt that those interred here were buried alive.

These houses and their occupants are important for an understanding of the royal cult of their time and its continuation in the ritual of Osiris at Abydos, and we should like to know more about them. To begin with, we may claim for these buildings the name of *ka* house. This would mean that the occupant of the house was not the person of the king concerned but rather that spiritual power of personality called the *ka*, which is not identical with the bodily appearance, but surpasses it in influence and permanence. The expression "*ka* house" occurs during the Old Kingdom and afterward as a designation of the royal cult center in temples of the gods, and especially in the royal temple at Abydos. We thus have here, formally and expressly, the starting point of a tradition that lasted through many centuries.

It is also certain that the cult and worship of the occupant of such a *ka* house was continued by his successors. Certain proof of this is given by cylinder seal impressions which derive from offerings and which bear the names of later kings.

There remains the question, In what form was the dead king or his *ka* present here? It seems very likely that it was as a statue; but apparently this statue did not show the ruler in his human shape. W. Helck surmises that the king was represented in the figure of the Great White One (that is, the great baboon).

Colorplate I. Shrine of Anubis. From the tomb of King Tut-ankh-amon (1347–1338 B.C.). Western Thebes, Valley of the Kings (Biban el Moluk). Late 18th Dynasty, New Kingdom. Cairo Museum.

This sacred animal died out early in Egyptian civilization, and we know of it only from a few ancient rites and textual allusions which reach back into the earliest historical period.

In the Berlin Museum there is a splendid statue of a half-erect baboon with the name of Narmer on it. Perhaps it is one of those royal representations from Abydos. Unfortunately, its provenance is unknown (it was bought from an art dealer). As this animal can be traced only in the final phase of prehistory and does not occur among the numinous animals of the historic period, its religious significance is doubtful.[6] An ivory tablet of King Den portrays a ceremony that took place before the Great White One on the occasion of the *sed* festival, the so-called jubilee of the king's accession. The king, wearing the white crown of Upper Egypt and with a bowl in his hand, runs toward the Great White One, who is squatting in a shrine. It is not clear whether this ceremony signifies a drink offering to the king's predecessor or some kind of transmission of power to his successor.

The "running out of Apis," a Memphite and therefore Lower Egyptian rite, is represented as a parallel. Here the king runs with the sacred bull across the fields in what is fundamentally a fertility rite. The two scenes could be understood as a reinforcement of the ruler and his rule. One reflects the nomadic-patriarchal tradition and the other the peasant culture, while both aim at a renewal of the king's reign. A small ivory figure in the British Museum of an unidentified king may illustrate the same ritual, since he is seen wearing the long robe characteristic of the *sed* festival and the tall white crown of Upper Egypt.

The sacred district of Abydos contained, accordingly, the royal cemetery itself and in front of it the *ka* houses as places of continuing worship. To these can be added a third site, the temple of the god Khentamenthes, the protector of the necropolis, whose name signifies "first of the westerners" (that is, of the dead). Originally he was represented as a lying dog. He is one of those dog-shaped gods who emerge in several places as deities of the necropolis (as a zoological identification is difficult, the name Canides has been generally accepted for the whole group). Those outside Abydos are mostly known under the collective name of Anubis—thus Anubis lord of the white land (the desert) at Gebelein; Anubis lord of the cave mouths; and so on. It is intelligible and consonant with a very ancient, quite concrete way of thinking that the protection of the necropolis should be entrusted to an animal that is at home there. Because this deity, in its animal form, is able to dig out corpses and destroy them, it quite obviously shows its power over them and therefore seems fit to be trusted with their protection. Similarly, the crocodile is the lord near the rapids on the river, while the lion is the numinous power at the mouths of wadies. In fact, the worship of these destructive beings is a means of escaping their pernicious power.

The temple of Khentamenthes was situated on the edge of the desert, in front of the site of the *ka* houses. There is no evidence that any of the remains derive from the prehistoric period, but some of the structures belong to the First Dynasty. The temple was built in two separate parts: the temple proper of the god and, to the northwest of it, the slaughtering yard. The core of the temple consists of a cella with two adjacent side rooms, while the outer buildings were enlarged several times. The slaughtering yard served for the preparation of the sacrifices, both for the deceased king and for the god Khentamenthes himself. A slaughtering yard remained afterward a necessary part of any temple. Temple and slaughtering yard open up toward the left side of the processional road, which then leads through a gate to the site of the royal cemetery. Today this cemetery bears the Arabic name Umm el Gaab ("mother of the sherds"). A procession coming from the cultivated land would have to pass the house of this protective deity, and the passing by was

Colorplate II. Landscape near El Kherbe, to the north of the temple of Sety I at Abydos.

undoubtedly connected with a ritual visitation of the god and with actions aimed at securing his protection.[7]

Near these buildings, in a pit and in a storeroom of the Old Kingdom, a great number of little figurines were found which may come from the temple of Khentamenthes. They are small and often crude representations of monkeys, hippopotamuses, crocodiles, birds, and children, probably votive figures which were brought to the temple of the god of the dead. It is not easy to understand their purpose. Quite possibly the supplicants thus requested the god to grant them physical fertility. Frog and hippopotamus, certainly, suggest deities subsequently connected with birth and fertility, and the figures of children instantly evoke such a meaning. The monkeys may represent the dead king. In ancient as well as in modern Egypt, the belief is found that the dead can help to bring desired fertility and progeny.

Under King Zoser, at the beginning of the Third Dynasty, the royal burial place was finally transferred to the north—first to Saqqarah and later to Giza. As a result, it would have been possible for Abydos, with its ancient royal cemetery and its ritual buildings, to become nothing but a magnificent memory. Nevertheless, a few vestiges show that the ancient Thinite royal ritual continued to be practiced. The cult of Khentamenthes persisted in his temple, and the kings of succeeding dynasties quite possibly built *ka* houses for themselves at Abydos. If this is true, they still became glorified in accordance with the ancient ritual of Abydos. For the *ka* was a form of existence that was separated from the bodily appearance as preserved in the corpse. Statues continued to be put up in the temple of Khentamenthes. By a strange accident, the only known sculpture in the round of King Cheops—a small seated figure a little less than two inches high (now in Cairo)—was found there. In spite of its small size, this little ivory figure is artistically a superlative work of art. As in all Egyptian sculpture, its greatness and excellence are independent of its measurable size. The king wears the so-called Lower Egyptian crown and is seated on a simple cubic stool. His right hand holds the whip and his left hand lies flat on his left thigh. His head is a little too big in proportion to his body, but in this way achieves a finer working of detail and a greater power of expression. That the ancient royal ritual continued to be practiced is, I think, proved by the fact that about the Sixth Dynasty the god Osiris was associated with Khentamenthes of Abydos (therefore the special cult of Khentamenthes must have existed at that time). Equally significant is the fact that the form of the so-called mysteries of Osiris of the Middle Kingdom (see below) is derived from the royal ritual. Royal seal impressions of Mycerinus and especially of Fifth Dynasty Pharaohs have been found in the temple of Khentamenthes; here is positive proof that he continued to receive regular offering gifts.

Preserved documents of two kings, Neferirkara of the Fifth Dynasty and Tety of the beginning of the Sixth Dynasty, prove beyond doubt that the temple of Khentamenthes was of outstanding importance. These are the so-called decrees of exemption, royal documents copied on stone and erected near the processional road leading from the temple of Khentamenthes to Umm el Gaab. Their content is revealing from the standpoint of economic history. According to them, the temple, or rather its inmates, are exempted from a number of taxes and burdens, which are enumerated in detail. In particular, the priests and bondmen of the temple are freed from all work for the state with the sole exception of their obligation to the temple.

THE GOD OSIRIS

All this in itself would not have sufficed to preserve the two peculiar cults of Abydos—the royal burial rites

22

Colorplate III. Osiris between *imy-ut* symbols. From the tomb of Sen-Nedjem. Western Thebes, Deir el Medineh, tomb 1.
20th Dynasty, New Kingdom (1186–1070 B.C.).

and the associated cult of the temple of Khentamenthes—from oblivion were it not for the fact that the cults were joined by the god Osiris, the divine embodiment of an essential aspect of the entire Egyptian religion. As a result, the sacred sites of Abydos did not become a historical memory, but gained rather a timeless ever-present importance, and the god Osiris himself achieved a historic and mythological crystallization of his complex nature.

At this juncture it is appropriate to reflect on the original nature of the oft-named Osiris; we must consider, too, his place of origin and the reason for his importance and veneration, which in the end reached far beyond the frontiers of Egypt. The task is certainly not easy. Ramesses IV described his nature as more mysterious than that of all the other gods, and this characterization remains fundamentally true even today, although for different reasons and from a different point of view. Scholars still disagree about him, and the following is therefore only an attempt to trace the history of the god and to say something about his nature. Especially as far as his supposed origins are concerned, only a suggestion is offered of a possible way of understanding. For it is particularly on this point that opinions differ: on the one hand, Osiris is placed with the Near Eastern gods of resurrection, such as Tammuz or Adonis; on the other hand, he is thought to have been a prehistoric chieftain or king who continued to live in a deified form. It is not difficult to discover reasons for these interpretations in the complex nature of the god. The following will serve to show how his complexity can be understood.

Osiris embodied the religiously experienced power of chthonic fertility. By this I mean the force which is active in the earth and causes corn and trees to grow from it. It is therefore closely related to the force which manifests itself in the inundation of the Nile, penetrating with the water of the inundation into the earth and finally proving its influence to the world at large through the burgeoning plant life of the soil. In itself the soil is not identical with the force, but merely provides it with a sort of habitation and living space; yet it is as closely related to it as to the Nile. In order to make this force intelligible and approachable, it has to be thought of as a human being—at least this idea is quite in line with the innate logic of all religious incarnation: human imagination and speech can work only with human concepts. When man tries to make some pronouncement about the divine, God necessarily assumes human traits. It is also quite in harmony with Egyptian ideas of heaven and earth that this chthonic power of fertility should take the form of a male being. For unlike most nations, even unlike the related Semitic civilizations, the ancient Egyptians always considered the earth as a male being, both grammatically as a noun and religiously as a god. And the sky was for them, quite naturally and inevitably, a female. The concept of the fertile womb of the earth is unthinkable in Egypt. On the contrary, the earth is represented as a man lying on the ground with the female sky bending over him; and plants are said to grow "on the back of Geb" (the earth-god). It is therefore quite consistent that the force which works in and out of the earth should be male. It was probably at the beginning of the historical period, at the time of the emergence of many other gods, that this force received the shape of a god. We do not know whether the god of chthonic fertility originally possessed the name Osiris. No written tradition about him is extant from that period. On the other hand, it is impossible to give a convincing etymological explanation of the name Osiris. Yet, quite apart from invocations, ritual procedures, and the like, we can recognize this peculiar aspect of his nature in a practice that appears occasionally in the New Kingdom, but may perhaps revert to the early dynastic period: it is the custom of placing in the tomb a wooden box in the shape of Osiris. This box is filled with earth into which seeds have been thrown, and the germination of

24

the seeds in the dampened earth symbolizes exactly that plantlike resurrection which Osiris incorporates.

A few tombs of the early dynastic period contain merely wooden frames with stretched-out mats—but not in human shape—on which corn seeds were spread. They may represent forerunners of the corn-Osiris, 15 which was put into tombs in a later period. In this way the fundamental idea of resurrection in vegetation would be expressed in a quite naturally concrete form.

It is obvious that this chthonic god achieved a special significance for the dead person who was embedded in the earth. There is a consoling analogy for man in the growth cycle of the seed corn, which is also embedded in the earth, then swells and germinates and rises up as a new plant. The cycle became for man the symbol of immortality, without granting deliverance from death or a resurrection of the body, but simply a continuity of life. In a chapter of the *Coffin Texts* the dead says:

> *I live, I die: I am Osiris.*
> *I have entered you* [or: as you], *and have reappeared through you* [or: as you].
> *I have waxed fat in you* [or: as you].
> *I have grown in you* [or: as you].
> *I have fallen upon my side* [this is a frequent expression for the death of Osiris].
> *The gods are living from me.*
> *I live and I grow as Neper* [this is the corn-god] *who takes out the Honored Ones.*
> *Geb* [the earth-god] *has hidden me.*
> *I live, I die, I am barley, I do not perish!*

In this way the two almost mutually exclusive main traits of the god Osiris are intelligible as characteristics of one and the same being—the fertility-god is at the same time also the god of the dead.

All this must have developed in a period before Osiris himself became known. Yet other even more decisive events must have taken place during the prehistory of the god.

The town of Busiris in the northern Delta is generally referred to in the texts as the "home town" of the god. Since ancient times he has been known as lord of Busiris. However, Osiris cannot claim to be an ancient local deity of that place. On the contrary, an anthropomorphic god with the name Anedjity, "he who comes from the Anedj waters," plays this role. We know him, in fact, almost only from his representations, and in these we are struck not only by his purely human shape but also by the insignia of a chieftain which he carries: a crook and a crown of feathers. One is prone to imagine—without being able to prove it—that this Anedjity had once been a chieftain who fell fighting against the eastern Bedouins and became deified after his death. However that may be, he is later on considered as a form of Osiris, as the double name Osiris-Anedjity indicates. Osiris then completely replaces him and receives from him the epithet lord of Busiris. To what extent the personality of Osiris in later mythology was shaped by the local legend of Busiris remains, however, an open question.

Wennofer is another personality who is appropriately recalled here as one who was completely absorbed by the god Osiris, although that happened only later on, most probably during the Middle Kingdom. His name means "he who is permanently perfect." Admittedly, it is impossible to prove the independent existence of a god of this name. The name is known as an epithet of Osiris and may emphasize a special aspect of the god's character. It is strange that long before this (during the Fifth Dynasty) "Wennofer" occurs as a personal name. It seems possible that we have here an early occurrence of the deification of a person (whatever the reasons for that may have been) whose form was subsequently absorbed *in toto* by Osiris. This case is mentioned only in order to demonstrate how difficult and complex the nature of the god had become even in a comparatively early phase of his development. The name Wennofer, as it happens, continued right into the Middle Ages in the form of Onofrio.

The decisive event, however, in the history of Osiris occurred when the chthonic god of fertility extended his sphere of influence, as mentioned above, and became also a god of the dead. Naturally, this god of the dead functioned in the nether regions and not in a heavenly other world of any sort. As fertility-god and god of the dead, Osiris represents two Egyptian concepts of life which have conspicuous counterparts in the world of Egypt. The chthonic concept of fertility, on the one hand, belongs naturally to the peasant part of the population. It was only in this sector that existence itself depended on the fertility of the soil which was brought about by the Nile inundation. It can therefore be maintained that Osiris is genuinely the most important and most highly esteemed god of the rural population. On the other hand, the idea of a beyond in the nether world represents only one side of Egyptian thought on life after death. It is opposed by the concept of a celestial afterworld which the dead hope to enter either by taking their place among the stars or else by traveling through the regions of light in following the sun-god Ra. Osiris is consequently cast in a role of ineffaceable antagonism to Egyptian sun worship, whatever name and form it may assume. A chthonic conception of this world and of the next is opposed by the radiant vision of a sunlit universe and the negation of everything dark and sinister; for the underworld too is illumined by the sun-god on his nightly journey. This opposition persists from the acme of the Old Kingdom until the Late Period; it polarizes two concepts of life in an enduring contrast. It is ineradicable because it corresponds with the two sources of energy that are historically united in the Egyptian nation: the peasant culture, which is tied to the Nile valley, and the culture of the nomads, which stands for domination and power.

All this should be borne in mind in any attempt to understand the significance of the victorious entrance of Osiris into the royal and general funerary worship. It happened in the Fifth Dynasty or thereabouts—naturally it is always impossible to give an exact date for spiritual and religious changes. What is of immense importance is that the worship of Osiris penetrated equally into the spheres of king and commoner alike, for this rebuts the frequent idea that the royal sphere was fundamentally different. Whether the ancient royal gods—Horus and Seth, the wolf-god Wepwawet, the crown-goddesses Nekhbet, Uto, and so forth—played a part in the religious imagination of the nation as a whole is extremely problematic. But it happens simultaneously that the god Osiris appears in the funerary prayers of the private tombs as dispenser of the offerings, and that the royal funerary literature, the Pyramid Texts, proclaims a transfiguration of the dead king as identified with Osiris. To be sure, the Pyramid Texts suggest at times that this reinterpretation did not always come about without contradiction and opposition. This emerges quite clearly in one section of the texts:

> *For he* [the sun-god] *has freed him* [the king] *from the "underworld" and he has not surrendered him to Osiris. He has not died a death, but he has become a spirit of light in the region of light; he has become enduring in the enduring land.*

26

Colorplate IV. King Ay completes the ritual of the opening of mouth on King Tut-ankh-amon, who is represented as Osiris. From the tomb of King Tut-ankh-amon (1347–1338 B.C.). Western Thebes, Valley of the Kings (Biban el Moluk). Late 18th Dynasty, New Kingdom.

In spite of this, the figure of the dead king was associated with the chthonic god of the underworld, and the king himself became Osiris. This development had consequences as grave for the royal cult itself as for the formation of the myth of Osiris. We shall study first the development of the myth.

IV Since ancient times the king had been the earthly incarnation of the falcon-shaped sky-god Horus. When the dead king became Osiris, the relation between the dead and the living king enforced the conception that Osiris should be the father of Horus. This is the decisive step on the way to the myth. For other royal gods are then necessarily drawn into the circle, above all Seth, the ancient god of the desert. Since time immemorial he has been considered the equal and brother of Horus. The original significance of this pair reaches far back into prehistoric times and escapes our knowledge. But the king incorporates in himself the powers of this
5 quarreling pair of brothers—he is Horus and Seth. Therefore Seth cannot remain outside this new grouping. The later interpretation explains the quarrel between Horus and Seth as a quarrel about the legacy of Osiris. In ancient times Seth, as an enemy of the gods, had not necessarily incorporated the powers of evil. He is rather a royal god whose antagonism toward his partner Horus cannot be resolved. In consequence, the conflict between them can really never be decided in favor of one or the other. Attempts to reshape the myth always lead to compromise solutions. One tries, for example, to divide their rule: Seth shall rule over Upper Egypt and Horus over Lower Egypt. This division, of course, stands in contradiction to the existing cult centers, since those of both gods are mainly situated in Upper Egypt. Or else one concedes to Horus the rule over Egypt and to Seth the rule over the desert. This distribution seems more realistic. For although the origin of Seth is uncertain, and although his sacred animal cannot be identified zoologically, it is obvious that strong ties connect him with nomadic prehistory. In historic times he appears especially as god of the western oases.

As one continues to humanize and elaborate the circle of Osiris-Horus-Seth, the question concerning the death of Osiris must logically be asked. Osiris embodied originally the chthonic element, or to express it anthropomorphically, the divine powers of the underworld and of fertility, and as such he assumed human shape. Therefore one must necessarily ask how he happened to achieve this other-world existence. Apparently the development did not start with a living god who met his death in one way or another. The process was the exact opposite of this. At the beginning stands a nether-world force to which human thought and supposition attributes death and therefore, before that, life. To give it a pointed formulation, one could say, Osiris is not a living, dying, and resurrected deity like the gods of the Near East, but he is from the beginning a dead god, to whom poetic thought later attributes a past period of life. Because of this the details that are given about his life remain colorless and general, and all his influence springs only from the underworld.

The myth explains in different ways the necessary event of his death. Once it was maintained that he was drowned. This idea, of course, derives from his role as the fertilizing water. Another version tells that he was slain. And here, of course, a slayer must be found. With a certain inherent logic and not quite unjustifiably, this part is ascribed to Seth; for as a god of the desert, Seth stands in a natural hostile opposition to Osiris as god of fertility. There are also several traditions concerning the manner of his death. According to one, Osiris was merely slain, and from the verb "to slay" a mythic place name, "Murder Place," is derived. It is sometimes said that this happened in the "land of the gazelles," apparently the region where the fertile land and the desert meet. A version describing the dismemberment of Osiris by Seth is perhaps not quite as ancient. Here, too, a meaningful symbolism finds expression. It explains on the one hand the ubiquitous influence of the dead god: he had to be present wherever the forces of fertility were active in the soil. This version was also connected with the custom of worshiping relics of Osiris in many different places. The existence of these relics could be explained without undue strain as a result of the cutting up of the body.

Although the attribution of this role to Seth seems to be meaningful in itself, it leads to almost insuperable inconsistencies within the associated circle of gods; and it becomes obvious that disparate elements had been conjoined.

The quarreling pair of brothers are now suddenly called Seth and Osiris. In fact, both are considered to be brothers as children of the sky-goddess Nut. It follows that the original pair of brothers, namely Seth and Horus, get into different generations. Seth becomes at one and the same time uncle and brother of his former partner Horus. This leads to a splitting up of Horus into two gods: an elder Horus (Haroeris), the royal god and partner of Seth, and a younger god called "Horus son of Isis and son of Osiris," or later simply Horus the child (Harpocrates). This younger Horus is the child-god sitting in the lap of his mother Isis with a finger raised to his mouth and usually naked. The name and image of this child-god retain and extend their importance over a very long period.

Female partners are early associated with the male gods of the Osirian circle. There are above all Isis and Nephthys, the divine sisters. The former is known as the wife of Osiris and the mother of Horus; the latter is designated as the consort of Seth. As far as we can judge, the origins of these two goddesses are widely divergent. The name Isis seems originally to signify the royal throne. The goddess may therefore have been the personification of a royal symbol of power. We find similar personifications of the crowns or of weapons. Possibly it is here that her role as mother originates, in the sense that she caused the one enthroned upon her to become a king. There is little that can be said about Nephthys. Her name signifies "mistress of the house." This is the general title of married women. She hardly ever occurs as an independent goddess, and it seems that even in more ancient times she was without a cult center of her own. Apparently she is simply a complementary figure to Isis, created in order to supply a second name in a female pair. Such a pair occurs earlier in the funerary cult in the form of two mourning women who shed tears for the dead at the funeral. They were often designated anonymously as two birds of prey, that is, "the two kites." This pair of mourning women may well be identical with Isis and Nephthys. One of them eventually received the name of a female royal symbol and the other a general female title, "lady of the house." In the myth of Osiris and later on in the so-called mysteries of Osiris it is their task to mourn and bury the dead.

The myth transmits a strange episode concerning the procreation of Horus. It is claimed that Isis conceived this her son only after the death of Osiris. Ancient sources already suggest this. It is said in the Pyramid Texts:

> *Your sister Isis comes to you* [that is, Osiris] *jubilant because of her love for you.*
> *You have placed her on your phallus.*
> *Your seed comes out into her, the sharp one as Sothis* [there is a word play with the words "sharp" and "Sothis," the dog star, which was considered to be the star of Isis].
> *Horus-Soped comes out of you as Horus who is in Sothis.*

Later pictorial representations show the mysterious event with Isis in the shape of a female sparrow hawk —perhaps a return to the primeval bird shape of the mourning woman—hovering over the body of her dead spouse and receiving the seed of her son from him.

This idea appears strange at first, but it is nevertheless meaningful and intelligible. According to ancient popular beliefs, it is precisely the dead who are able to grant fertility to the living, and this general idea of life emerging from death may have here found its mythological expression. Furthermore, the event seems to be an almost inevitable conclusion in the logic of the Osiris myth. We started with the statement that at first the god embodied chthonic fertility and that therefore his active force proceeded from the nether regions. If this thought is personified in the figure of a dead god, it is only consistent that his most lasting effect, the creation of new life in his son, should proceed from the dead. From all that has been said it should be evident that Osiris is in no sense a resurrected god. It is not he himself who wakes to a new life; his force works from the nether regions, hidden in darkness but sending up new life to this world.

This then in essence is the god who became dominant in Egyptian belief and faith, while his influence also reached in time and space far beyond the borders of Egypt. Before we return to Abydos to show his significance there, it is worth pointing out how one should understand such Egyptian myths, or else how one should not understand them. It should be evident by now that many inconsistencies are to be found in this complex myth, for example, variations concerning the family connections of the gods, concerning the kind of death suffered by Osiris, and concerning the characterizations of the gods: Isis as mourning woman, mother of Horus, and throne goddess and Seth as royal god and murderer. In all this our description has consciously chosen the dominant traits and excluded at first all accretions of local origin or variants which were added in the course of time. It is obvious, nonetheless, that the aspects thus included can hardly be rendered in the form of a continuous mythological tale. It would be more fitting to speak of the personification or epitomization of fundamental religious concepts and experiences. It is noticeable that differences in these experiences have not been erased for the sake of forming a consistent whole, thus achieving a literary sequence of events. In principle, this is applicable to all statements concerning the influence and nature of the gods in Egypt, and it clearly contrasts with the form of transmitting tales about the gods which was possible in Greece since Homer. Admittedly, in Egypt too there exist rudiments of such tales about the gods. But the fact remains that statements concerning the truly mythic events do not belong to literature. For this reason their religious reality is much more direct and much more closely tied to special cult traditions. Scholars state again and again, and with a certain amount of regret, that the earliest extant narrative of the legend of Osiris is that of the Greek Plutarch. It is certainly true that the story written down by Plutarch was not his own creation but that he transmitted it as something that had been handed down to him. Nevertheless, the form of the story is without doubt a Greek product which used Egyptian and other elements and cast them in a literary mold alien to Egypt. We have no right to expect an Egyptian narrative that records the legend of Osiris.

OSIRIS AT ABYDOS

Now back to Abydos and the question of how it happened that the royal cult there was connected with the god.

30

At the outset stands the fact that probably since the Fifth Dynasty the concept of the king's life after death was influenced by the figure of Osiris and the particular afterworld which he represented. As always in Egypt, a new idea is linked to one that is older and seemingly incompatible. Side by side with the vision of ascent to heaven and of life with the sun-god Ra stands now the idea of existence in the underworld as Osiris. The dead king will now reign over the realm of the spirits as Osiris, king of the dead, and his son, the "living" King Horus, will rule in his place on earth. Through the link with the dead king, Osiris is identified with Khentamenthes, the ancient Abydene god of the dead, and becomes Osiris-Khentamenthes, and he is thus evoked in the funerary prayers. Although the actual burial of the king continues to take place in the north (at Saqqarah), his way into the next world proceeds through the ancient royal ritual at Abydos. The texts make it quite clear that they are modeled on the ancient rites, which by now have been reinterpreted to suit Osiris. Thus it is said: *"The great landing pole greets you as the one who stands without fatigue* [that is, Osiris], *who is at home in Abydos."* Furthermore, the text actually hints at a performance of the ritual of Abydos. "The great landing pole" and "the one who stands without fatigue... in Abydos" are at one and the same time real objects in a ritual play and persons in its mythological interpretation. The superficial interpretation hints at the fastening of a moving object that "stands without fatigue" on a "landing pole." Quite obviously this object is the nome symbol of Abydos, a high polelike object that carries something resembling a beehive. We have therefore to do with the description of a processional voyage on the 13 Nile. The strange nome symbol was certainly later on, and apparently already then (in the Pyramid Texts), conceived as Osiris, in the sense that the "beehive" is supposed to be a reliquary for the head of the mutilated god. In other funerary rituals, the landing pole symbolizes Isis. The tying of the ship to the nome sign at the landing pole means, mythologically speaking, the meeting between Isis and the king who is borne to his funeral, that is, Osiris. One is entitled to recall here the dead ruler's original journey to Abydos, his burial site. The text now presupposes the application of the same event to Osiris. Another time it is said: *"If you walk, Horus walks; if you speak, Seth speaks. You are coming to the lake, you approach Thinis, you are passing through Abydos. The gates of heaven toward the horizon are opened for you."* These sentences really encompass the whole royal image that is related to Osiris. The walking and speaking mentioned in the first sentence are actions which characterize the living king. Insofar as he is alive, he is Horus and Seth. But it is as a dead person that he travels to the Thinite nome and passes with the funerary procession through Abydos and enters the ancient burial place.

In this way the ancient royal necropolis has received a renewed importance. Osiris is not only the dead V king or the royal god of the dead; he represents the faith of an essential part of the whole nation. Through him participation is possible—if only indirectly—in the festivities of Abydos, which are now reinterpreted on Osirian lines.

Two political and historical events that do not immediately concern the history of religion doubtlessly helped to strengthen the importance of Abydos during the late Old Kingdom. Toward the end of the Fifth Dynasty the office of superintendent of Upper Egypt was created, apparently in order to establish some kind of governor over the nomarchs who were dispersed over the long stretch of the Upper Egyptian Nile valley. The intention was to create a center of cohesion to prevent the parts from becoming independent. The fact that this attempt proved unsuccessful in the long run belongs to a different context. It seems that Abydos was the administrative center of this newly created superintendent. One holder of this office, Uni, is historically well known. He lived from the time of Tety to the reign of Mernera and provided a burial place for himself near his place of office. His tomb was situated to the south of the road which led from the ancient temple of Khentamenthes to the royal necropolis at Umm el Gaab. This location can hardly be accidental: the festive procession passed on this road in imitation of the royal funerary procession, and it must have been the wish of Uni to take part in it, as it were, from his tomb.

King Pepy I married the two daughters of a nobleman from Abydos named Khui, whose original office is not known. Both of them received the name Ankhnes-Merire, "Merire [that is, Pepy I] lives for her." They became the mothers of the later kings Mernera and Pepy II. Under the latter king their brother Djau held the office of a vizier, but he too was buried at Abydos. Although from the middle of the Sixth Dynasty it was the custom of provincial officials to be buried near the place of their activity, this did not apply to Djau, who as a vizier belonged to the central administration at Memphis. But the ancient holy site possessed a great power of attraction, and those who were buried here expected to take part forever in the cults of Abydos.

Here, for the first time, the position of Abydos as the favorite burial place becomes apparent. Anticipating events which happened after the Old Kingdom, one sees that it was practically impossible for all private persons and kings of the following centuries actually to be buried here. Private persons were prevented for economic reasons; and the kings had to choose their burial place near the contemporary capital. If one desired, nevertheless, to be present at Abydos in some kind of form, several possibilities were open. During the Middle Kingdom especially, hundreds of private persons erected stelae carrying their name and a prayer to the god, placing them near the processional road from the temple of Khentamenthes to Umm el Gaab.

6,7 For the Egyptian a stela was more than a memorial or a token of recollection. Rather, it represented a part of the person who was pictured and named on it. At the place where the stela had been erected the individual was himself present in a part of his being. The statues set up in a temple have a similar significance. The painted image, too, is a form of the person depicted. Similarly, a possible substitute for the desired burial is the erection of a cenotaph. Many kings of the later period made use of this possibility, and their monuments will be treated below in detail. The mental basis for this practice lies in a conception of man's personality and its media of appearance which is quite foreign to us. After a man's death there remains more than the mummified body which is revived through offerings and somehow has still a part in life. Alongside the body and independent of it there exist other manifestations of personality, for example, the bird-shaped *ba* soul, the *ka* soul, and the *akh*, which are able to appear on earth and live and be active. Therefore a second tomb may be meaningful if it is considered as a dwelling place for a part of man other than his body. A later magical story reveals something of this belief. It tells how a man who is buried in Memphis, while the body of his wife and child lie in a tomb at Coptos, is nevertheless able, in a mysterious way, to have both of them with him in his own tomb.

There was yet another possible means of allowing the dead a temporary visit at Abydos. This one too is connected with the special conception of the multiform manifestations of the dead which are not tied to the tomb. According to a primeval burial rite, the dead should be taken for his interment to the holy places of prehistory, namely Sais and Buto in the Delta. For here existed in early historic times, according to Egyptian tradition, a Lower Egyptian kingdom that corresponded to the Upper Egyptian kingdom of Hierakonpolis-Nekhen and Abydos. This is not the place to examine the historic content of the tradition. But the role

32

Colorplate V. Maat, Ramesses I, Ptah, Horus, Ramesses I, Anubis. From the tomb of King Ramesses I (1306–1304 B.C.). Western Thebes, Valley of the Kings (Biban el Moluk). Beginning of the 19th Dynasty, New Kingdom.

which the two places played in the consciousness of the Egyptians is important. In historic times such a funerary journey was desirable but impracticable, just as was burial at Abydos. Therefore, instead of enacting the real thing, symbolic holy stations were erected on the path of the funerary procession. They suggested the desired holy places in the manner of scenery on a stage and were passed by the procession. It was customary to request for the dead, or rather for one of his free-moving souls, a repetition of this singular event which happened at the time of the burial, that he should visit the holy places. Since the late Old Kingdom a journey to Abydos was also desired for the dead. Thus a funerary prayer for a priest buried at Giza asks that he may receive offerings on all great festivals of the dead, that these "*may be granted to him in the necropolis* [that is, where he himself is buried], *at Busiris* [the presumed home of Osiris], *at Abydos, and in the pyramid city of Khephren* [Giza]." This means that the dead will be able to take part in the great offering feasts of the sacred places.

II. ABYDOS AT THE END OF THE OLD KINGDOM AND THE CHANGES DURING THE FIRST INTERMEDIATE PERIOD

During the Sixth Dynasty such methods were considered expedient to enable people to respond to the attraction of the sacred town of Abydos.

New temple buildings naturally helped at that time to extend and renovate the site. Our knowledge of these unfortunately has to depend on architectural fragments and scant remains of ground plans. Not one of the buildings is well enough preserved to provide a lifelike impression of the plan of the cult center, nor do they enable us to re-create the ceremonies that took place in them. It is known that Pepy I built a temple for Osiris-Khentamenthes to the west of the ancient temple of Khentamenthes. According to its position, this too was intended as a temple of passage, and it may have contained an image of the king as Osiris-Khentamenthes. During the Eleventh Dynasty it was renewed by Mentuhotep III (Se-ankh-kara), who speaks of it as his *ka* house. In addition, the king built a new surrounding wall and probably also outbuildings, which were used for managerial and administrative purposes.

The subsequent kings also promoted the cult. The number of statues consecrated by the king and the royal family must have been considerable. A decree of Pepy II regulating the offering gifts for the statues of himself and of his relations was written on a stela, a fragment of which has been preserved. Its wording is here recorded because it shows clearly the economic and administrative side of all those cult institutions. It reads thus:

> *My Majesty commanded them to give:*
> *One thigh of an ox and one jug of milk in each festival there for the sacrificial service of the chief priest and the priests of this temple, protected like an offering of a god. I do not allow the royal offering and the offering for which I provide to be carried away for ever and ever.*
> *My Majesty commanded them to give:*
> *One-eighth of an ox and one jug of milk in each festival there for the statue of Neferkare [Pepy II] which is in the temple of Khentamenthes.*

One-eighth of an ox and one jug of milk in each festival there for the statue of the king's mother Ankh-nes Pepy from Men-anch-Neferkare [that is, the pyramid town of Pepy II] *which is in the temple of Khentamenthes.*

One-eighth of an ox and one jug of milk in each festival there for the statue of the vizier Djau.

The priests and the funerary priests of their endowment shall do sacrificial service, it being protected like the offerings of a god. I do not allow the royal offering and the offering for which I contribute to be carried away for ever and ever.

Sealed in the presence of the king himself, in the fourth month of the shomu *season, eighth day.*

This decree is only one of many which show the interplay of ritual and economic needs. The food offerings mentioned are to be taken from the provisions set aside by the king for the use of the temple. On each festival day they are to be placed before the specified statues, while at the same time they serve as a stipend for the officiating priests. This appears to be a very realistic and sober way of employing the offerings in kind, for which the nominal receiver (a statue or a god) has only an imaginary use. One should not forget, however, that this paying off in kind, in addition to its immediate use, serves also an ulterior purpose: it enables a bodily participation in the meal of the gods. These problems still wait a thorough examination, but one should beware of a too one-sided interpretation. One recalls, for example, the communal meals and celebrations in the Theban tombs of the New Kingdom. Here also the survivors take part in a meal at which the deceased is also "present." In a wider sense, the custom of presenting sacred bouquets to the god in the temple in order to receive his blessing belongs probably also to the same circle of ideas.

At the end of the Old Kingdom we must imagine the sacred district of Abydos as a popular place of pilgrimage situated in the vicinity of the temple of Khentamenthes and filled with temples, *ka* houses, and administrative buildings. From here the processional road led through monumental gates in a southwesterly direction to the ancient royal cemetery at Umm el Gaab. At its side stood tomb buildings of noblemen and stelae of those who were not able to be physically present. On festival days a procession of priests equipped with statues of the god, of kings, and of private persons moved from the temple to the necropolis. The favored ones permitted to take part in the procession in this way are called "companions of the god." To belong to this privileged group was in this period the desire of all the nobility. Concrete allusions to these "mysteries" exist only from the Middle Kingdom onward, but we may take it for granted that the object of the festival, exactly as in the ancient royal ritual, was the renewal of life after death.

Pepy II ruled for ninety-four years and was followed by a few kings of the same dynasty who were short-lived and obscure. The unity of the kingdom broke down and there began a period which we call the First Intermediate Period. This era is characterized by local feuds of single nomarchs. Uncertainty, famine, deeds of violence, and distress are quite naturally commonplace in such a situation. These conditions are described in the *Admonitions of an Egyptian Sage*, a well-known literary work:

Is it not so? The Nile floods, yet one does not plough. Everybody says: we do not know what has happened in the land.

Is it not so? The women are barren and there is no conception. Khnum no longer fashions men, because of the condition of the land.

Is it not so? Poor men now possess treasures. He who could not make sandals for himself has become a lord of riches....

Is it not so? Many dead people are buried in the river. The stream is a tomb; and the place of embalmment is in the water.

Is it not so? The noble lament, the poor rejoice. Every town says: Let us expel the mighty from our midst!

But this era became also a period of spiritual restlessness and of a new self-examination. After all, the collapse of the Old Kingdom had not only a political, revolutionary, and social significance; it was also the outcome of a new and compulsive self-assertion. All the ancient concepts of the world, the ideas about creation, the influence of the gods in this world, and the position of man in the world and before god were revised. A copious literature, now mainly lost to us, reflected the intellectual struggles.

Among other notions that were newly formed in this period, the idea concerning the judgment of the dead is of decisive importance for our study. Even this concept is not a complete novelty but represents a much older conception filled with new life and new meaning. Many inscriptions of the Old Kingdom can be quoted to prove that even at that time the Egyptians believed in a posthumous court of judgment. The identity of the presiding god is not always clear. Frequently he is merely called "the great god" and this name may be simply a designation for the dead king. The underlying idea may be as follows: as the living pharaoh embodied right and justice here on earth, it was hoped that in the beyond too his transfigured personality might be able to grant legal protection. In many cases this role may also have been ascribed to the sun-god Ra as lord of the universe. The idea of the judgment of the dead is part and parcel of a picture of the life beyond which was based on the experiences and needs of this world. One conceded that man would have the same needs in life after death as in the present life: that he would possess a house and need food and drink. Consequently, one imagined the whole of the next world more or less in terms of this one. The expected court of justice was a legal institution that could vindicate a plaintiff or that could, alternatively, avenge the wrong done to the dead and his possessions. Thus one could threaten the violator of a tomb or the person who harmed the firmly contracted offering gear of the dead that one would take him to court "at the place of judgment" or "in front of the great god." This court could therefore be approached in the same way as a court on earth, and it was not a place where the righteousness of the dead himself was examined.

In an era as disturbed as the First Intermediate Period, it is quite natural that the ideas concerning the future life should also be re-examined. Men saw that tombs were destroyed or despoiled; that the special stipulations of the contracts concerning the funerary offerings were no longer honored; that dead persons remained unburied or were carried away by the river. All of these events necessarily led them to question whether the conventional ideas concerning life after death were really sufficient. Did a continuance of life really depend merely on a ritual burial and the bestowal of offerings? Was the life to come only a continuation of this miserable and unhappy life on earth? There can be little doubt that the debates devoted to these questions were much stronger and livelier than can be recognized from the remnants of literature which by chance have come down to us. As a rule only a few sentences, isolated fragments, or scraps of dialogues have been preserved, and because of their brevity and lack of coherence, much of their content is not fully intelligible. Nevertheless, the literature of the period does give an answer to the very question about the nature of the afterworld and the conditions for man's existence there. And this answer shows clearly how the ideas concerning this place changed. It probably derives from a dialogue between man—or perhaps Osiris as representative of suffering mankind—and the creator-god who is responsible for the world. The creator says incisively: "I have put spiritual glory in place of sexual pleasure, magnanimity in place of greed, peace of mind in place of belly-filling."

In the life to come, therefore, man will not be troubled by human and earthly needs, but he will be able to exist in a state of real transfiguration, far from the wants and worries of this world. Theoretically it would have been possible to start from here with a completely new form of funerary cult, if there was need for one at all. But in fact, the ancient customs continued and with them the mummification of the body, to preserve its form in this life, the offering meals for the dead, and the recitation of spells for the protection of the 3 deceased against many dangers in the afterworld. If one recalls the longevity of cult usage, one will not be surprised at this. It should, of course, also be taken into consideration that continuing customs are susceptible to new interpretations which an outsider cannot easily apprehend.

In these struggles for an image of the afterworld the god Osiris played a central part. On entering the royal funerary cult he was strongly committed to the royal dogma by his mythological role as father of the Horus king. But side by side with this idea persisted the consciousness of his all-pervading "natural" character as a chthonic power that could transmit life from the depths of the earth. The quotation given above (p. 25) about Osiris as the barley which does not die reveals the god's premythological significance; but this text is preserved only from a period after the Old Kingdom and therefore it shows that the original nature of the god had not been forgotten. The power of this god was naturally experienced anew in a period when faith in the traditional funerary beliefs and customs had been lost; and one hoped to find in him a new security in the midst of the great uncertainty about the last things.

Another quotation may be given from the same collection of texts, the Coffin Texts, which contain a 4 comprehensive treasure of sayings from different sources. Since the end of the Sixth Dynasty these sayings were inscribed on coffins, and more rarely on tomb walls. The quotation interprets the relation of the dead believer to Osiris in a kind of mystic way. The dead says: *"Osiris has taken my place, my* ka *is high. He has repeated my name* [that is, he has taken my name]. *I do not die in his manner* [that is, I do not suffer death like him]. *I am Osiris!"*

The union with the god is accepted as a promise of life which goes far beyond all safeguards of an ever extending funerary cult.

This heartfelt turning toward a god whose life is encompassed by death also indicates, without strain, how Osiris now becomes the lord of the judicial court of the dead: he is the true sovereign of the realm of the dead. This court, however, is no longer an institution that can be used by the individual for his own legal claims, but has become, rather, a supreme scrutinizing court; anyone who wants to share the life under the aegis of the god must subject himself to its decisions.

The "classical" form of the judgment of the dead is admittedly to be found first only in New Kingdom versions of the Book of the Dead, and it is quite likely that this canonical form was in fact fixed at a late stage, although its spiritual suppositions reach back into much earlier times. Now we see Osiris as supreme judge of the dead seated on a throne and surrounded by forty-two other judges. In front of him stands the

pair of scales on which the heart of the dead is weighed against a feather, the symbol for righteousness and order (Egyptian: *maat*). The ibis-headed Thoth, the god of writing and calculation, functions as keeper of the balance. Anubis, the conductor of the dead, leads the deceased person to it, while near it a monster, the "devourer," threatens to swallow and destroy those of the dead who are condemned. This certainly is a pleasing and picturesque image of a great thought, but nothing more. The same is true concerning the con-
8,9 nected 125th chapter of the Book of the Dead, the "negative confession." The chapter is, essentially, a full statement of all the offenses, faults, and sins which, according to the deceased, he has not committed. This text too does not antedate the New Kingdom, and it is not likely that it is older in its stereotyped form. The rigid form of picture and text should not be taken too seriously. The fact that a living and decisive thought is here represented in an unchangeable form shows that it has evidently already lost its vital spirit. Above all, it is bereft of its real significance by the fact that the possession of this spell of the Book of the Dead tries to force an entrance into the afterworld of Osiris by magic means. In order to pass the examination it is enough, according to its claim, to take this "lip-service confession" in written form into the other world. This has nothing more to do with the reality of a possible confession of guilt or generally with an individual sense of guilt.

We cannot treat here in detail the place which magic and ethic take in Egyptian religion, not even in their relation to the judgment of the dead. Something, however, must be said to enable the facts to appear in the clear light of reality. Admittedly, we possess no pictures or detailed texts concerning the judgment of the dead from the early period, the First Intermediate Period, or the early Middle Kingdom; and the official funerary literature of this time—the Coffin Texts just mentioned—is mainly magical in character. Basically there doubtless stands the idea that a truly transfigured existence after death can be obtained only under certain conditions. It will suffice to quote the well-known saying concerning the judgment of the dead from the *Instructions for King Merikara* (see below, p. 39): "*Put not your trust in length of years! They* [the judges] *regard your lifetime as an hour. A man remains after death and his deeds are placed beside him in heaps. Yet it is for eternity that one is there, and he is a fool who complains. But the one who comes to them without a fault, he will be there like a god, stepping boldly forward like the lords of eternity.*" It cannot be denied that the suppositions were not only of an ethical nature. Demands of class and society, reversion to ancient funerary customs, magical means where human power and thought had failed, all play their part. Yet there is indubitable evidence from this period to prove that there was an urgent search for a new relation between world and existence. We should be simplifying the circumstances quite unduly if we merely took refuge in the panacea "magic." Behind magic there exists a problem of verbal expression. When we hear that the dead wants to be cleansed, freed, solved of impurity, disorder, and evil, who can give the right interpretation and tell us how far in every single case these conventional expressions cover a "magical" or an "ethical" meaning? Only very much later, after the time of Amenhotep IV (Akhenaten), were special forms of expression created to convey the confession of guilt and the consciousness of failure, punishment, and redemption. But it is quite obvious that we should do injustice to a more distant era if we let the existence of such a consciousness depend on whether or not we are able to trace an unambiguous verbal expression of it.

This awakening of a new understanding of the world and the new ideas concerning the life after death are, of course, only indirectly connected with Abydos; but they are directly linked with the god Osiris. Because his nature brings him so close to human fate, he is able to foster the emergence of new human thoughts and to incorporate them in himself. Insofar as the god who is worshiped becomes the center of new movement, he imbues the holy places with new, up-to-date life and this, in turn, also influences the history of Abydos itself.

Between about 2120 B.C. and 1900 B.C. the town of Abydos played, in fact, a recognizable role in the political events of the period. In about the year 2120 two places arose out of the general chaos as rallying points of political and spiritual power, and for one hundred years they wrestled for supremacy: Heracleopolis and Hermonthis. Heracleopolis, which is situated near the entrance to the Fayum, was the capital of the rulers of the Ninth and Tenth Dynasties, the successors of the Sixth Dynasty. We know too little about these kings, with the exception of the last one, to be able to say anything concrete about their activities and their art. In name they seem to have ruled over the whole of Egypt; in fact they dominated at least the Delta and Middle Egypt. In their spiritual make-up they continue the traditions of the Old Kingdom, and literature in the widest sense reached a considerable height. We possess nothing of their plastic art and architecture. The nomarchs of Hermonthis, on the other hand—they are mostly named Intef—freed themselves from the dynasty of Heracleopolis and extended their rule toward the north. One of them, Uahankh Intef, vividly maintains on a stela that he has conquered the Thinite nome and has taken possession of the "sacred valley," the holy sites of Abydos. But during the strife of the following decade Abydos was again submerged in obscurity. An "insurrection of Thinis" is mentioned under the reign of Mentuhotep III (Se-ankh-kara). But the "union of the kingdom" under Mentuhotep II (Neb-hepet-ra) was apparently no longer seriously threatened.

One detail from these struggles for Abydos deserves to be specially mentioned because it illuminates the spiritual significance of the place. Under the predecessor of the last king of the Heracleopolite dynasty, Merikara, some fighting for the site took place, and it happened that the tombs—most likely the tombs of the kings and the nobles from the end of the Old Kingdom—were destroyed and pillaged. This king, probably Akhtose III, left an "instruction" for his son. It is obvious that this written document was posthumously composed as some kind of political testament, so that the son could profit from the political and human experience of his predecessor. In it the king mentions the events in the Thinite nome and says of them:

> Behold, a calamity happened in my time. The necropolis of Thinis was violated. This happened as something that I have done, although I only knew it after it was done [therefore it happened under his responsibility, although it was not really his own deed]. Behold my punishment for what I have done. Evil is he who destroys. It is no use for him to restore what he has overthrown, to build again what he has shattered, to repair what he has brought to ruin. A blow is avenged with a like deed. This is the coherence of all deeds!

The king does not depict the event as a despicable deed, but although he was not present himself, he expressly assumes the responsibility for it himself. In consequence, an equivalent punishment has hit him. "I did the like and there happened to me what is done to him who leaves the god's path [that is, the right way]." We do not know the nature of this punishment. Possibly the king died an unnatural death or his tomb, too, was destroyed. But this incident and its consequences, which were fateful for the person responsible, prompt the king, or else the author of this document, to generalize reflectively on the relation of deed and effect. This is one of a few cases in Egyptian didactic literature where a concrete experience leads to the statement of a generally valid rule. The fact that the causal connection of events in historical actions is here explicitly emphasized deserves special notice. Even the king, in spite of his godlike role, is morally responsible for his deeds and does not stand outside or above the interlacing of cause and effect.

This passage is unique in Egyptian historiography. Even later, and in some sense more progressive, times can show nothing like it. It is one of the astonishing feats of this period that in all spheres of life problems are examined anew, new cognitions are formulated which reappear only much later, if at all, and determine the mental attitude. It is perhaps more than a mere chance that this thought concerning the responsibility for historical action was sparked by an occurrence in Abydos.

The Upper Egyptian kings of Hermonthis-Thebes erected buildings in Abydos even before the reunion of the different parts of Egypt in the Middle Kingdom: sanctuaries for the royal statues as well as renovations of the temple of Khentamenthes. Mentuhotep III (Se-ankh-kara) pulled down the old temple of Pepy I and replaced it with a new building. This suffered the same fate at the hands of Sesostris I. Unfortunately, the archaeological remains are again so sparse that neither the exact extent of separate buildings nor the form of the ground plan can be reconstructed with any amount of certainty. We derive our sole knowledge from chance discoveries of foundation deposits, isolated parts of architecture, and occasional allusions found on the monuments of private individuals. It is evident, therefore, that the kings of the Eleventh and Twelfth Dynasties continued, in buildings and ornamentations, the cultural tradition of the Old Kingdom. Here, as well as elsewhere in Egypt, the peculiar tradition can be observed that apparently each king felt obliged to raise a new building, or at least a partially new building, even if that necessitated the pulling down of edifices erected by his predecessors. This continuous inauguration of new buildings may have had its roots in the idea that a new world era began with each king, and therefore a new king felt an obligation to set up new sanctuaries.

III. ABYDOS DURING THE MIDDLE KINGDOM
THE MYSTERIES OF OSIRIS

Abydos apparently achieved its greatest splendor in the Middle Kingdom when the sacred character of the place and its festivals took definite shape. A great part of the population could now participate in the rites and therefore receive the Osirian transfiguration. These people are represented by stelae, cenotaphs, and little clay figures hidden in the ground. The stelae were put up near the processional road, and they suggest the special nature and significance of the rites, which are commonly known as the mysteries of Osiris. It remains questionable how far the term "mysteries" is applicable to these celebrations and to ancient Egyptian festivals in general. In the history of religion, this term is derived from ceremonies found in Greek and Roman religion, and it presupposes the presence of "initiates" in the mysteries—their "transformation" is suggested, as well as their nearness to God, and so on. We cannot take for granted that these aspects characterized the Egyptian rites in the same degree. Leaving this question aside, we must ask, rather, what concrete facts are ascertainable concerning these celebrations, what actually took place here, and what significance the Egyptians attached to the ceremonies. We must reconstruct the mysteries at Abydos from a number of isolated remarks, from wishes expressed in offering prayers, and from laconic statements concerning the soul. Only thus is it possible to differentiate between separate phases of the festival and to make some inferences concerning their significance.

In the center of the proceedings stands a statue of the god Osiris. In accordance with Egyptian custom, this cult image was replaced fairly frequently, just as the renewal of the cult was also expressed in the rebuilding of the edifices. The treasurer Ikhernofret was sent to Abydos in the nineteenth year of Sesostris III by royal command in order to arrange the preparations for the mysteries of Osiris and to supervise them himself as the king's representative.[8] He reports: *"The royal decree for the treasurer Ikhernofret: My Majesty commands you to go to Abydos in the Thinite nome to raise there a monument for my father Osiris-Khentamenthes and to complete his sacred image out of the gold which he had ordered my Majesty to bring from Nubia in victory and power."* In addition to the royal decree, Ikhernofret received the ritual qualification by the bestowal of the title "the Beloved Son." This priestly title derives from the family funerary cult and signifies the son who has been charged with the funeral of his father. From here it was meaningfully transferred into the cult of Osiris.

> *I played the "Beloved Son" for Osiris-Khentamenthes. I built his large eternal boat. I created for him a sanctuary "which elevates the beauty of Khentamenthes," of gold, silver, lapis-lazuli, copper, sandalwood, and ebony. I fashioned the gods of his following and renewed their shrines. I installed the priests and the hour priests in their tasks and gave them daily orders on the calendar feasts. I supervised work on the* neshemet *barque* [the name of the god's sacred barque] *and made its shrine* [the shrines mentioned above and here are locked boxes that enclose the images of the gods and are put on portable barques]. *I decorated the god's breast with lapis-lazuli and turquoise, gold, and all precious stones as protection for the divine members.*

After these general preparations, the inscription of Ikhernofret mentions the particular acts of the festival for which he was responsible. For details we have to rely on pertinent statements from other reports.

The first part of the festivities consists of the "departure of Wepwawet." In connection with this, Ikhernofret says: *"I performed the departure of Wepwawet, as he went to help his father. I repulsed those who attacked the* neshemet *barque and threw down the enemies of Osiris."* What is the meaning of this? The wolflike god Wepwawet, who in contrast to Anubis is represented as a standing animal, is grouped in historical times with those powers who protect the king from the front at his public appearances. He "opens the way" for the king (this is the meaning of the name Wepwawet). We know from ancient rituals of the coronation and royal festivals that, at the same time, the god is identified with Horus as an embodiment of the living young king in contrast to his deceased father. It is the departure of this Wepwawet that is referred to here in Abydos, as one can clearly see in a text like the following: one wishes "to see his [Wepwawet's] beauty here in his first departure as triumphant Horus." This departure of Wepwawet-Horus as successor to the throne is a rite intimately connected with the accession to the throne; and the procession originated in a "race" for possession of the throne. The throwing down of the enemies mentioned in this context may have been enacted in a symbolic form. Thus the first part of the mysteries of Osiris signifies the seizure of power and the beginning of a new king's rule.

The next part is described by Ikhernofret in the following words: *"I performed the 'great departure' and accompanied the god on his way. I caused the boat of the god to proceed and Thoth caused the voyage to progress well."* From the last sentences one infers that what happened was a voyage on water, and not a procession on land in which the barque was carried. The expression "the great departure" may signify the funerary procession of the dead king, the predecessor of Horus king; for this had to proceed from the capital—in the Old Kingdom from Memphis—to Abydos. Quite naturally, this has become a voyage of Osiris, and most probably it was enacted in Abydos itself. Unfortunately, nothing else is reported concerning this funerary journey. Perhaps it was accompanied by choirs of mourners, such as those referred to in late times (see pp. 47–48). The meaning of "great departure," which is in itself a noncommittal expression, is assured by its rendering in Greek as "great mourning" (μεγα πενϑος).

After this follows that part of the ceremony which was apparently of the greatest importance for the public: the procession across the "great valley" to the necropolis of Umm el Gaab, a region for which the unexplained name "region of Poqer" has been transmitted. The image of the god was carried in the *neshemet* barque and was accompanied, it seems, by images of other gods and the statues of kings. To be able to take part in this procession to the sacred necropolis was the wish of all those who had a tomb or a stela erected for themselves near the processional road. For such participation enabled them to join the dead god-king in his journey to the next world.

Ikhernofret's account of this procession shows clearly that in his time it was understood as related to the Osiris myth. He mentions here the epithet of Osiris-Wennofer and his mythical place of death Nedit ("Murder Place"; see p. 28). *"I sanctified the god's way to his grave in Poqer. I helped Wennofer on that day of the great battle and threw down all his enemies on the water of Nedit."* Perhaps one should not imagine that there was a combat, but rather that during the procession songs and incantations were sung with the intention of dispelling all hostile spirits and evil powers.

Naturally, the funeral in the necropolis came next. In some form an actual interment must now have taken place, either of the god's image itself or else of a copy of it. But apparently the act belonged to the most secret events of which nothing is reported. It does not seem impossible that we shall be able at some future date to deploy pertinent texts from other sources. For there exists an abundant ritual tradition referring to this act, including allusions which may reveal their significance to the Egyptians. According to Ikhernofret's meager sketch, the divine image was then carried back and reinstated in the temple.

The next episode is as mysterious as the interment of the god. It is called "the night of sleeping," also "the sleep of the fighter Horus," or the festival of *haqer*. According to an attractive suggestion by W. Helck, the *haqer*, the name of a festival, represents the beginning of a hymn which was sung at the time and can therefore be translated "come to me" or "descend to me." These are details that can reveal something of the significance of this mysterious action. The fighter Horus, the successor to the throne, sleeps, and a being is called upon to descend. A further allusion on a private stela gives an additional hint: it desires "to hear the rejoicing at the appearance of the *sem*," the last word being a priestly title which is known from primeval rituals. It designates special functions of the beloved son, that is, the successor to the throne, who is also the fighter Horus. We may with certainty refer the three titles to one and the same person, whose role is fairly accurately indicated by them. This night of sleeping apparently signifies a mysterious act of reanimating the god's statue. We know the ritual of which it was a part. It is the ritual of the "opening of the mouth." Its purpose is the calling to life of the statues of kings and the images of gods; it therefore implies a magic

42

action which aims at giving life and soul to an originally inanimate object. According to the testimony of the texts, the essence of the ritual reaches back to very ancient times, perhaps to the Thinite period. A strange scene forms its nucleus. The *sem* priest (= son) sleeps on a low couch in front of the statue which is to be revived (= father). In his dream he meets the soul of his father, catches it as one might catch a night bird, and instills it into the statue which now has a soul and is alive. The sparse allusions to the *haqer* festival probably involve this: the fighter Horus sleeps in the temple of Osiris. He calls upon the soul of Osiris, which is hovering in the night air: "Descend to me!" and he "animates" the statue. In the morning he is able to announce to a jubilant crowd that the buried god has been resuscitated.

This interpretation of the mysteries of Osiris at Abydos in the Middle Kingdom admittedly leaves many details still indistinct and uncertain. Nevertheless, it represents its essential nucleus. What is completely impossible is to bring back the fullness of life and ritual and the colorful scenes which were witnessed by the participants. Neither can we reconstruct the religious feeling in the believer who followed the rites. On the stela of a woman we find greater detail as to how the events appeared to those who received the favor of a burial in Abydos: "*She arrived at Abydos on the day of which one speaks. She entered the temple, she saw the mystery. She climbed into the* neshemet *barque and crossed the river in the divine barque. So she came out into the fields of Ra with reviving flowers on her eyes, nose, and ears and scented flowers on her body. She was dressed by Tayt* [goddess of weaving] *and received the garments of the great Horus on the day when he seized the crown.*"

It is obvious that this description does not refer to a living person who takes part in the celebrations, but conveys the wishes of the dead who was transfigured at Abydos. Naturally, true ritual data are here intermingled with events that are possible only in the religious imagination. The latter is doubtless true of the journey in the "divine barque" with the god. The "vestments" and "flowers," on the other hand, probably imply real customs, for these objects embellished the festival of the god; they were hallowed by him and are now given to the favored dead persons.

One thing in these mysteries is especially revealing for us in our effort to follow up the growing myth of Osiris and the development of his cult at Abydos. Certain actions still reflect quite clearly those of the royal ritual at Abydos: the seizure of power by the successor to the throne, the funeral procession of the dead king, his interment at Umm el Gaab, and his resuscitation in a statue in the temple. It seems that all this was preserved for more than a thousand years in the form of a ceremony; but a new interpretation relates the same rites to Osiris and thus covers the original meaning. Now it is the dead god who is being carried here to his grave, and his statue represents new life. The procedure thus gains a new and far-reaching meaning: not only does it secure the continuance of the dynasty and its rule and implicitly, too, in the end, the continuance of the whole world and of each individual, but it also now appeals directly to the individual human being. It is his death and his resurrection that are here enacted and guaranteed.

Apparently several more centuries were needed for the myth of Osiris to create its own ritual.

Abydos maintained its importance in the subsequent era until the time of the Hyksos, and even the politically weak kings of the Thirteenth Dynasty continued to build on the site, nor did the urge for a burial at Abydos diminish in any way. From this period comes a stela which reaffirms the boundaries of the sacred precincts, apparently in order to keep it free from the pressure of those who wished to be buried directly inside it. It is only one of a number of stelae which express a delimitation of boundaries in all directions.

The king calls this boundary stela "*a monument which he makes for his father Wepwawet, the lord of the royal land*," and he declares categorically: "*If anyone is seen inside the area of the erected stelae, with exception of the priests at their duties, he shall be burnt* [as a punishment this means for the Egyptian the irrevocable form of destruction]. *Furthermore, any official who makes himself a grave inside the royal precinct shall be reported and punished. But outside the prohibited area people may build tombs for themselves and be buried there.*"

One king of this dynasty, Neferhotep, became especially noted for his solicitude on behalf of Abydos. He has left a detailed description of his arrangements. He ordered the learned men in his palace to let him know the sacred books with all their regulations in order for him to begin a "great revision" of all ritual institutions. One leads him into the "house of books" and there he finds "the documents of the temple of Osiris-Khentamenthes, the lord of Abydos." It seems to him most important to do something for this god. Is he not his son and has he not received the kingship from him? Also, it is stated, devoted ministering to the god would benefit the whole land and all its inhabitants. The king then sends a messenger before him with the direction: "Hasten upstream with a ship's crew. Sleep not, neither day nor night, until you reach Abydos!" The messenger who is sent in advance fetches the divine image out of the temple and sends it on the Nile to meet the king. After the encounter of king and god the king boards the divine boat and he himself rows it back to Abydos. Then god and king move in a great procession in front of which runs Wepwawet, "who opens the way against the enemies." After that the god rests in the "golden house" and the king himself directs the work in connection with him and his ennead. What actually happened may have been concerned with the reanimation of the images of the god and his companions by means of the accepted magical technique, and this time the king himself acted the part of the son and *sem* priest. It is not necessary to assume that all the statues were in fact completely renovated. They may have received new ornaments, but the important thing was that they were consecrated anew and reanimated by the king himself.

From the same period—perhaps even from the reign of the same Neferhotep—derives an architectural innovation that decided the direction of ritual institutions for several centuries. In much the same way as the royal inscription just quoted, it indicates a very intense and close relation between god and king. For it was at this time that the first royal cenotaph was built at Abydos. It is situated on the westernmost border of the valley plain, about eight hundred yards behind the temple of Sesostris III, and for that reason it was once thought to be a cenotaph of this king. However, as O. Firchow has shown, architectural details of the construction and the date of seal impressions discovered there link the edifice securely with the Thirteenth Dynasty. The superstructure of the tomb, which is now destroyed, may have had the rectangular shape of a mastaba. In the substructure a long subterranean passage lined with limestone led from a shaft first in a westerly and then in a northeasterly direction. The tomb chamber contained a large sarcophagus of red granite, but it was without inscriptions or reliefs. We do not know with certainty which king ordered the cenotaph to be made. But the basic idea is obvious: for the identification of the dead king with Osiris the presence of a statue in a shrine—as with the former kings—is not enough. It must be fortified with a special tomb at Abydos.

44

IV. ABYDOS DURING THE NEW KINGDOM AND THE LATE PERIOD
ABYDOS DURING THE EIGHTEENTH DYNASTY

It is here that the first rulers of the Eighteenth Dynasty resume the thread after the Hyksos period. In about 1560 B.C., the Theban prince Kamose, and after his death his brother Ahmose, succeeded in freeing Egypt from its dependency on the Hyksos kings who were reigning in the northeastern Delta. Politically this struggle stood at the beginning of the New Kingdom, the historical era during which Egypt, after emerging from the domination of the Hyksos, expanded beyond its natural frontiers and, in competition first with the Mitanni of Asia Minor and then with the Hittites, became a major power herself. The initiative for this, as we have already seen, came from the Theban princes who had apparently ruled under the Hyksos over some kind of feudal state. Following their victory over the Hyksos and as a result of it, they established themselves as the new ruling dynasty after first disposing of the other dynasties in Middle Egypt. But power needs legalization before it can be lastingly valid. Every change of dynasty in Egypt bears, fundamentally, a double face. On the one hand stands the factual seizure of power, be it by force, marriage, or inheritance, and on the other the legalization and the consolidation of the seizure in harmony with the royal dogma. At the beginning of the Eighteenth Dynasty, the legalization seems to have taken place by consciously forging links with the cult of Osiris and the royal cult at Abydos. It might have been more obvious to start in Thebes itself and imply a succession of King Mentuhotep, who had united Egypt at the beginning of the Middle Kingdom. But an appeal to the first, half-legendary union under Menes seemed, after all, to guarantee a higher degree of legitimacy.

At Abydos, Ahmose erected for himself a large tripartite monument south of the Middle Kingdom buildings.[9] Some of it still remains: a terraced temple near the western mountain ridge is preserved in ruins; in front of it lies the spacious cenotaph, and almost on the borderline of the cultivated land stands a pyramid. It was the monumental burial site of Mentuhotep on the west side of Thebes that provided ultimately, of course, the pattern for those structural elements, if not their spatial arrangement or their architectural accomplishment.

In addition, the king ordered a shrine to be raised on the road between his pyramid and his cenotaph for his grandmother Teti-sheri, the mother of the princely pair Sekenenra and Ah-hotep. The great prominence attributed here, at the beginning of the Eighteenth Dynasty, to the king mothers is surprising. Queen Ahmes-Nefertari, the wife of Ahmose, is the mother of Amenhotep I, and together with her son she played for several centuries a semidivine role in the Theban necropolis. The worship of the king mothers seems to have mainly been characteristic of the period of transition from one dynasty to another. The custom was prominent in the transition from the Third to the Fourth Dynasty, and then again from the Fourth to the Fifth Dynasty; and it seems to have helped to legalize the new dynasty, especially, of course, if it could be proved that the king mother descended from the old dynasty. An inscription in the offering room of the cenotaph tells how the king and his wife Ahmes-Nefertari were sitting together:

One spoke to the other about the quest of what is useful for those who are in the beyond.... Then his sister said answering him: "Why does one remember it and why does one talk thus? What has come into your mind?"

45

Then the king himself said to her: "It is I who remember the mother of my mother and mother of my father, the great royal wife and king mother Teti-sheri, the deceased and justified. Her tomb and her cenotaph shall now be on the soil of Thebes as well as of the Thinite nome. I have told you this because my Majesty has the wish to build a pyramid and a mortuary temple for her in the 'sacred land,' near the monument of my Majesty. Its lake shall be dug, its trees shall be planted, its bread offering shall be established: it shall be provided with men, donated with fields, invested with herds, while the funerary priests and the lector-priests are doing their duty and each of them knows his order." His Majesty spoke and it was already achieved. But his Majesty did it because he loved her more than anything. Never before have ancestors done such a thing for their mothers. His Majesty stretched out his hand and bent his arm [the gesture of offering] *and brought her a sacrifice....*

It was therefore the personal wish of the king to provide for his deified ancestress, in addition to her tomb at Thebes, a cult center on the sacred site of Abydos. In fact, the buildings of this dynasty at Abydos were much more extensive and magnificent than the relatively modest beginnings at Thebes itself, in spite of the fact that their remains have not preserved their monumental size.

This certainly marks the end of the royal cenotaphs at Abydos. It may not be accidental that this is also the beginning of the powerful building activity of this dynasty at Thebes: the progressive enlargement and embellishment of the temple of Amon, the richly endowed and highly decorated tombs in the Valley of the Kings, and the series of mortuary temples in the western town of Thebes. The kingdom of the Eighteenth Dynasty stood decidedly under the protective power of Amon of Thebes, and as a token of gratitude the building activity of the rulers was dedicated to this god.

But the solicitude for Abydos does not cease completely. Amenhotep I erected there a shrine for his father Ahmose. Under Tuthmosis I the *neshemet* barque of Osiris was renewed again. Tuthmosis III enlarged the temple of Osiris there and built for himself a shrine for his statues. From the inscriptions of architects and priests, we have reports during the whole period until the time of Amenhotep III of buildings, restorations, and endowments. Statues and ritual implements were also made for the gods who were worshiped together with Osiris. For according to the tradition, the main god and lord of the temple is here joined by a company of gods worshiped together with him, the "guest gods" (σύνναοι θεοί), who are also called the ennead. The last-named conception probably comes directly from Heliopolis, where all the principal gods are comprehended as an ennead, beginning with the creator god Atum and including the gods of the Osiris circle.

Standing on its own the ennead represents the gods in general and need not be limited to nine. Their joint veneration in the temple of a god signifies that all the gods of the country are present under the rule of the special lord of the temple. Here in Abydos the evidence for the composition of the ennead differs so considerably with regard to both the number and the names of the gods that one is inclined to doubt whether this ennead existed at all in any form in the cult. A treasurer of the time of Tuthmosis I enumerates the following gods as the "great ennead of Abydos" and claims to have "formed" them, which means apparently that their statues were made by him: Khnum of Herewer (in the fifteenth Upper Egyptian nome), Khnum of Kebehu (the god of the first cataract), Thoth of Heseret (a cult place in the fifteenth nome), Horus of Letopolis (a Horus of the western Delta), Horus the defender of his father (that is, Horus the son of Osiris), Wepwawet

46

of Upper and of Lower Egypt (the dualized person of the Upper Egyptian royal god). This enumeration, which as we have already said may be different in other records, makes a very casual impression, and one can no longer recognize the reasons for the choice. But it may well be that in this era the ennead contained many more gods and that only those members were named whose statues were made at the time.

In any case, it is obvious that religious activities at Abydos continued in the ancient mode even in the middle of the Eighteenth Dynasty. We hear of buildings, endowments, and performance of the mysteries.

Only toward the end of the Eighteenth Dynasty do we get to know something concerning a question which up to now we have left untouched, namely, where exactly was the tomb of Osiris believed to be. It is certain that it was located to the southwest of the temple of Khentamenthes and Osiris, at Umm el Gaab, the necropolis of the early dynastic kings. It is possible to be even more precise. One particular site was evidently regarded as the tomb of Osiris: this was a hill in front of Umm el Gaab, which Petrie, who excavated it, called "hill of Heka-reshu," after the man whose funerary figurines were found there. Offering gifts continued to be deposited at the site. But at least since the end of the Eighteenth Dynasty the actual tomb of an ancient king was chosen instead, namely that of King Zer, the successor of King Menes, who united the kingdom. And the finds testify that this place was regarded until the Late Period as the tomb of Osiris.

The finds at Abydos, which are, of course, incomplete, might give the impression that the cult declined in importance during the Eighteenth Dynasty. And perhaps this was true to some extent, since the material expenses involved in its upkeep did not much exceed those for any other provincial temple. But the situation conceals the fact that the importance of the god himself, quite independently of the local cult, continued to grow. In the Theban district likewise, no funerary prayer could do without the favor of Osiris, although Amon was eminently the god of the dynasty and of the kingdom; and none of the Books of the Dead of this period renounced, for example, the 125th chapter containing the Osirian judgment of the dead. All these ideas had penetrated deeply into the consciousness of each individual, and the belief in a continued existence 10–12 in the next world was unthinkable without the figure of Osiris. Even the royal funerary texts of the period, which were recorded in the royal tombs at Thebes, could not have existed without Osiris, since they were based on his religion. Still more does the hymnology of the period convince us of the god's far-reaching importance, for the invocations of these hymns dwell on the dignity and influence of Osiris as well as on his mythological significance. They differ, nevertheless, fundamentally from the "stories about the gods": the invocation of the hymns is set in the present time and happens now and always, while the narratives about the gods refer to some seemingly historical event, something that has happened, even something unique. The statement embodied in a hymn constantly refers, at the same time, to some ritual presence. In a hymn to Osiris of the Eighteenth Dynasty, the god is first evoked in his numerous cult centers:

> *Hail to thee, Osiris, lord of eternity, king of the gods, with many names and of hidden form in the temples: He it is who has the noble soul in Busiris, who is rich in Letopolis, lord of exultation in Anedjt, who has many victuals in Heliopolis... lord of eternity in Abydos, who has his throne in the sacred region!*

Everything is subjected to him:

> *The ennead adores him, they that are in the underworld kiss the ground before him, and the dead make an obeisance; the ancestors rejoice, when they see him.... Geb entrusted to him this land, its water, its air, its*

herbs, and all its cattle; all the birds, all the fowls, all the creeping things, and all the wild beasts of the desert were made over to the son of Nut [Osiris].

Of Isis it is said in the same text:

Isis, the beneficent, who protects her brother, who seeks him without wearying, who traverses the land in mourning, without taking rest until she has found him; she who affords him shade with her wings and creates air with her feathers; who rejoices and brings her brother to land [that is, the drowned god]; *she who revives the faintness of the weary one and receives his seed* [these two phrases refer to the posthumous procreation]; *who provided an heir and rears the child in solitude, no one knows where.*

Then follows praise of Horus, who seizes the power. The text clearly demonstrates that the elements of the myth of Osiris are vitally persistent and at the same time that they belong to the present; for the narrated event happens now and is repeated evermore. Further, it illustrates the universal importance of Osiris: he is not only the god of the nether world but also the chthonic dispenser of fertility whose active force pervades everything on earth.

If it is right to speak of an antagonism, mostly latent, between sun worship and the worship of Osiris (p. 26), this tension comes into the open toward the end of the Eighteenth Dynasty during the "reform" of Amenhotep IV (Akhenaten). The sources show clearly that his doctrine of the one and only god Aton was historically linked to the cult of Ra at Heliopolis. The more violent opposition to Amon of Thebes, who under the form of Amon-Ra was himself a sun-god, probably lies on a different plane. The sun-god of Amenhotep IV was to be free of any animal or human guise and similarly of all mythological admixture. But the Theban cult of Amon was inescapably involved in it. In addition, there existed real economic contrast between the richly endowed priesthood of Amon and the claim of their god to rule the world, on the one hand, and the quite different conceptions of the king on the other. The opposition to the cult of Osiris had different and perhaps still more dangerous consequences. The latent split in religious thought here becomes an open gulf: on the one side stands the god of light, whose rays create all life, and on the other side the chthonic god who dispenses life from the underworld and from the midst of death. They are mutually incompatible, like the day and night division of the world. And what kind of answer had the professing follower of the Aton religion to the question, What would happen after death to those who live under the care of the Aton? The well-known hymn of the king, in which he expounds the fundamental ideas of his doctrine, does not give the answer. On the contrary, we find here the words:

When thou goest down in the western horizon,
The earth is in darkness, as if it were dead;
The sleepers are in their chambers, their heads covered up,
One eye cannot see the other.

These lines emphasize in only slightly veiled form how distant from God are creatures without light. Did not such a doctrine necessarily imply damnation and despair for all those who were looking forward VI to a transfigured life under the ruler of the dead, Osiris?

We do not know whether at Abydos, destruction and effacement of the names of the gods took place under

Colorplate VI. Sen-Nedjem and his wife praying and the goddess of the sycamore. From the tomb of Sen-Nedjem. Western Thebes, Deir el Medineh. 20th Dynasty, New Kingdom (1186–1070 B.C.).

the rule of Amenhotep IV, as certainly happened elsewhere. Neither do we possess any written document with an explicit "discussion" between the Aton and Osiris. From the reaction to the Amarna period, the period of Amenhotep IV, we may assume with certainty that the worship of Osiris belonged to those forces that were mortally hit by the doctrine of Aton, after whose elimination they emerge more powerful than before. But the cult of Osiris received now—in contrast to the cult of Amon—a new and probably final shaping of its ritual.

A NEW START DURING THE NINETEENTH DYNASTY

New building activities in Abydos were again connected with the rule of a new dynasty, the Ramessides of the Nineteenth Dynasty. Its founder was Ramesses I, who came from an officer's family in the Delta—we do not know any details—and ascended the throne after the death of Horemheb. He himself reigned for only a year and a half. He was followed by his son Sety I, after whom came Ramesses II. It is the name of Sety that is specially and irrevocably connected with Abydos. He was the founder here of the first large mortuary temple of the period, the only temple which has been almost entirely preserved until today. In addition, he erected a smaller temple for his father Ramesses I, whose short reign, apparently, did not allow him to build a temple of his own. It is situated in the northeastern corner of the temple precinct of Sety I and was also, it seems, connected with it in economic and administrative matters. It is distinguished by the same elegant workmanship found in the temple of Sety I. The little temple contained the statue of the king to whose memory it was dedicated, as well as statues of other members of his family. In a dedicatory inscription, Sety I says: "*I built for him a resting place for his* ka... *his mother is beside him and those who preceded him are not separated from him but are united before him. The beloved royal brother is before him.*" If the temple had been preserved with its whole equipment, we would know more about the family history of the dynasty. Another sentence of the inscription is meaningful, however, because it shows that a fundamental change has taken place in the celebration of the mysteries of Osiris: "*I let a statue remain in it, provided like the* [other] *kings. When the Majesty of the sacred god Wennofer came in order to rest there, he greeted my father as he did the ancestors....*" The meaning of this is that the god Osiris-Wennofer visited the king's temple during his procession and stayed there with them in the same way as Amon used to stay inside the Theban mortuary temples during the procession on the occasion of the valley festival. This addition to the procession of Osiris was doubtless an imitation of the Theban ritual customs, and the reason for its introduction in the reign of Sety I was to give to the mortuary temple at Abydos a ritual similar to that found in the Theban temples.

In view of its exquisite decoration, the building of Sety I is quite rightly regarded as one of the most beautiful temples of the country. The elegance of the delicate, only slightly raised, relief, with its occasional traces of paint, implies a new formal restraint which seems to contrast consciously with the exaggerated and pathetic outlines of the art of Amarna. A direct development can be traced from the artistic style of Amenhotep II to the not too numerous works of art from the time of Horemheb, for example, the reliefs from his tomb at Memphis, to the works of Sety I. Certainly Sety I's temple does not show the greatness and restraint of the reliefs of the period of Hatshepsut and Tuthmosis III, for example. Compared with those, the reliefs appear somehow effeminate and academic. Nevertheless, they must be appreciated as the mature

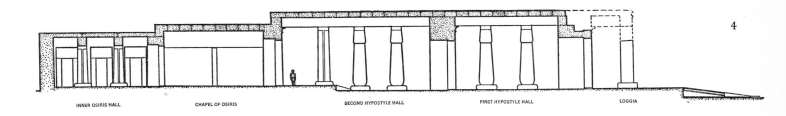

**TEMPLE OF SETY I
ABYDOS**

SCALE

0   25   50   75   100   125   150 feet

3

Figures 3 and 4. Temple of King Sety I (1304–1290 B.C.) at Abydos. 3: Ground plan. 4: Vertical section. The vertical section begins on the right with the ramp that leads from the second courtyard to the pillared hall (loggia) and meets the median of the two hypostyle halls, the chapel of Osiris, and the inner Osiris hall. On the northwest wall of the inner Osiris hall, as indicated, are the doors to the smaller chapel rooms, which were dedicated to Horus, Osiris, and Isis. After Alan H. Gardiner, 1933.

4

INNER OSIRIS HALL   CHAPEL OF OSIRIS   SECOND HYPOSTYLE HALL   FIRST HYPOSTYLE HALL   LOGGIA

expression of a new style, which was abandoned again as early as the reign of Ramesses II. Under him we see the beginning of those typically Ramesside representations; their execution is much coarser, often schematical, and, in addition, their relief is deeply sunk under the surface, in a strange way, without achieving the impression of real depth. As Ramesses II continued the work of his father on many sites, it is often possible to observe the two phases of style side by side in the same building.

At Abydos the name of the temple of Sety I is preserved in a form indicating that it was considered to be the mortuary temple of the king. It runs: *"The house of millions of years of the king Men-Maat-Ra, who is contented at Abydos."*[10] In its special arrangement it differs considerably from the Theban temples, as also from the mortuary temple of the king himself. Apparently this arrangement of the rooms was exceptional even at Abydos. We must probably regard it as a singular creation following the wish of Sety himself.

Externally the breadth of the ground plan is conspicuous, and it is determined by the number of chapels of gods to which the plan leads. And that exactly is its peculiarity. As a rule the holy of holies is set apart for the one lord of the temple, at most for a trinity of gods; but here the nucleus of the building is formed by seven chapels which lie side by side and are therefore of equal importance. The seven gods actually represent the religious dogma of a state religion. In a north-south sequence we see here the adjacent abodes of Horus, Isis, Osiris, Amon, Harmachis (Ra), Ptah, and the king. This septet can be subdivided without difficulty into three groups. First, of course, there are the three principal gods of the circle of Osiris: Osiris, Isis, and Horus. Then come the three main gods of the country, Amon of Thebes, Ptah of Memphis, and Ra of Heliopolis. They represent, above all, the politically and religiously dominant sites of the country: Thebes, the capital of the Empire, which apparently already under the Ramessides was given up in favor of the Delta capital of Ramesses town; Memphis, the capital of the Old Kingdom; and Heliopolis, the town of sun worship and of the classical ennead (see p. 46). But these three gods do not only represent a recollection invoking religion and history; in addition, they mysteriously form a trinity which is also a unity, and in them all the gods as a whole are embodied. This statement may at first sound somehow absurd, but it is based on Egyptian theology and may be understood as follows: the conception of the triad means here the plurality of the gods as such. Three is the first number to signify a plural. But the number three contains at the same time the three components that express the essential qualities of a god—name, appearance, and essence. Amon, Ptah, and Ra embody in this sense all the gods, and at the same time, they are only aspects of *one* god. From a hymn of the Ramesside period we learn this meaning of the triad: *"Three are all gods: Amon, Ra, and Ptah. He who hides his name is Amon, he who is visible is Ra, and his body is Ptah."* The two triads Osiris-Isis-Horus and Amon-Ptah-Ra are joined by the king himself, the original owner of the mortuary temple. In this way is reached the otherwise uncommon number seven. Probably the Egyptians would have gone still one step further and explained the seven as a triad, that is, the gods around Osiris, the gods of the country, and the king.

These seven chapels, side by side, reveal in their decoration and their architectural details important information about the cult. They are fairly extensively ranged, and they are divided by small projections into a front and a back room. Apparently each of them contained two cult objects that were kept and worshiped here at least during the celebrations. One would have been the statue of the deity and the other a portable barque to carry the statue out during the procession.

Another peculiarity is added, which is a rare element in the temple of the gods though a regular item of the royal mortuary temples. The back wall of each chapel is formed as a false door on which the king is represented worshiping the god of the chapel. On the other hand, the false door at the back of the king's chapel shows the king himself, followed by his *ka*, stepping out of the door. Here the function of the architectural elements follows the mode of the royal mortuary temples, since the false door is a typical element of tomb architecture. Fundamentally it is but an imitation of a door in stone; technically the door can, of course, be formed in differing ways with differing degrees of accomplishment. In the tombs it signifies from the Old Kingdom onward the place where offerings and prayers were dedicated to the dead. It is therefore an intermediary between this world and the next. In the temples of the pyramids, too, the false door forms the ritual link between the temple of worship in the east and the king who is buried in the pyramid. We meet it again in the mortuary temples at Thebes; here it is quite logically in the room set aside for the worship of

Colorplate VII. Isis, Sety I as Osiris, and the *yun-mutef* priest. Temple of King Sety I (1304–1290 B.C.) at Abydos. From a small chapel dedicated to Osiris, the middle one of three chapels to the northwest of the hall of Osiris.

the dead king. As all the offerings need a transubstantiation to reach through the door to the other world and to the dead, an actual connection in space with the burial chamber is not necessary. Here in the temple of Abydos, too, the doors represented the link of communication between the gods of the chapel who were present during their worship and the unearthly world of the dead. Instead of a false door, the chapel of Osiris has a real door, leading into a transverse set of rooms, which occupies the whole rear of that part of the temple: these are the rooms in which the special mysteries of Osiris (see pp. 58ff.) took place.

Still another detail of the temple should be mentioned because of its basic significance and because of its special role in the history of research: this is the royal list of Abydos. In the passage leading from the second hypostyle hall to the south, King Sety I is represented bringing an offering before the names of his predecessors from Menes onward. The names written in the royal cartouches represent the kings themselves; for according to Egyptian belief, the name too is among the powers of the personality, which like the body or the *ka* can take the place of the person itself. Therefore, the named kings are also present in this form in the temple and take part in all the ritual proceedings. The words uttered by Sety concerning the temple of his father Ramesses I are also verified here: *"Those who went before him are not separated from him but are united in front of him."* A similar royal list, but of lesser size and less well preserved, is to be found in the temple of Ramesses II.

The idea of a mortuary temple is further confirmed by the fact that the enormous cenotaph of the king stands behind the temple to the west, so that all the false doors are directed toward it. This cenotaph is often called the Osireion. But in fact it is intended as the king's false tomb, as expressed in its name, "useful is Men-Maat-Ra [Sety I] for Osiris." Therefore it is no more the tomb of Osiris than the temple is a temple of Osiris. Only in its architectural form does it imitate the god's tomb, for it is, after all, the tomb of the dead king as Osiris. Essentially it consists of a subterranean hill surrounded by water-carrying canals: this is the island on which the tomb of Osiris was thought to be situated. It is the canal flowing under the temple that made the artificial island a reality.

Neither temple nor cenotaph was finished during the king's lifetime. Ramesses II as well as Merenptah continued the task of building them, the former having taken over the work at the temple even during the lifetime of his father, whose funerary temple he also continued at Thebes.[11] This probably happened after he had been elected co-regent. Ramesses II left a detailed dedicatory inscription at Abydos concerning his activities on behalf of his father, partly during the lifetime of Sety I and partly after his death. In its form the description is without doubt literature, but it also contains some not unimportant remarks. When he came to Thebes he *"created statues of his father, the king Men-Maat-Ra [Sety I], one in Thebes and another in Memphis, in chapels which he erected for them. But the most beautiful was the one for the statue in Abydos, in the Thinite nome, the region which he loved and for which he longed ever since he lived on earth, the land of Wennofer."* When Ramesses himself came to Abydos, *"in order to sacrifice to Wennofer … he found the mortuary temple of the 'sacred land' of the kings, the predecessors, and the cenotaph at Abydos in decay. Part of it was still unfinished* [their walls hidden] *in the ground, the walls not yet ready. Nor did the bricks hold each other. The material on the building place had fallen into dust. Nobody had finished the building* [?] *nor kept the place* [?] *as soon as their lord ascended to heaven* [that is, after the old king had died]." The king then expressed before his courtiers the wish to complete the unfinished buildings of his father and to equip them.

The temple of Sety I at Abydos was a splendid ritual foundation that revived the local cult and united all

54

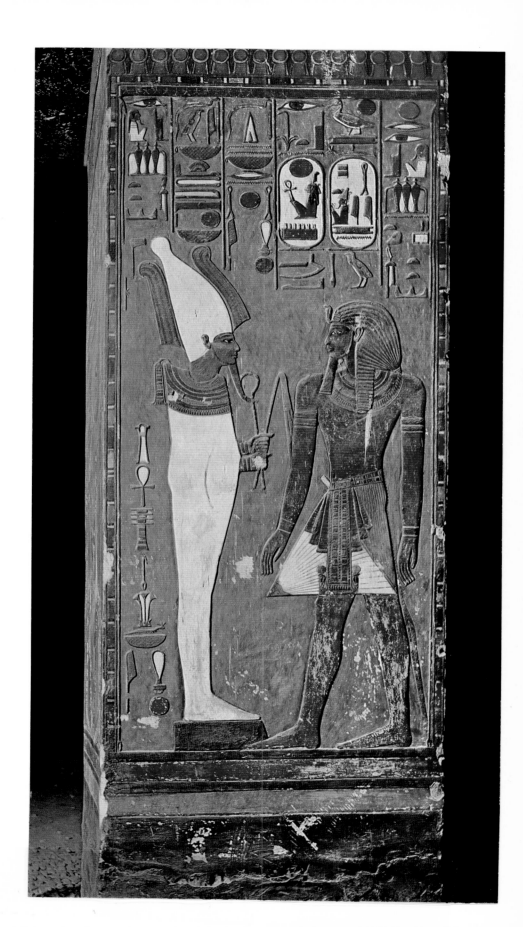

Colorplate VIII. King Sety I in front of the mummy-shaped Osiris-Khentamenthes. From the tomb of King Sety I (1304–1290 B.C.). Western Thebes, Valley of the Kings (Biban el Moluk).

the gods of the country. Moreover, its religious significance was equaled by its economic importance. The possession of fields, herds, and men was transferred to it, especially in Nubia, and above all the products of the gold mines. Several decrees of the king are preserved which aim at safeguarding the economic power of the temple. The pertinent institutions, material, values, and working power are withdrawn from all interference by state authorities, and infringements are severely punished. If there occurred, for instance, loss of cattle or the like, the responsible official had to replace the damage with its tenfold value. If anybody hindered the working men of the temple—which probably means if he employed them for other tasks—he was punished with one hundred strokes of the rod and five bleeding wounds. In other cases corporal punishment was linked with loss of office and removal to the forced-labor unit.

In one of the decrees is the following colorful description of the temple itself:

You [the king] *have built his* [the god's] *temple like the horizon of heaven, with its splendor shining on the face. The cult images of the lord of the Thinite nome are of gold and the figures of the gods rest in their proper places while their forms are right, as at the time of Ra; jewels are fitted into their barques.... A "palace"* [probably the temple proper] *is in it, profusely adorned with genuine* djam-*gold of the best that is to be had in the foreign countries. If one sees it, the heart rejoices and all glorify it. For his power gave it an appearance like the horizon of Ra, when he rises. In it are steps of silver-earth which shine when one looks at them. Its enormous doors are made of wood from the Lebanon, while they are gilt with* djam-*gold and overlaid behind with copper. One feels refreshed seeing their form. The great pylons are made of limestone from Tura, the passages are of granite. Their beauty is united with the height of heaven and they fraternize with Ra in the horizon. A lake in front of the temple is like the sea; looking on it one does not recognize the land around, for it is clear like the color of lapis-lazuli. Its middle consists of papyrus and reed and lotus flowers in abundance, every day; its flock of birds comes down to earth—surrounded with trees which join the sky, as though they have grown like a pine tree in its mountain country....*

The hyperbole of this description belongs, of course, to the style of the Ramesside period, and it can be paralleled in other literary works. Yet for us it may replace all that we can no longer see and admire in an Egyptian temple: its embellishment with statues, metals, dazzling jewels, and precious wood. In addition, VIII one has to imagine that a number of these adornments are fitted inside the temple, in apartments, therefore, which were mostly in semidarkness. Their sparkling splendor became the more alive when during cult procedures the rooms were lit by torchlight.

Ramesses II, too, built for himself his own mortuary temple to the north of his father's, but only a little of it is preserved. The whole temple was much smaller, and it seems that besides the king himself and his father only the triad of the Osiris circle—Osiris, Isis, and Horus—were worshiped here. Like the temple of Sety I, this temple also contained a list of kings (see p. 54), enabling the royal ancestors to participate in the cult.

During the following centuries the number of sacred buildings increased while existing edifices were continually altered. A mortuary temple of Ramesses III contains a long enumeration of his works for the temples. Ramesses IV left a stela recording his deed in the place itself. These details certainly belong to the cult topography of Abydos, and they could be made more complete by enumerating the high priests, who are partly known by name, and their works. But it may suffice here to note that until the Late Period, the sacred site was a showplace for royal buildings and the *mise-en-scène* of the festivals of Osiris.

One detail from the time of transition to the Late Period is worth noting because it indicates the effect of Abydos on people who were not originally Egyptians. After the rule of the Ramessides, Egypt was divided into an Upper Egyptian divine state of Amon of Thebes, of which Abydos too was a part, and a Lower Egyptian state with Tanis as the capital. In Lower Egypt a number of Libyan tribesmen had enlisted as mercenaries and had settled in many towns, and their chieftains established a territorial rule in relation to which the Pharaoh of Tanis was not much more than a *primus inter pares*. One of these chieftains, Sheshong of Heracleopolis, made himself king and founded the Twenty-second Dynasty. Even before he usurped the royal power Sheshong wished to put up a statue of his deceased father Nimrod at Abydos. A text which is historically and culturally most revealing gives full details of this plan. The procedure is complex, and the statue is richly endowed with land, cattle, and men in order to ensure the offering gifts. From this it is apparent that the endowment signified much more than the arrangements commonly made for private statues. It was necessary, in this case, to receive the approval of the king, probably Psusennes II, the last king of the Twenty-first Dynasty. But in addition, the approval of Amon was requested, because as the real "king" of the divine state he was, in fact, co-regent of the Lower Egyptian king. The statue was consequently introduced to Amon at Thebes, and the god through the medium of an oracle consented to have it put up at Abydos. Only then was it sent to Abydos with a rich escort, including Sheshong I himself. There the resuscitation ceremonies ("the opening of the mouth") were performed for four days, and at last the statue was erected in the temple. The inscription contains a detailed enumeration of the property. We shall not be far from the mark if we assume that this donation, again, has something to do with the legalization of power, although at the time Sheshong was apparently not yet king. The whole of the solemn ceremony gives the impression that the pretender fortified his claim to the throne by giving the ancestor of his house a place on the sacred site of the ancient kings.

The later dynasties of the Ethiopians and the kings of the Libyan Twenty-sixth Dynasty and their successors have also left traces at Abydos, and during these centuries tombs continued to be established by people of non-Egyptian origin, such as Nubians and Libyans. The mysteries of Osiris, likewise, continued to be celebrated until far into the Ptolemaic period. It is remarkable, however, that the official royal building activities stopped after the Thirtieth Dynasty, as far as we can ascertain. It seems that neither the Ptolemaic kings nor the later Roman emperors built in Abydos, in spite of the fact that otherwise the biggest temple buildings in the country derive from that period. All the same, it is certain that the cult of Osiris did not itself diminish even during these latest eras; quite to the contrary, the god increased in importance, and from the late Ptolemaic period we have detailed instructions concerning his festivals, even for those at Abydos. The surprising decrease of the power of Abydos has perhaps two explanations: first, the Ptolemaic rulers, descendants of the Macedonian general Ptolemaeus, may have had different ideas about the divine right of their dynasty, even if they tried to identify themselves with Egypt; and a connection with the royal cult of Abydos had no meaning for them. Assuredly, there did exist a Hellenistic divine kingship, but this was based on different foundations from those posited by the Pharaohs. The other reason may be sought in the development of the cult of Osiris since the Nineteenth Dynasty. Even before that Osiris had been worshiped under many names and forms in many ritual centers where he received special cults. The new form he assumed in the Nineteenth

Dynasty put a stronger accent on the general human traits of the cult, and in consequence the pre-eminence of Abydos and the original link with the ancient cult diminished. Certainly the town continued as a holy place and attracted tombs and monuments. But the awareness gained in strength that it was possible in other places, too, to connect personal immortality with that of the god and to experience the Osirian rites of resurrection. In the Ptolemaic period, certainly, and perhaps even earlier, a festive ritual existed which encompassed the whole of the country.

THE LATER RITUAL OF OSIRIS

In order to understand the last phase of the Osiris cult we must revert once more to the time of Sety I and ask what knowledge can be gathered from his period concerning the cult of the god.

We have already discussed in detail the seven cult chapels in the king's temple at Abydos. They all end in a false door which leads to another world; only the chapel of Osiris opens up into rooms which can be entered. And here we find the secret rooms in which the resurrection of the god is experienced. The crucial representations are to the left in the southern part of the complex. At its extreme end are three small chapels, the middle one of which is dedicated to the worship of the god's resurrection. Although the representations are partly destroyed, the preserved remains can be restored and understood with the help of the related and similar pictures in the king's mortuary temple at Thebes. The main representation is concerned with life

17-20 emerging from death, mythologically expressed as the posthumous procreation of the son: Osiris is lying on a bier decorated with lion heads and lion feet. On both sides stand, or rather squat, mourning women. On top of his body hovers with outspread wings the female kite—Isis—and she receives from him the seed of the son. The same idea is expressed in a pictorial representation, of which we possess only later examples,

15 showing plants sprouting out of the dead Osiris. We may imagine that the ancient symbol of the corn-Osiris (see pp. 24–25) has here become a rite. Although descriptive texts exist only from much later times (see p. 59), the nucleus of the action must have been the same in both contexts. It concerns the preparation of the bed of Osiris, or garden. This is a coffin-like vessel of granite which stands on supports in a greater basin. In it lies the golden image of the god. The vessel is filled with earth, which is intermixed with sacred material—incense, precious stones, and so on. Seeds of differing kinds are embedded into this mixture, and their germination and growth signify the revival of the dead.[12]

This in plain words is the nucleus of the procedure. But we are insufficiently informed about the accompanying ritual actions. Naturally purification, sacrifice, prayer, and song form part of the ceremonies. The songs are well exemplified in the "Laments of Isis and Nephthys" preserved in a later papyrus. The text gives the following details with regard to ritual preparations: *Beginning of the book roll with verses of the festival of the 'two kites'* [that is, Isis and Nephthys as mourning women] *that is celebrated in the temple of Osiris-Khentamenthes, the great lord of Abydos, on 22nd to 26th* Khoiak [month of the mysteries of Osiris]. *The whole temple shall be cleaned; there shall be fetched two women of pure body, virgins; the hair of their body shall be removed, their heads shall be decorated with wigs... with tamborines in their hands, their names written on their arms as Isis and Nephthys, and they shall sing verses of this book in front of this god."* The songs that follow are sung by the women, partly as solos, partly as duets, and alternating sometimes with the song of the priests. They contain mytho-

58

logical and ritual allusions and also lamentations for the dead husband, which are closely connected with the mourning of the dead at funerals.

Isis sings: *How I long to see you!*
I am your sister Isis, who loves your heart,
[I long] for your love, you distant one.
I inundate the land today [with tears].

Both sing: *Come, beloved one, to us!*
Life escapes us, when we are deprived of you;
Come in peace, O our lord, that we may see you,
Lord, come in peace!
Dispel the mourning from our house,
Associate with us as a man! ...

Isis: *I am a woman who is useful to her brother,*
Your wife and sister of the same mother;
Hasten to me!
Since I desire to see your face, after not seeing it [any more].
There is darkness here with us before my face, even when Ra is in the sky!
The sky has intermingled with the earth and [thus] has shed shadow over the land.
My heart is burning through being parted from you,
My heart is burning because you have turned your back on me,
Although there is no guilt that you have found against me!

Other texts, too, relate to the ceremonies concerned with the "body" of the god, although it is not easy in every single case to infer from the invocations and songs the nature of the pertinent rites. From an "order concerning the transfiguration of the god" comes an invocation which apparently belongs to a later phase of the ceremonies:

O Osiris-Khentamenthes! The gods and the goddesses sit with their heads on their knees [as a sign of mourning] *and long for you to come to them. The people are full of woe, because you are not seen. Come to us, soul which is valiant in eternity! Perfect is your body, your suffering is healed, all evil is driven away, you are made perfect and you are protected, while nothing is missing* [in you]! *Your members are complete, none of them is left out!*
O Osiris-Khentamenthes! Perfect is your head, you with raised arms and high crown, whose hair is real lapis-lazuli!
O Osiris-Khentamenthes! Perfect are your eyes, so that you can see with them like the two maat-goddesses, who protect you!
O Osiris-Khentamenthes! Perfect are your ears, which listen to the prayers of millions!
O Osiris-Khentamenthes! Perfect is your nose, your nose breathes air!
O Osiris-Khentamenthes! Perfect is your mouth, so that you can speak with it. Horus has given you your mouth!

It is clear that the litany names all the parts of the god's body in order to show that he is made whole again. The words at the end suggest the appearance of an image of the god in which he has become present once more.

The god had now found a form of cult congenial to his nature, and this cult form was no longer necessarily linked with the royal cemetery at Abydos, although Abydos, naturally, remained even in later times the scene of the mysteries of Osiris. The great granite bed of Osiris in Cairo, which probably belongs to the Twenty-fifth or Twenty-sixth Dynasty, came from the tomb of Zer, which was regarded as the god's tomb. It shows the dead god on a lion-headed bier, while Isis in the form of a sparrow hawk hovers over his lap receiving the procreative seed. The other squatting birds represent the mourning women.

Since time immemorial the cult of Osiris was spread through the whole of the country; the two ritual procedures discussed were celebrated not only at Abydos but in many great temples of the country during the month of *Khoiak*, the fourth month of the season of inundation.

We are now able to examine the end of the development: in the late Ptolemaic temple of Hathor at Denderah, ritual prescriptions relating to the ceremonies have been recorded in the rooms of Osiris on the temple roof. Unfortunately, we do not possess the ritual texts themselves, that is, a co-ordinated collection of the rites and of the concomitant words. However, we do have the instructions for the preparation of a garden of Osiris, from which we have here reproduced Figure 5. In addition, the instruction contains the relevant dates, and above all the places where the resurrection is celebrated. What emerges is that the cult of Osiris, with certain variations, now encompasses the whole of the land like a net. In Denderah as well as in other contemporary temples, for example in Edfu, there are lists enumerating the relics of Osiris which are dispersed all over Egypt. Thus the left leg is supposed to be in the first Upper Egyptian nome, the right

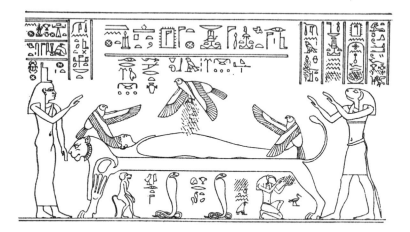

Figure 5. The posthumous procreation of Horus. Relief in the temple of Hathor at Denderah. Isis in the form of a sparrow hawk hovers over the ithyphallic body of Osiris, which is lying on a lion-shaped bier. At the head and foot bird-shaped deities protect the body. Other deities that confer protection and power are pictured under the bier: an ibis-headed god, two serpents, a baboon. At the head of the bier stands "Isis, the great, the mother of the god, the mistress of Denderah who protects her brother." At the foot stands "Horus, the avenger of his father, the son of Isis, who raises his hands over [his] progenitor." Above the body the name of the god is written in a horizontal line: "Osiris-Khentamenthes, the great god, lord of Abydos, the divine god, who rests in Denderah." Underneath are notes concerning the material and the size of the object: "Sycamore wood, covered with gold, the images of the gods made of gold; height one arm length [about 2 feet]." After Mariette, V, Abydos II.

leg in the sixth nome, the jaw in Eileithyaspolis (the third Upper Egyptian nome), the heart in Athribis (the tenth Lower Egyptian nome), and so on. In the course of this worship of the relics of Osiris, unrelated ancient cult symbols are often reinterpreted as relics. This happens, for example, in Letopolis (the second Lower Egyptian nome), where the unintelligible nome sign is interpreted as the god's shoulder blade. In Busiris, the *djed* pillar, probably a kind of sheaf of corn, is said to be the backbone of Osiris; and finally Abydos itself claims to possess his head in the form of its beehive-like nome symbol. But this doctrine applies not only to parts of his mutilated body; the god himself is supposed to be present in many forms in various parts of the country. Long litanies praise his omnipresence and the multiplicity of his forms of appearance. In spite of it all, Abydos remains the most favored place of worship. For, as a late document in the Louvre states: "*Abydos is your town in Upper Egypt; you live there every day, O Osiris-Khentamenthes, you great god, lord of Abydos!*"

V. PLUTARCH'S ACCOUNT OF THE MYTH OF OSIRIS

From the very ancient holy site of the first kings a great stream of vital conviction had risen which fed the whole nation with a belief in another world. But meanwhile the belief in Osiris had extended far beyond Egypt itself. During the last centuries before Christ the eastern world of the Mediterranean as well as the Greeks got hold of Egyptian and Near Eastern beliefs and deities, mingled them with their own religious traditions, and created from it all a new system of beliefs and doctrines to interpret the world. The myth of Osiris was among them. Then and only then did it become a story about gods, a myth in the classical sense of the word. The Greek philosopher-theologian Plutarch used the myth in order to demonstrate the differing ways of interpreting traditional spiritual treasures. The myth of Osiris as he knew it contained a number of non-Egyptian traits alongside Egyptian material. In particular, the journey of Isis to Byblos originates apparently in this mixture of Egyptian and Near Eastern traditions. Nevertheless, we shall end our account with the story as transmitted by Plutarch. The reader himself will be able to judge how it still enshrines Egyptian conceptions, which are clearly recognizable although they are dressed up in a foreign mode.[13]

They say that when Nut secretly had intercourse with Geb, Ra came to know about it and set on her a curse that she should not give birth in any month or year. Then Thoth, falling in love with the goddess, became intimate with her, and then played draughts against the moon-goddess [Selene]. He won the seventieth part of each of her illuminations, and having put together five days out of the whole of his gains, he added them to the three hundred and sixty [days of the year]; these five the Egyptians now call the "additional days" [epagomenai] and on them they celebrate the gods' birthday. For they say that on the first day Osiris was born and that as he was delivered a voice cried out that the Lord of All was coming to the light of day.... On the second day, it is said, Haroeris was born, whom some call Apollo and the elder Horus; and on the third Seth was born, not in the right time or place, but bursting through with a blow he leapt from his mother's side. On the fourth day Isis was born near very moist places and on the fifth Nephthys.... They say that Osiris and Haroeris were the offspring of Ra, Isis of Thoth, and Seth and Nephthys from Geb. For this reason kings used to regard the third of the epagomenal days as unlucky and on it they did no public business nor did they attend to their own persons until night. They say that Nephthys married Seth and that Isis and Osiris, being in love with each other even before they were born, were united in the darkness of the womb....

It is said that Osiris when he was king at once freed the Egyptians from their primitive and brutish manner of life; he showed them how to grow crops, established laws for them, and taught them to worship gods. Later he civilized the whole world as he traversed through it, having very little need of arms, but winning over most of the peoples by beguiling them with persuasive speech together with all manner of song and poetry. That is why the Greeks thought he was the same as Dionysus. When he was away Seth conspired in no way against him since Isis was well on guard and kept careful watch. But on his [Osiris'] return he devised a plot against him, making seventy-two men his fellow conspirators and having as helper a queen who had come from Ethiopia, whom they name Aso. Seth secretly measured the body of Osiris and got made to the corresponding size a beautiful chest which was exquisitely decorated. This he brought to the banqueting hall, and when the guests showed pleasure and admiration at the sight of it, Seth promised playfully that whoever would lie down in it and show that he fitted it should have the chest as a gift. They all tried one by one, and since no one fitted into it, Osiris went in and lay down. Then the conspirators ran and slammed the lid on, and after securing it with bolts from the outside and also with molten lead poured on, they took it out to the river and let it go to the sea by way of the Tanitic mouth, which the Egyptians still call, because of this, hateful and abominable. They say that all these events occurred on the seventeenth day of the month of Athyr, when the sun passes through the scorpion, in the twenty-eighth year of the reign of Osiris. But some state that this was the period of his life rather than of his reign.

The first to hear of the misfortune and to spread the news of its occurrence were the Pans and Satyrs who live near Chemmis, and because of this, the sudden disturbance and excitement of a crowd is still referred to as "panic." When Isis heard of it she cut off there and then one of her locks and put on mourning garment; accordingly the city is called Coptos to this day. [A play on words with the Greek Κόπτειν, "to cut off"; in fact, the name is derived from the Egyptian word *Gbtyw*.] ... *Isis, when she was wandering everywhere in a state of distress, passed by no one without accosting him, and even when she met children, she asked them about the chest. Some of these had happened to see it, and they named the river mouth through which Seth's friends had pushed the box to the sea. For this reason the Egyptians believe that children have the power of divination, and they take omens especially from children's shouts as they play near the temples and say whatever they happen to. When Isis found that Osiris had loved and been intimate with her sister while mistaking her for herself, and saw a proof of this in the garland of melilot which he had left with Nephthys, she searched for the child [of this union]. For Nephthys had exposed it instantly upon giving birth to it, in fear of Seth; and when Isis found it with the help of dogs which had led her on with difficulty and pain, it was reared and became her guard and attendant, being called Anubis. He is said to keep watch over the gods as dogs do over men.*

They say that she learned afterward that the chest had been cast up by the sea in the land of Byblos and that the surf had brought it gently to rest in a heath tree. Having shot up in a short time into a most lovely and tall young tree, the heath enfolded the chest and grew around it, hiding it within itself. Admiring the size of the tree the king [of Byblos] cut off the vaulted part of the trunk which encompassed the coffin, which was not visible, and used it as a pillar to support his roof. They say that Isis heard of this through the divine breath of rumor and came to Byblos, where she sat down near a fountain, dejected and tearful. She spoke to no one except the queen's maids, whom she greeted and welcomed, plaiting their hair and breathing upon their skin a wonderful fragrance which emanated from herself. When the queen saw her maids she was struck with longing for the stranger whose hair and skin breathed ambrosia; and so Isis was sent for and became friendly with the queen and was made nurse of her child....

They say that Isis nursed the child, putting her finger in its mouth instead of her breast, but that in the night she burned the mortal parts of its body, while she herself became a swallow flying around the pillar and making lament until the queen, who had been watching her [once], gave a shriek when she saw her child on fire, and so deprived it of immortality. The goddess then revealed herself and demanded the pillar under the roof. She took it from beneath with the utmost ease and proceeded to cut away the heath tree. This she then covered with linen and poured sweet oil on it, after which she gave it into the keeping of the king and queen. To this day the people of Byblos venerate the wood, which is in the temple of Isis. The goddess then fell upon the coffin and gave such a loud wail that the younger of the king's sons died. The elder son she took with her, and placing the coffin in a boat, she set sail.... As soon as she happened on a deserted spot, there in solitude she opened the chest and pressing her face to that of Osiris, she embraced him and began to cry. She then noticed that the boy had approached silently from behind and had observed her, whereupon she turned round and full of anger gave him a terrible look. The boy was unable to bear the fright, and dropped dead....

Having journeyed to her son Horus who was being brought up in Buto, Isis put the box [with the body of Osiris] aside, and Seth, when he was hunting by night in the moonlight, came upon it. He recognized the body, and having cut it into fourteen parts he scattered them. When she heard of this, Isis searched for them in a papyrus boat, sailing through the marshes. That is why people who sail in papyrus skiffs are not harmed by crocodiles, which show either fear or veneration because of the goddess. From this circumstance arises the fact that many tombs of Osiris are said to exist in Egypt, for the goddess, as she came upon each part, held a burial ceremony. Some deny this, saying that she fashioned images and distributed them to each city, as though she was giving the whole body, so that he [Osiris] might be honored by more people and that Seth, if he overcame Horus, when he sought for the true tomb, might be baffled in his search because many tombs would be mentioned and shown. The only part of Osiris which Isis did not find was his male member; for it had been instantly thrown into the river and the lepidotus, phagrus, and oxyrhynchus had eaten of it, fish which they most of all abhor. In its place Isis fashioned a likeness of it and consecrated the phallus, in honor of which the Egyptians even today hold festival.

Afterward Osiris came to Horus, it is said, from the underworld, and equipped and trained him for battle. Then he questioned him as to what he considered to be the finest action, and Horus said, "To succor one's father and mother when they have suffered wrong." Osiris asked him again what he considered to be the most useful animal for those going out to battle. When Horus replied, "The horse," he was surprised and he queried why he did not name the lion rather than the horse. Horus answered that the lion was helpful to someone in need of aid, but that the horse routed the fugitive and so destroyed completely the force of the enemy. Osiris was pleased on hearing this, thinking that Horus had adequately prepared himself. When many were coming over, as they say, to the side of Horus, there came also Thoueris, Seth's concubine; and a snake which pursued her was cut in pieces by the followers of Horus, for which reason they now throw out a piece of rope in public and cut it up. The battle then lasted for many days and Horus won. When Isis received Seth tied in bonds, she did not kill him, but freed him and let him go. Horus did not take this at all calmly, but laying hands on his mother he ripped off the crown from her head. Thoth, however, put on her instead a cow-headed helmet. When Seth brought a charge of illegitimacy against Horus, Thoth helped Horus, and the latter was judged by the gods to be legitimate. Seth was defeated in two other battles, and Isis, having sexual union with Osiris after his death, bore Harpocrates, prematurely delivered and weak in his lower limbs.

Plutarch's "divine story" represents a contamination of Egyptian and Near Eastern elements. It has freed itself from the cult actions and ritual celebrations in which the myth originally grew. Plutarch here speaks for a type of priestly attitude that was possible only in the late era. For him the myth has become a profound record of prehistoric events, and he used the record in order to demonstrate the exegetical methods which he regarded as applicable to traditional myths. In all this we recognize the far-reaching difference between the Egyptian and the Greek attitude. In Egypt, the story of Osiris was a continually repeated event; it was always contemporary and therefore it was always amenable to change. For the Greeks it had become an unchangeable tradition, and its significance for life derived from interpretations and speculations of various kinds. It was by way of these that the Occident first became acquainted with Egyptian ideas and Egyptian gods; the latter enriched Occidental thought with many a concept and kept alive an admittedly uncertain knowledge of ancient Egypt, which ultimately contributed to the growth of the science of Egyptology.

NOTES

1. The name Abydos belonged originally to a town near the Hellespont. The Greeks transferred it to the Egyptian town whose Egyptian name, in their time, sounded something like "Ebot." To the Greek ear this seemed similar to the name Abydos, with which they were familiar.

2. The place Naqada, after which the prehistoric cultures have been named, is also situated in the region where east-west communications were active.

3. The reading "Sekhen" has recently been suggested instead of an earlier reading "Ka." Both of them are uncertain, and the meaning of the name is not known in either case.

4. Theoretically one must differentiate between the royal necropolis, the administrative center, and the residence, of which we know nothing in this period.

5. The reading and interpretation of most names of this period are uncertain.

6. The sacred baboon is to be basically distinguished from the apes, who appear in groups, for example, those who worship the rising sun, and also from other apelike creatures who are seen occasionally in the company of gods.

7. The situation of the temple of Khentamenthes is not unlike that of the temple of King Snofru at Dahshur in its relation to the ascending road leading to the pyramid: here too the temple lies at right angles to the path and opens to it. As a result, a procession on its way to the pyramid must pass in front of it.

8. In theory, all essential ritual actions in the cult of the gods were executed by the king himself. In practice, suitable officials and authorized persons had to represent him as the need arose. The idea of the priest as a representative who acts for the king underlies the theory of priesthood right up to the Late Period.

9. The general sequence of buildings is here from north to south, as with the royal mortuary temples of the New Kingdom in the western town of Thebes.

10. The title "house of millions of years" is the special name assigned to the mortuary temples, as we well know from such temples of the New Kingdom at Thebes.

11. It is interesting to note that during the lifetime of his father he had the work executed in the style of the Sety period. Only afterward did he use the style of his own period, that is, the Ramesside style, the main characteristics of which we have briefly enumerated.

12. Smaller and more modest imitations occasionally found in tombs convey an impression of these beds of Osiris. The example here (plate 15) comes from the tomb of Tut-ankh-amon, but similar objects have also been discovered in private tombs.

13. The Greek text sometimes uses the names of Greek gods. These I have replaced with their Egyptian equivalents. Short digressions in the story have been left out here.

NOTES TO THE COLORPLATES

Colorplate I

SHRINE OF ANUBIS. From the tomb of King Tut-ankh-amon (1347–1338 B.C.). Western Thebes, Valley of the Kings (Biban el Moluk), tomb 62. Late 18th Dynasty, New Kingdom. Guide T.447, Cairo Museum.

The god of the dead Anubis lies on a shrine which stands on a sledge. The animal is made of wood, and eyes, ears, nostrils, and neck decoration are inlaid in different materials. The jackal-like animal, who was regarded as guardian of the cemetery, shows by his watchful head and the strained attitude of his body that he is wide awake. The wooden shrine in the form of a pylon is covered with gold and carries inscriptions on the edges as well as groups of symbols, the *djed* pillar and the "blood of Isis." The *djed* pillar, originally perhaps a sheaf of corn, was treated as a symbol of eternity. The bow, which is called "blood of Isis," probably belongs to the numerous group of knot amulets whose main meaning is the idea of tying, holding, and strengthening. Only from the time of the New Kingdom was it accepted in Egypt as a symbol of Isis; the connection with the blood of the goddess is not evident.

Colorplate II

LANDSCAPE NEAR EL KHERBE, TO THE NORTH OF THE TEMPLE OF SETY I AT ABYDOS.

The picture shows the undulating desert landscape between the modern village of El Kherbe and the mountain slope in the west. The dark brick walls in the right of the picture belong to the ancient buildings of the 1st Dynasty behind the temple of Khentamenthes at Abydos. The temple itself was situated behind the sand hills, which begin on the left.

Colorplate III

OSIRIS BETWEEN *IMY-UT* SYMBOLS. From the tomb of Sen-Nedjem. Western Thebes, Deir el Medineh, tomb 1. 20th Dynasty, New Kingdom (1186–1070 B.C.).

Under a baldachin, which is held up by wooden plant-shaped columns, stands Osiris on a pedestal shaped like the hieroglyph for "truth"; in front of him is an offering table with a water jug and a bunch of flowers. To his right and left are the apotropaic eyes which keep evil away. On both sides of the columns stand two *imy-ut* symbols, each represented as a stick with an animal skin tied to it and standing in a basin. The original meaning of the name was probably "he who is in the wrapping." But the meaning of the object is quite uncertain. Among other things, it is connected with jackal-shaped gods of the cemetery and with funerary gods.

Colorplate IV

KING AY COMPLETES THE RITUAL OF THE OPENING OF THE MOUTH ON KING TUT-ANKH-AMON, WHO IS REPRESENTED AS OSIRIS. From the tomb of King Tut-ankh-amon (1347–1338 B.C.). Western Thebes, Valley of the Kings (Biban el Moluk), tomb 62. Late 18th Dynasty, New Kingdom.

The walls of the king's burial chamber are decorated with scenes of offerings and ceremonies of transfiguration. Among them is the representation of the "opening of the mouth," reproduced here. This is a ritual that aims at reviving a statue or a mummy. To the left is Tut-ankh-amon in the form of Osiris, and in front of him is his successor Ay completing the ritual. As a king, Ay wears the blue crown, and as an acting priest he wears the leopard skin. He holds with both hands an adz, a joiner's tool that plays a great part in this ritual, which has its ultimate origin in the work of craftsmen. On a table between the two figures more ritual objects are displayed, among them another adz and an ostrich feather, while beneath these is a feather-like symbol that may originally have been a flint knife; above them are five cups with grains of natron.

Colorplate V

FROM THE TOMB OF KING RAMESSES I (1306–1304 B.C.). Western Thebes, Valley of the Kings (Biban el Moluk), tomb 16. Beginning of the 19th Dynasty, New Kingdom.

On the left wall in the picture stands Maat. The transfigured king has his back to her and turns to the god of Memphis, Ptah, as the lord of the truth; behind Ptah is the *djed* pillar, a symbol of duration and immortality. On the right wall Ramesses is led by the god Anubis (in front of him) and the god Horus (behind him), so that he may enter the underworld as a king who has become Osiris.

Colorplate VI

SEN-NEDJEM AND HIS WIFE PRAYING AND THE GODDESS OF THE SYCAMORE. From the tomb of Sen-Nedjem. Western Thebes, Deir el Medineh, tomb 1. 20th Dynasty, New Kingdom (1186–1070 B.C.).

To the left the deceased and his wife pray before five gods under a starry sky with sun disk. On the right they receive food from the goddess of the sycamore. The theme is often represented in the tombs of Thebes, but the bond between tree and goddess is rarely depicted as convincingly and impressively as in this tomb painting.

Colorplate VII

ISIS, SETY I AS OSIRIS, AND THE *YUN-MUTEF* PRIEST. Temple of King Sety I (1304–1290 B.C.) at Abydos. From a small chapel dedicated to Osiris, the middle one of three chapels to the northwest of the hall of Osiris.

The deceased King Sety, decorated as Osiris, receives the incense offering from the *yun-mutef* priest. Behind the priest stands Isis wearing the crown of Hathor on her head and holding the sistrum and *menit* necklace of Hathor in her hands.

Colorplate VIII

KING SETY I IN FRONT OF THE MUMMY-SHAPED OSIRIS-KHENTAMENTHES. From the tomb of King Sety I (1304–1290 B.C.). Western Thebes, Valley of the Kings (Biban el Moluk), tomb 17. From the left of the two rear pillars in the hall of the six pillars.

NOTES TO THE BLACK-AND-WHITE PLATES

Plate 1

KING CHEOPS. Seated ivory figure. Height 2 inches. From Abydos. 4th Dynasty, Old Kingdom (2600–2480 B.C.). Cairo Museum.

This figurine is the only completely preserved piece of sculpture of the builder of the largest pyramid. It was found by Flinders Petrie in 1902 in the district of the temple of Khentamenthes at Abydos. The king is wearing the red crown, the upper part of which is broken away; his right hand holds the whip, his left hand being extended on his thigh. He wears a short kilt. His name is engraved on the front of the cubic seat. In spite of its smallness, the work expresses something of the energy and enterprise that one would like to ascribe to this ruler. In a general way it recalls the statue of Mentuhotep II (Neb-hepet-ra) from Deir el Bahari (Colorplate IX).

Plate 2

SQUATTING BABOON. From Abydos. Archaic Period, c. 3000–2778 B.C. Cairo Museum.

This is one of the offering gifts found in the precincts of the temple of Khentamenthes. Quite apart from its religious significance, it is an impressive example of the art of rendering the typical features of an animal in a simplified but convincing form, an art that is especially characteristic of the Archaic Period.

Plate 3

FALSE DOOR IN THE TOMB OF MEHU AT SAQQARAH. 6th Dynasty, Old Kingdom (2350–2190 B.C.).

The false door acts as an intermediary between the offering person in this world and the dead in the other world. A much-diminished doorway with door jambs to the right and left bearing the names of the deceased is all that is now left of the imitation of the door itself. Below the names on each side is a representation of the deceased. His name stands also above the entrance; and above this again is a representation of the deceased at the offering table. Here he is shown sitting before a table that is covered with upright palm leaves. Parts of the offering list with names and titles are written above it. The false door and the offering list are two elements usually combined in tomb decoration. They are here enclosed in a bigger framework of three horizontal lines with offering prayers and four vertical lines, right and left, with offering prayers, titles, names, and two additional pictures of Mehu on each side.

Plate 4

FROM THE TOMB OF THE CHANCELLOR HARHO-TEP. Western Thebes, Deir el Bahari, tomb 314. 11th Dynasty, Middle Kingdom (2133–1992 B.C.). From the coffin of Harho-tep. Guide 300, Cairo Museum.

The limestone sarcophagus and the walls of the burial chamber to right and left are covered with prayers and spells of the Coffin Texts. Under the richly decorated cornice a horizontal line gives the name of Harhotep and the funerary prayer. Beneath it the Coffin Texts are inscribed in cursive writing. The spells themselves are written in vertical columns, while their titles are given in a horizontal line above, at the beginning of each spell. The titles here pictured read from left to right: "The fetching of the ferry boat"; "The coming out by day"; "The transfiguration in heaven."

Plate 5

HORUS AND SETH. From the funerary temple of the pyramid of King Sesostris I (1971–1928 B.C.) near Lisht. 12th Dynasty, Middle Kingdom. Relief on the throne of one of the ten seated statues of the king. Exh. 301, Cairo Museum.

The two gods tie the heraldic plants of Upper and Lower Egypt around the hieroglyphic sign which signifies "unite." On top of this sign is the king's name ring, or cartouche. The picture symbolizes the union of the two countries, that is, Upper and Lower Egypt, as an achievement of the ruler. Therefore the two gods represent the two halves of the country; Horus stands for Lower Egypt (its symbol is the papyrus plant) and Seth for Upper Egypt (its symbol being the lotus plant).

Plate 6

STELA OF AMEN-EM-ONE, THE SUPERVISOR OF THE CRAFTSMEN OF THE LORD OF THE TWO LANDS. Limestone. Late 18th Dynasty, New Kingdom (second half of the 14th century B.C.). Inv. 11732, Cairo Museum.

The composition and theme of this stela are typical of its era. The upper part of the outer frame comprises two symmetrical scenes in a horizontal line which show in the corners the deceased and his wife adoring (the invisible) Osiris, while the middle part is taken up by symbols of good luck. On each side there are two vertical lines with inscriptions; they contain the offering prayer four times and name the gods Ra-Harakhte-Atum, the god of heaven; Hathor, mistress of the sycamore, the Memphite protective goddess of the dead; Ptah-Sokar-Osiris, the Memphite funerary triad; and "the great ennead of the necropolis." The reliefs inside the frame are again subdivided. The upper scene shows on the right the deceased and his wife worshiping Ra-Harakhte-Atum, the sun-god and creator-god; and on the left the deceased and his wife are worshiping Osiris-Khentamenthes, the god of the dead. In the lower register husband and wife are shown sitting comfortably on chairs. A monkey squats under the seat of the wife beside a fruit basket eating a fruit. The couple receive offerings and gifts from eleven persons, of whom the first three are named as their sons. An inscription under the seats of the parents names the son Ptahmose as donor of the monument. The whole work must be regarded, in view of its beauty and meticulous execution, as one of the masterpieces of the 18th Dynasty.

Plate 7

STELA OF IPUYA, CHIEF GOLDSMITH. Limestone. From Abydos. 19th Dynasty, New Kingdom (1306–1186 B.C.). Inv. 11751, Cairo Museum.

The upper scene shows the deceased and his wife in front of Osiris; by the erection of this monument in Abydos they hope to share in his resurrection. In the lower scene they themselves receive prayers and offerings from their three sons. The composition and theme of this stela are the same as those in the stela of Amen-em-one (Plate 6). But a comparison of the two works shows clearly that the artistic perfection of the late 18th Dynasty was beyond the reach of this 19th Dynasty piece.

Plate 8

JUDGMENT OF THE DEAD. From the temple of Deir el Medineh in western Thebes, begun under Ptolemy IV (Philopator; 221–204 B.C.), completed under Ptolemy VIII (Euergetes II; 145–116 B.C.). The southern sanctuary. (The representations are divided into two intersecting halves.)

This little Ptolemaic temple gives more attention to the afterlife and to the gods of the dead than any other temple on the western bank of Thebes, more even than the royal mortuary temples. The fact indicates clearly the final victory of Osiris over the royal god Amon even here in Thebes. We find here a representation of the judgment of the dead that corresponds in all details with the pictures of the Book of the Dead (cf. Plate 9). Above each scene, divided into two rows, are the forty-two demons of judgment, with a deceased person before them. Underneath are two *maat*-goddesses who introduce the deceased. Anubis and Horus are weighing the heart; Thoth stands with writing palette and reed; a nameless child-god is sitting on a scepter; there is also the "devouring" deity, and finally Osiris himself on his throne with the *imy-ut* symbol of the embalming god before him, as well as a lotus flower with the four gods of the canopic jars (which contain the intestines): Hapi, Amset, Dua-mutef, and Kebeh-senuf.

The whole representation is so divided that the figure of the god Thoth appears twice, once in the right-hand corner at the end of the upper picture and then again at the beginning in the left corner of the lower picture.

Plate 9

FROM THE BOOK OF THE DEAD OF ZOSER, PRIEST OF BASTET AT MEMPHIS. From Saqqarah. Ptolemaic Period (323–30 B.C.). Exh. 6335, Cairo Museum.

The papyrus leaf shows the scene of the judgment of the dead in front of "Osiris Khentamenthes, the great god the lord of Abydos, the lord of infinity and the ruler of eternity," who is shown on the left enthroned in a shrine. The whole scene takes place in a pillared hall, which the Egyptians name the "hall of the two truths." In the upper register forty-two demons are represented who are faced by the deceased. On the right of the main scene appears the deceased, who is led into the hall by Maat, the personification of justice and truth. Then follows the scene of the weighing, in which the heart (left) is weighed against the figure of Maat (right) on a huge standing pair of scales. The weighing is supervised by Horus and the funerary god Anubis. Thoth, "the twice great, the lord of Hermopolis, lord of the divine word, who satisfies the gods," records the result with reed and palette. At his side is the tiny figure of an unnamed god, who is squatting on a scepter. The demon "devourer" sits on a high bench; those who do not pass the examination fall into his power. The picture belongs to Spell 125 of the Book of the Dead, which consists mainly of the "negative confession," a long enumeration of transgressions and crimes, of which, according to his claim, the deceased is not guilty.

Plate 10

FROM THE TOMB OF PASHEDU. Western Thebes, Deir el Medineh, tomb 3. 20th Dynasty, New Kingdom (1186–1070 B.C.). Pashedu before Osiris.

The picture is dominated by the figure of Osiris, who is sitting in front of a mountain ridge; he is called "king of the living, lord forever, ruler of eternity." Behind his throne kneels the deceased in adoration. Above him is the healing eye, which is equipped with arms to hold a vessel with two burning wicks. On the far left is an excellently drawn falcon. Before Osiris squats a demon with a vessel that is identical with that of the eye. This scene signifies the lighting of the torch, a ritual action which is transferred into the other world for the benefit of Osiris and the dead.

Plate 11

FROM THE TOMB OF SEN-NEDJEM. Western Thebes, Deir el Medineh, tomb 1. 20th Dynasty, New Kingdom (1186–1070 B.C.). Sen-Nedjem and his wife before the gods of the underworld.

In the rounded vault above are two decorated jackals. Beneath them the deceased and his wife worship the gods of the underworld, who are squatting in two rows on little pedestals inside a shrine. The upper row is led by Osiris, the lower by Ra. An invocation is written between the two rows with the purpose of giving the dead power and greatness with the gods and free movement in the underworld.

Plate 12

FROM THE TOMB OF INHER-KHA. Western Thebes, Deir el Medineh, tomb 299. 20th Dynasty, New Kingdom (1186–1070 B.C.).

Above: The deceased in the rich festival garment of his period, with a long curly wig, kneels in prayer before four jackals "which draw the barque of Ra." They are supposed to grant him participation in the journey of the god and in his offerings.

Below: The deceased prays before three gods with jackal heads, who are called the "souls of the hidden world"; he asks for safety and security in the afterlife.

Plate 13

FROM THE TEMPLE OF KING SETY I (1304–1290 B.C.)

IN ABYDOS. FROM THE CHAPEL OF OSIRIS. Processional barque *(above)* and processional shrine with standards *(below)*.

Above: The nome symbol of the eighth Upper Egyptian nome appears on top of a shrine in the processional barque. At this time the beehive-shaped symbol was interpreted as the reliquary of the head of Osiris. It is crowned with the head of a god and high feathers. The bow of the barque also ends in the head of a god, and the stern in a lotus flower. Little figures of gods stand on top of the barque and on top of the shrine. Below the barque and in front of it stand tables with flowers and offering gifts. Behind its bow and stern are two big fans with ostrich feathers.

Below: The nome symbol appears as in the other picture, but without human head and not on a barque, but on a portable stand in a shrine. It is here called "Osiris-Khentamenthes, lord of Abydos, in the temple of King Men-Maat-Ra [that is, Sety I]." In front of the symbol are five upright standards, which were carried before it during a procession, and displayed images of the gods Wepwawet of Upper and Lower Egypt, Thoth, Horus, and Onuris. They prepare the way for the sacred object. The king approaches from the left offering water and incense.

Plate 14
THE SO-CALLED OSIREION NEAR THE TEMPLE OF KING SETY I (1304–1290 B.C.) IN ABYDOS.

The cenotaph of Sety I was built in imitation of the tomb of Osiris. It lies behind the temple of Sety I, the rear wall of which can be seen in the background. The part here visible was originally underground. The row of pillars surrounds the central hall, which was planned as an island containing the god's tomb.

Plate 15
CORN-OSIRIS. From the tomb of King Tut-ankh-amon (1347–1338 B.C.). Western Thebes, Valley of the Kings (Biban el Moluk), tomb 62. 18th Dynasty, New Kingdom. Exh. T. 1064, Cairo Museum.

A wooden figure imitating the outline of Osiris is filled with earth and seed corn. The germinating seed symbolizes the resurrection of the god of fertility.

Plates 16 and 17
FROM THE SOKAR ROOM IN THE TEMPLE OF KING SETY I (1304–1290 B.C.) IN ABYDOS.

Plate 16. SOKAR-OSIRIS. The god "Sokar-Osiris, who is in his barque," lies ithyphallic on a lion-headed bed. The Memphite earth-god Sokar was regarded as a form of the subterranean fertility-god Osiris because of his connection with agriculture and especially with sowing. For this reason he appears here in the form of the dead god in the moment of awakening, with Isis clasping his head and Horus approaching his feet. Under the bed King Sety I is represented four times presenting a jar to each of the gods of embalming (the gods of the canopic jars: Hapi, Amset, Dua-mutef, and Kebeh-senuf).

Plate 17. OSIRIS-WENNOFER. It is here said of the dead god: "Osiris-Wennofer in the Sokar room; may he give life and happiness to King Men-Maat-Ra [that is, Sety I]." He is lying ithyphallic on a lion-headed bier; above his body hovers Isis as a sparrow hawk in the process of conceiving her son from him. The same goddess stands in human form behind his head, and Horus at his feet. Four protective deities are represented under the bed. (Isis and Nephthys also appear as the two kites behind his head and feet.)

Plates 18 and 19 *top*
OSIRIS BED WITH ISIS AS A SPARROW HAWK CONCEIVING HER SON HORUS FROM OSIRIS. Black granite. From Abydos. Late Period, probably Saitic Period (26th Dynasty, 663–525 B.C.). Exh. 621, Cairo Museum.

This monument was found by Amélineau in Abydos in the tomb of King Zer of the 1st Dynasty. The inscription which runs around the top of the bed assigns a number of epithets to Osiris. The name of the king who dedicated the monument is destroyed, and an exact dating is therefore impossible. But there can be little doubt that it belongs to the Late Period. The god lies on a bier which has lion heads and lion feet. On his body rests Isis in the form of a sparrow hawk in the process of conceiving her son Horus. At the feet and head of the god are four more birds who protect him with their wings.

Plates 19 *below* and 20
FROM THE INNER ROOM OF THE OSIRIS CHAMBERS ON THE ROOF OF THE HATHOR TEMPLE AT DENDERAH. Begun under Ptolemy X (Alexander I; 80 B.C.), completed mainly under Cleopatra VII, the Great (47–44 to 30 B.C.).

Two sets of rooms on the temple roof served for the performance of the god's resurrection festival. The objects employed during this celebration are depicted on the walls, and inscribed texts indicate their use.

Plate 19 *below*. The four sides of the shaftlike dormer window in the roof are each decorated with a representation of the divine mummy on the bier. Above it are inscribed the beginnings of hymns to the god, which praise his fertile power even in death.

Plate 20 *top*. The picture shows the ithyphallic mummy of the god lying on the lion bier; above him hovers Isis in the form of a sparrow hawk. Two figures of the mourning Isis and Nephthys kneel at his head and feet. The inscription points out that these reliefs do not represent the three gods themselves but only imitations made of gold with inlaid eyes (cf. the text with Figure 5).

Plate 20 *below*. Theme and picture are fundamentally the same as above. The Osiris shown here, also a golden figure, is especially the Osiris of Coptos. The festive ritual of Denderah includes the special rites for all important centers in the country, which differ from each other only in details.

PLATES

Plate 1. King Cheops. Seated ivory figure. Height 2 inches. From Abydos. 4th Dynasty, Old Kingdom (2600–2480 B.C.). Cairo Museum.

Plate 2. Squatting baboon. From Abydos. Archaic Period, c. 3000–2778 B.C. Cairo Museum.

Plate 3. False door in the tomb of Mehu at Saqqarah. 6th Dynasty, Old Kingdom (2350–2190 B.C.).

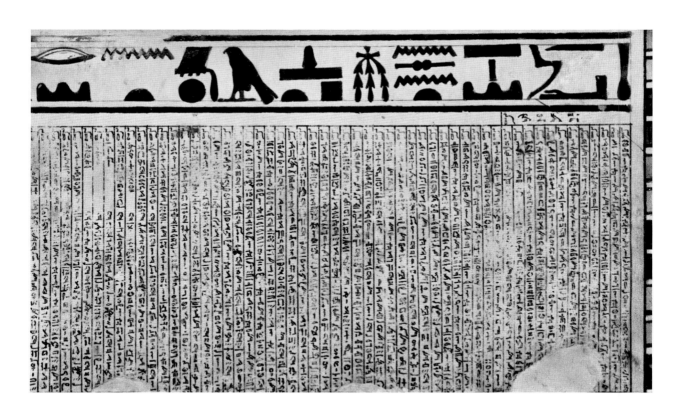

Plate 4. Funerary prayer and Coffin Texts from the coffin of the chancellor Harhotep. From his tomb in Western Thebes, Deir el Bahari. 11th Dynasty, Middle Kingdom (2133–1992 B.C.). Cairo Museum.

Plate 5. Horus and Seth. From the funerary temple of the pyramid of King Sesostris I (1971–1928 B.C.) near Lisht.
Relief on the throne of one of the ten seated statues of the king. 12th Dynasty, Middle Kingdom. Cairo Museum.

Plate 6. Stela of Amen-em-one, the supervisor of the craftsmen of the lord of the two lands. Limestone. Late 18th Dynasty, New Kingdom (second half of the 14th century B.C.). Cairo Museum.

Plate 7. Stela of Ipuya, chief goldsmith. Limestone. From Abydos. 19th Dynasty, New Kingdom (1306–1186 B.C.).
Cairo Museum.

Plate 8. Judgment of the dead. From the temple of Deir el Medineh in western Thebes, begun under Ptolemy IV (Philopator; 221–204 B.C.), completed under Ptolemy VIII (Euergetes II; 145–116 B.C.). The southern sanctuary. (The representations are divided into two intersecting halves.)

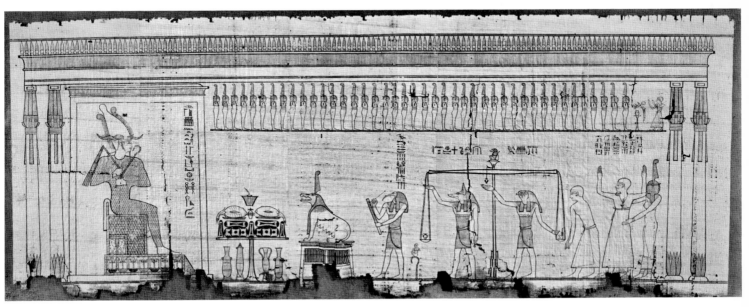

Plate 9. From the Book of the Dead of Zoser, priest of Bastet at Memphis. From Saqqarah. Ptolemaic Period (323–30 B.C.). Cairo Museum.

Plate 10. Pashedu before Osiris. From the tomb of Pashedu. Western Thebes, Deir el Medineh. 20th Dynasty, New Kingdom (1186–1070 B.C.).

Plate 11. Sen-Nedjem and his wife before the gods of the underworld. From the tomb of Sen-Nedjem. Western Thebes, Deir el Medineh. 20th Dynasty, New Kingdom (1186–1070 B.C.).

Plate 12. From the tomb of Inher-kha. Western Thebes, Deir el Medineh. 20th Dynasty, New Kingdom (1186–1070 B.C.). *Above:* The deceased in front of four jackals "who draw the barque of Ra." *Below:* The deceased in front of three jackal-headed gods, the "souls of the hidden world."

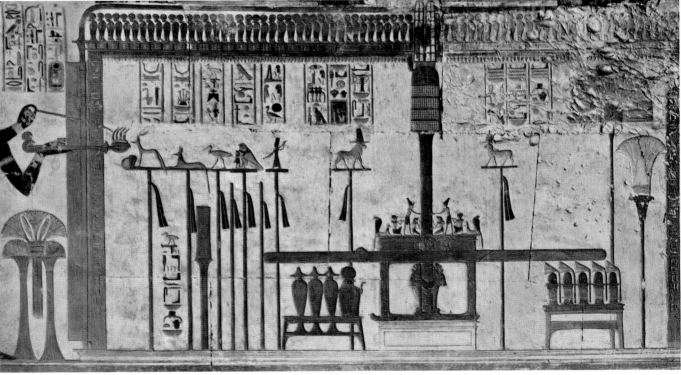

Plate 13. From the Osiris chapel in the temple of King Sety I (1304–1290 B.C.) in Abydos. *Above:* Processional barque. *Below:* Processional shrine with standards.

Plate 14. The so-called Osireion near the temple of King Sety I (1304–1290 B.C.) in Abydos.

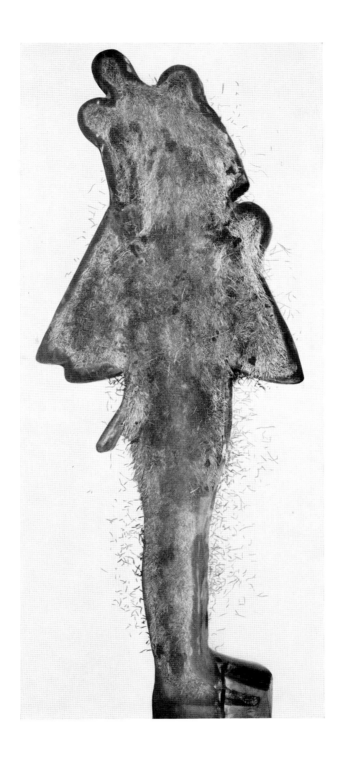

Plate 15. Corn-Osiris. From the tomb of King Tut-ankh-amon (1347–1338 B.C.). Western Thebes, Valley of the Kings (Biban el Moluk). 18th Dynasty, New Kingdom. Cairo Museum.

Plate 16. Sokar-Osiris. From the Sokar room in the temple of King Sety I (1304–1290 B.C.) in Abydos.

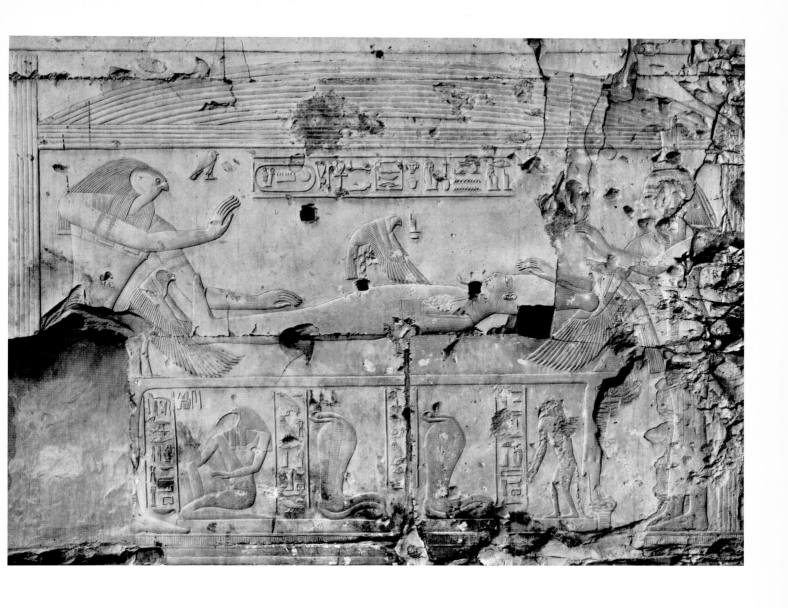

Plate 17. Osiris-Wennofer. From the Sokar room in the temple of King Sety I (1304–1290 B.C.) in Abydos.

Plates 18 and 19 *top*. Osiris bed with Isis as a sparrow hawk conceiving her son Horus from Osiris. Black granite. From Abydos. Late Period, probably Saitic Period (26th Dynasty, 663–525 B.C.). Cairo Museum.

Plate 19 *below*. Osiris. From the Hathor temple at Denderah, begun under Ptolemy X (Alexander I; 80 B.C.), completed mainly under Cleopatra VII, the Great (47–44 to 30 B.C.).

Plate 20. Osiris with Isis as female hawk. From the Hathor temple at Denderah, begun under Ptolemy X (Alexander I; 80 B.C.), completed mainly under Cleopatra VII, the Great (47–44 to 30 B.C.).

PART TWO

AMON

I. HISTORICAL SURVEY
PREHISTORY OF THEBES

"Thebes of a hundred gates" arose in a part of the country which was practically indistinguishable from any other Nile landscape, and no special reason seems to have existed which could predestine it to achieve its later greatness. Toward the east the river valley extends for about six miles before it reaches the desert plateau. In the distance three distinctive mountain tops limit the view. The western river side is narrowed by the curved limestone massif, which withdraws in a westerly direction toward the south, while it keeps an even distance from the river toward the north until it reaches Denderah. Near Gebelein, twenty miles to the south of Luxor, the valley narrows noticeably. It seems only natural that the administrative power of the Theban nome should have terminated here in historical times. But in the northern direction the landscape is completely open.

According to the ancient Egyptian division of administration, the region was counted as the fourth Upper Egyptian nome, and its capital was Armant-Hermonthis, which is situated about eight miles south of Luxor.

There is nothing particularly distinctive in the landscape; nor does anything emerge in the historical past until the end of the third millennium B.C. to suggest or justify the later importance of the name of Thebes.

The presence of man can be noticed early in this region. Flint tools found in the western mountains attest the presence of Paleolithic men, who here eked out a living at a time when the bottom of the valley was still higher than it became in the historical period and when the valley plain was boggy and uninhabitable. An extensive late prehistoric cemetery (fourth millennium B.C.) was excavated west of Armant in 1926 and afterward, and single finds testify also to Neolithic settlements.

But what do we know of the historic foundation of this region? Above all, what do we know of its cults during the Old Kingdom, when the center of government as well as the royal residence were in the north near Memphis and when the first pyramids were built?

Like all other administrative regions of the kingdom (the nomes), the fourth Upper Egyptian nome had a heraldic sign: it was a hooked stick, possibly a shepherd's stick (rather like a crook). Its name was phonetically the same as the Egyptian word for "happiness." Perhaps we may conclude from this that a pastoral economy was characteristic of this district when it first came under the central administration. The relatively broad expanse to the northeast and southwest of Luxor would offer a fitting locale for such an economy. Another element of the later cult tradition may also be considered in this connection, namely, the sacred cow of Deir el Bahari, with its cavelike sanctuary between the later mortuary temples of Mentuhotep and Hatshepsut. It may seem a strange idea to worship a cow in a mountain cave; but an explanation is forthcoming if we think of the sacred site as the offering place of a cattle-breeding people. During the summer when the pastures of the west had dried out, these people may have driven their cattle to graze in the well-watered valley. Conditions of this kind may still have existed during the fourth millennium. The oasis roads which end here would have kept open the connection with the western desert. Finally, a sacred white bull may also be claimed for this oldest religious stratum. In historical times it was worshiped at Armant, Tod, and Medamud, and it was regarded as the sacred animal of the god Monthu, in the same way as the Apis was the sacred animal of the god Ptah at Memphis.

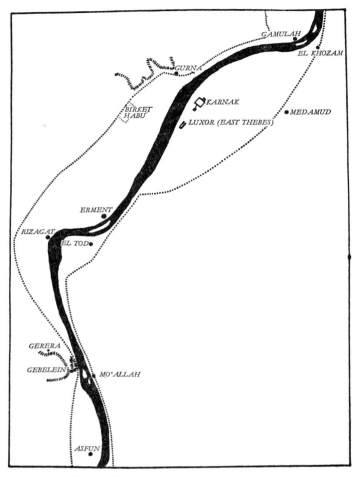

Figure 6. The district of the Theban nome. After E. Otto.

Over this oldest prehistoric stratum there accumulated during the Old Kingdom a second stratum, which in some ways was the historical basis of all that followed. Now we get to know Monthu of Armant-Hermonthis as a nome god, a falcon-god. The meaning of his name and his original significance are unknown, but he is worshiped in several parts of the nome. In Armant there stands at his side a goddess, Tanenet, and later, in the New Kingdom and afterward, a second goddess, Rat-taui, "the female Ra of the two lands." Very little can be ascertained about what happened during the Old Kingdom in the district of the later town of Thebes. Recently doubts have arisen as to whether the vulture-goddess Mut at the lake of Asheru is really an ancient local goddess (see p. 90). Possibly the god Khonsu was already worshiped in the vicinity, but we are unable to dwell with any certainty on his significance and his original shape. From a relatively early time he was regarded as a moon-god.

And what existed on the western bank of the river where the funerary temples of the rulers of the New Kingdom were later to rise? The possibly very ancient sanctuary at Deir el Bahari has already been mentioned. In front of it, near El Khokha, are very modest tombs belonging to the end of the Old Kingdom. The precinct of the later temple of Medinet Habu was also perhaps a sacred site; it is possible that from ancient

76

times a snake was worshiped here in a sanctuary, a deity connected in Egyptian thought with the concept of the primeval and the pre-existent.

There is very little, therefore, that can be said about the "prehistory" of Thebes, and nothing of it predestined the region for its later fame. Not even the name of the town or its sanctuaries occur in the lists or other documents of the more ancient period.

THE FOUNDING OF THEBES

The existence of the town of Thebes is due to a certain historical situation; this statement can be briefly explained as follows: After the Sixth Dynasty the kingdom dissolved into an Upper Egyptian part, where independent nomarchs were fighting with each other, and a northern half, ruled by the weak kings of Heracleopolis. According to the testimony of contemporary inscriptions, this state of affairs caused famine, social unrest, and disorder tantamount to civil war. This was especially true of the long stretch of Upper Egypt, where power was divided and where the parts were dependent, more so than in Lower Egypt, on provisions from other areas. After about a century the nomarchs of Armant-Hermonthis succeeded, step by step, through fighting and through alliances with rivals, in gaining domination first over Upper Egypt and then over the whole of Egypt. The conclusion of the new "union of the land" was the work of the later King

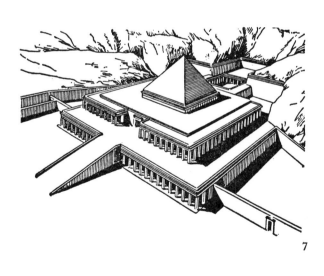

7

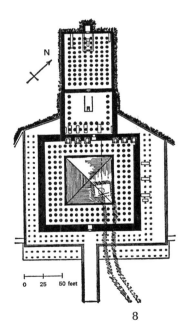

8

Figures 7 and 8. The mortuary temples of Mentuhotep (Neb-hepet-ra) on the mountain slope of Deir el Bahari. *Figure 7:* Western Thebes, reconstruction. After Koepf, 1955. *Figure 8:* Ground plan, relating to three planes. In the southeast: The lowest plane with the front hypostyle hall, which is intersected by the ramp as a median line. Attached is the plan of the temple building proper and the hypostyle halls, which surround it on three sides, as well as the small pillared courtyard to the northwest and the hall with sanctuary which is situated inside the rock. The pyramid is on the uppermost plane. Based on Naville and Hall, 1903–7.

IX Mentuhotep II (Neb-hepet-ra; the first name contains that of the god Monthu) about 2050 B.C. He must be considered as the real founder of the town of Thebes, which received its name from the nome. We do not know why the king preferred not to keep Armant-Hermonthis as his center, transferring the capital instead to the northern frontier of the nome. Yet the forerunner of the later temple of Karnak must have been founded during this period, although no archaeological remains of it are known. The name of the temple occurs for the first time on a stela from Qurneh which must probably be dated from the time of Mentuhotep. Opposite it, on the western bank on the mountain slope of Deir el Bahari, Mentuhotep built his mortuary

XIII, Figs. 7, 8   monument. Two kings of the same name who succeeded him reigned for only a short time; the tomb of the penultimate Mentuhotep was begun south of the site of Deir el Bahari, but remained unfinished. In addition, another site about two and a half miles north of Deir el Bahari, which is called the temple of Thoth, may be his work. It is situated on top of a rock beyond the way to the Valley of the Kings. About ten years after the death of the Mentuhotep who united the kingdom, a new dynasty ascended the throne that was perhaps connected with the last viziers of Mentuhotep's era. This was the Twelfth Dynasty. Its kings, who bear alternatively the names Amenemhat and Sesostris, transferred the residence to the north for political reasons. It was here, in the region of Lisht, that they built their mortuary monuments in the form of pyramids. They continued, nonetheless, to build at Thebes as well, and their names express their feeling of belonging to this town: Amenemhat has the name of the god Amon as its first element, while Sesostris includes the name of a Theban goddess.

THEBES DURING THE MIDDLE KINGDOM

The few known facts concerning the foundation of Thebes in no way justify the later importance of the town. Why did it not sink back again into the state of an unimportant provincial town after its rise in the Eleventh Dynasty? It does not seem to have played an eminent part in the political life of the Middle Kingdom, and its role during the time of Mentuhotep, although it was important for the whole of Egypt, could easily have remained an isolated episode.

There exist varying reasons for the contrary development of events, but we are able to grasp only a few of them. Most important is the fact that the new foundation of the kingdom after the collapse proceeded from here. This was not so much a political event as the repeated fulfillment of a religious demand for the new organization of the world and the restitution of the cosmos. To the Egyptians their kingdom was never merely a political formation, but the nucleus and center of the ordered world in accordance with the intention of the creator-god. The fact that this event proceeded from Thebes must have given an exceptional importance to the place. When, about three centuries later, the liberation from Hyksos rule (see p. 82) was again completed by a king who resided in Thebes, this must have appeared as a confirmation of the beginning made by Mentuhotep. It is possible that in the end very ancient considerations of nationhood played a part which can hardly be explained historically. It is a striking fact that since the beginning of the historical period it was Upper Egypt that always took the leading part on each occasion when the recollection of nationhood and of national unity had to be promoted.

Here, indeed, remained the heart of the country even during those times when international events attracted the main political activities to the north. In the periods when the north took the lead or when it was divided

Colorplate IX. King Mentuhotep II (Neb-hepet-ra) (2060–2010 B.C.). Sandstone, painted. Complete height 6 feet. 11th Dynasty, Middle Kingdom. Cairo Museum.

from the south, it was in danger of becoming but a pawn in the power game of the Mediterranean nations.

But it must be added that Mentuhotep—or else the men who were acting together with him—showed great foresight in preparing the ground for something new.

The king's mortuary monument appears to symbolize a link between an ancient tradition and a new start. He takes over the shape of the pyramid, the royal symbol of the Old Kingdom, but he places it on top of a terraced construction in front of the rocky slope of the valley gorge. The long rampart, too, has been taken over from the royal tomb buildings of the Old Kingdom. At its lower end must have been some building similar to the valley temple of the pyramids, to receive the funerary procession. The pyramid itself has, in fact, a symbolic value. For the tomb of the king is not in it or under it, but behind it in the rock, with a long down-sloping passage leading to it. The Bab el Hosan, on the other hand, with its entrance standing in the forecourt of the temple and leading under the pyramid, was apparently only a cenotaph. Like the pyramid proper, the terraced building and the rock tomb are nothing new in themselves. These individual forms had been developed during the preceding two centuries by the Upper Egyptian nomarchs. But an act of creative imagination was required to dare to connect these parts and plant them together as a monument on the majestic solitude of the mountains. Again we do not know the names of the builders, architects, and artists who in a comparatively short period succeeded in leading the rather primitive workmanship on Theban soil to such a height. Any other stelae, paintings, and the like which we know from the time of Mentuhotep must in all fairness be called provincial and unskilled. We may, however, assume that after his victory over the Heracleopolitan dynasty the king fetched the artists and craftsmen, who had themselves continued the tradition of the Old Kingdom, from the former residence southward to Thebes. This we know for certain about at least one of them. A supervisor of the sculptors from the time of Mentuhotep tells on a stela, which comes from his tomb in Thebes, that he had occupied this office in the "House of Kheti [that is, the royal house of Heracleopolis] at a time when it was still the royal house."

The tombs of officials and courtiers of this time lie in front of Deir el Bahari in the Asasif, the plain before the village of Dra' abu'l-Naga and halfway up the mountain slope. They are all empty today.

The most invaluable spiritual achievement of this time—although we cannot tie it down to a definite moment—is the conception of the god Amon of Karnak. We can ascertain with some confidence that up to then he had not possessed a cult center on Theban soil. He belongs to a number of timeless—and in the beginning perhaps even cultless—conceptual divinities who play a part in the religious picture of the world. His name means "invisibility," or, more personally, "the invisible one." With similar beings like "darkness," "pathlessness," and so on (see p. 124), he must be grouped with those abstract concepts that connote the negative qualities of the chaos before the creation and emergence of the ordered world. It was, in fact, an act of genius to select this god from an abundance of divine possibilities and to create for him a place of worship in the new town.

The idea of an invisible god answered precisely the religious need of the period. The preceding era, which we call the First Intermediate Period, was characterized by the loss of order in political, economic, and spiritual fields. The main achievement of the Old Kingdom had been the centralization of all forces: the country was highly organized even as far as the most distant provinces, and all was related to the godlike kingship at its center. Even if the general wealth was modest, the consciousness that one belonged to one great organism pervaded everything. The strict order imposed was identical with the world order that was the will of God, and this order, in the form of regular ritual usage and doctrine, extended even into the afterlife. The disturbance of this closely knit order started when the regions gained more independence politically, economically, and spiritually. In politics this happened when the official administrators of the provinces, or the nomes, became nomarchs who isolated themselves from the central power. At the same time, signs of cultural and spiritual independence became apparent. Provincial necropolises were created; the tombs of the nobles increased in size, splendor, and richness. The catastrophic consequences of the change in the political structure of the country can be most easily judged in the economic field. The strength of the central state was based on the interrelation and central organization of production and need. The moment when regional members of the whole became independent, the central power could no longer make efficient adjustments, and danger threatened the provisioning of those regions that were more densely populated or were less productive. Insufficient inundations of the Nile, which are mentioned several times in the inscriptions of the period, worsened the situation. There resulted famines, turmoils, and the formation of gangs. At the same time, it was possible for the individual to find new and hitherto unknown outlets for his energies. But for the greater part of the population the period brought need, uncertainty, and separation from the ancient ordered ways of living. As the ancient order had been the will of the creator-god, and had been supported also by the other gods, the breakdown of the order of the state resulted in a deep-seated skepticism vis-à-vis all institutions. Even the traditional forms of faith were smitten by it, and a text reproaches the gods for continuing creation. The sun-god Ra, who was somehow identified with the rule of the Old Kingdom, had become "old" in the mythological parlance of the period. At the same time, believers felt unable to imagine a world without a divine creator and divine influence. Amon was now a deity who in a sense was without an incriminating past. His mysterious nature connected him with all conceptions of primeval times, giving him also the possibility of being unseen and ubiquitous. Admittedly, he too was to find visible forms of appearance in the course of time; for the faith of different social classes has differing needs—the simple man wished to see his god and to meet him face to face. Many ritual phenomena on Theban soil testify to this, and it was possible also to connect Amon with these. His nature always offered enough possibilities for speculative theology to embody its changing thoughts. Finally, as he was not tied to a place, he was especially suited to become the lord and ruler of a kingdom whose frontiers were expanding. His final official name became (from the Eighteenth Dynasty) "Amon-Ra [that is, Amon who is also Ra], king of the gods, lord of the thrones of the two countries [therefore the god of the kingdom], residing in the one who counts the sites [that is, Karnak as mistress of all the sacred sites]."

The god's oldest temple was built in Karnak at that time, but we know nothing of its character. Opposite Fig.11 it, at Deir el Bahari, was the king's monumental mortuary site, and the two sacred places were axially related. Thus were determined the focal points for the further development of Thebes. They were also ritually connected: once a year the god went to Deir el Bahari, during the festival of the valley (p. 116), and visited the XIII, Figs. 7,8 king's temple. We do not know whether this festival originated with Mentuhotep. Possibly an earlier festival of the dead, with visits to the tombs, had received a special significance by connecting it with the cult of Amon. But the name of the festival and its principal forms are known since the Middle Kingdom; in the New Kingdom it gave the name of *Payni* to the tenth month of the year.

It is impossible to understand the architectural development of Thebes in the following centuries without a survey of Egypt's political development, and especially of the role played by Thebes. Just as its foundation was due to a political situation, so too did its destiny remain closely connected with the political development of the kingdom.

As has already been noted, the kings of the Twelfth Dynasty abandoned Thebes as an administrative center and moved again to the borderline between Upper and Lower Egypt in the vicinity of Lisht. Nevertheless, Thebes was probably more than a mere provincial town, although Armant-Hermonthis remained the capital of its nome, a fact attested by a unique monument of the time of Sesostris I. It is the reconstructed limestone kiosk to the north of the first pylon; it was found in 1927–34 in the filling of the third pylon, and its original site is uncertain. It is certain, however, that the building served during the *sed* festival, the jubilee of the king's accession. Its double entry is characteristic. This was not a shrine or a sanctuary to keep a sacred object, but an edifice with the special purpose of enabling someone to pass through it: one was expected to enter it, walk through it, and leave it again on the other side. At the time of Sesostris I, Thebes was not the residence proper; we may therefore assume that the king himself celebrated the festival in Lisht or in Memphis, while a statue had to represent him in Thebes (so H. Kees). This alone would be enough to prove the importance of Thebes-Karnak even during the Twelfth Dynasty. The inscriptions on the base of the kiosk are important intrinsically and symbolically. For here is some kind of assessment register of the country as a whole. Lists on its north and south sides state the nomes of the two halves of the country, their capitals and gods, the amount of ground under cultivation, and other statistics. There is no need to explain the scientific value of this assessment, although we cannot be sure whether this is a contemporary document or a copy of a more ancient list. But it is also significant in connection with the statues of the temple. If we consider the purpose of these dry statistical enumerations, the Egyptian mode of thought reveals that these lists imply the presence of the whole of the country in the king's jubilee building. The items noted here are the achievements of the king's reign; they are really present and surround him when he or his picture is seated in the building. As early as the Old Kingdom, processions of nome gods and personifications are depicted as surrounding the temples of the kings—this is only another form of the same idea—and the convention persists in later periods.

Other architectural remains of the Middle Kingdom are less important, save for the fact that they show that other kings of this dynasty were active here. Unfortunately, they cannot help us to gain a picture of the oldest temples.

At the end of the Middle Kingdom several kings were apparently buried again in western Thebes. The inscription on the statue of a vizier, which was put up in Thebes, mentions the mortuary temple of a King Sebekhotep.

THEBES DURING THE NEW KINGDOM

Another historic turning point was needed for Thebes to emerge again. It was here that the struggle for freedom against the Hyksos began. About 1660 B.C. Egypt had fallen under the rule of a conglomeration of people who were superior in military and political affairs and whom the Egyptians called the Hyksos, "lords of the foreign countries." We have to do here, in fact, with the backwater of an Asiatic movement of nations, whose representatives in Egypt were predominantly of Semitic and Hurrian descent. About 1550 B.C. Kamose, and after his death his brother Ahmose, descendants of the Theban princes, attempted to break the rule of the Hyksos in Egypt. They conquered Avaris, the capital of the enemy in the northern Delta, and carried the war into the south of Palestine. Amenhotep I, the son of Ahmose and his sister Ahmes-Nefertari, is counted as the first king of the Eighteenth Dynasty.

Now begins that period of "world domination," with Thebes as its center, which produced an abundance of outstanding personalities and great actions. It lasted for about two centuries. Its kings (Tuthmosis, Amenhotep, Hatshepsut; for details see the chronological table) built monuments at Karnak and on the west side of Thebes. Its officials and priests were the possessors of richly decorated tombs. Then Amenhotep IV transferred his residence to Tell el Amarna after a short reign in Thebes and opposed the cult of Amon. This meant at first a standstill in the development of Thebes. His peculiar way of life expressed itself also in a distinctive style of art, the "Amarna art." Its beginnings, however, belong to his Theban period. Thousands

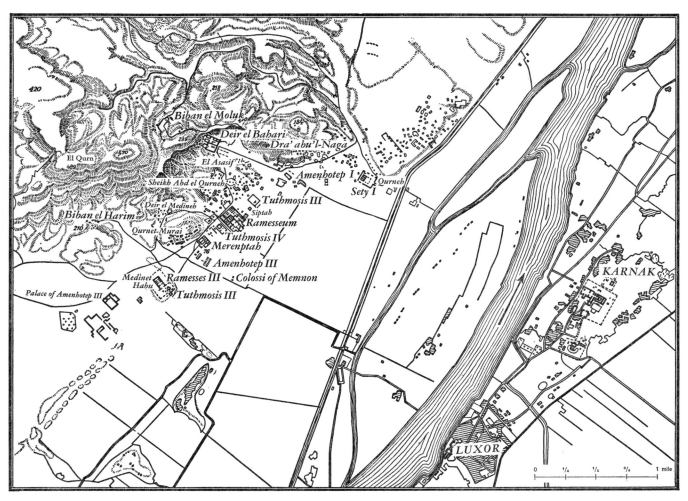

Figure 9. Map of Thebes. On the eastern bank of the Nile are the present-day Luxor and Karnak; on the other side, adjoining the cultivated land, is the necropolis of western Thebes. The names of the kings are added to their mortuary temples. Biban el Harim = Valley of the Tombs of the Queens; Biban el Moluk = Valley of the Tombs of the Kings. The most important burial places of the nobles of Thebes are situated near the present-day settlements of Qurnet-Murai, Deir el Medineh, Sheikh abd el Qurneh, El Asasif, and Dra' abu'l-Naga.

83

of relatively small stone slabs decorated with reliefs in the new style have come from a building that was probably situated east of the temples at Karnak. Statues of the king which had been erected here are now in the museum in Cairo. A striking example of the sudden break in style between the art of Amenhotep III and that of Amenhotep IV is preserved in the unfinished tomb of Ramose (no. 55), a vizier who held office under both kings. The reliefs in the left half of the antechamber of his tomb in Sheikh Abd el Qurneh show the perfection and delicacy of the style that prevailed before the Amarna era; but on the right rear wall of the same room we now meet the "new style" with all its peculiarities.

In the "period of restoration" the kings returned once more to Thebes. Tut-ankh-amon and the rulers of the Nineteenth and Twentieth Dynasties (Ramessides) prepared their tombs and mortuary temples once more in Thebes and enlarged the temples of Karnak and Luxor. But Thebes did not regain its status as a political capital. Because of Egypt's involvement in the world politics of the Near East, it seemed more appropriate to establish the royal residence at a place nearer to the focus of events. This led to the foundation of the "Ramesses town," Tanis, in the north of the Delta. When the kingdom broke down once more in about 1085 B.C., after the reign of Ramesses IX, the last of the Ramessides, the political center remained finally in Lower Egypt. For about a century (until 984 B.C.) a Lower Egyptian dynasty ruled in Tanis, while Thebes was at the same time governed by a succession of priest-kings who were simultaneously high priests of Amon. In the Twenty-second Dynasty descendants of Libyan mercenaries occupied the throne of the Pharaohs. They ruled over the whole country, but their center and residence remained in the Delta.

For more than three centuries (1085–751 B.C.) Thebes did not take part in the main political events of the time. It had to give up its leading role also in cultural matters and could easily have degenerated to the position of an insignificant provincial town. Building activity in Thebes was, in fact, relatively inconspicuous during this period, although it must be remembered that because of economic and political reasons the kingdom as a whole was unable to produce anything like the achievement of the past centuries. In spite of all this, Thebes now became the holy city par excellence. A mourning song for Osorkon II, a king of the Twenty-second Dynasty who was buried in Tanis, expresses the wish "that he may go to Thebes, to the divine nome beloved by his soul" (H. Kees), as if a real royal funeral could take place only there. During these centuries, above all, the divine state of Amon was created both as an idea and as an institution. Eduard Meyer calls it "the oldest, the most naïve, and also the most consistent formation of theocracy known in history." The early concept of Amon as a heavenly king was here fully realized. It means that Amon was the real king of the country and that the earthly ruler was only commissioned by him to administrate the country, or particular regions of it, in his place. The Upper Egyptian kings of the Twenty-first Dynasty, Herihor and his successors, were enthroned by means of an oracle of the god. The king carried out his rule, because the main offices, the high priesthood of Amon, the vice-kingship of Kush (that is, the repository of military power), and the viziership (that is, the civil power), were united in him. This is not just a whimsical fiction made up on the spur of the moment; its roots reach back over centuries into the Eighteenth Dynasty. The idea was already present then that the king was elected by Amon, but in practice only the legitimate heirs had the right to be elected. The institution of the oracle, too, developed, spread, and gained in strength during a long space of time.

In Middle and Lower Egypt the situation was somehow different. The dynasties that evolved from the garrisons of the Libyan mercenaries (the Twenty-second to Twenty-fourth Dynasties) acknowledged the

84

divine state as such; at the same time, they tried to link it with the dynasty by conferring the office of high priest on a royal prince. Regarded as a whole, the rule of the king became a purely secular sovereignty which could accept the possibility of several "kings" ruling legitimately side by side. How far, then, did the factual power of Amon's rule extend? This is a question we cannot answer. The transference, however, of royal power to the god doubtless helped to secularize the sovereignty of the mundane rulers, with all the consequences that such a process involved.

At the turn of the eighth to the seventh century Thebes experienced once more a short period of political importance under the Ethiopian kings. Lower Nubia had been for centuries an Egyptian colony, and eventually it had been administered, at least in name, by the divine state. During the period 1000–800 B.C. it was lost, but the continuous infiltration of Egyptian customs and religious ideas had left their mark on a deeply religious and impressionable people, so that finally a mixed culture was created whose single elements were at first mostly Egyptian, though its spirit was quite foreign. The capital of the kingdom was situated near Napata, at the fourth cataract, where a temple of Amon had already been built by Tuthmosis III. Obscurity shrouds the origin of the Nubian royal dynasty. Apparently it felt authorized by Amon himself and connected with this authorization the claim to rule over Egypt. The Ethiopian prince Piankhy moved against Egypt about 750 B.C. in the spirit of a holy war. He purified himself and his army in Thebes before Amon and then conquered the land after a number of battles. The rule of the Ethiopians was broken in 671 B.C. by the invasion of the Assyrians under Assarhadon, and Assyrian troops pillaged Thebes. This event evoked a widely resounding echo throughout the Eastern world. The prophet Nahum (*Nahum*, 3:8ff.) warningly points to the fall of Thebes as a visible example of divine judgment.

During the short period of the Ethiopian rule a new form of control over the divine state was realized. Its head was now a female regent, the divine consort of Amon, a priestess who was also a member of the ruling royal family, first of the Ethiopians and then of the Saite kings of the Twenty-sixth Dynasty. This female dynasty propagated itself through adoption and continued until the end of the Twenty-sixth Dynasty (525 B.C.). The end of the divine state also meant the end of the history of Thebes, for the Persian conquest probably inflicted here, as elsewhere, much destruction. Ptolemaic kings and Roman emperors still continued to build in Thebes, but the remaining historic role of the city was that of a leader of reaction and insurrections, especially against the Ptolemaic and Roman regimes. Eventually Christianity and Islam took hold of the ruined sites and gave a new interpretation to the traditional holiness of the temples and tombs.

II. BUILDINGS AND CULTS

This short survey of the history of the city was necessary in order to show how the importance of Thebes as a sacred site was closely and indissolubly linked with the history of the country. Its origin was really due to a historical event, and its history remains permanently linked with the historical development of the country. One could even maintain that the history of Thebes faithfully reflects the fate of the kingdom. The monuments of Thebes and the works of art erected within them are for us the petrified relics of historical epochs and rulers. The kings of the Eighteenth, Nineteenth, and Twentieth Dynasties were themselves buried beyond the western mountains of their city and hoped to survive forever in their inaccessible, richly decorated tombs.

We are dealing here mainly with the sacred architecture of Thebes, since almost nothing is left of the secular buildings, and we shall study in particular how these monuments can be understood as a form and expression of their cults. From the beginning, as stated earlier, there existed two main centers: on the east side the temples of the gods and on the west side the tombs with their mortuary temples. From the start the two parts were closely related to each other. The western temples were more or less exactly oriented toward the temple of Karnak; and the same gods were worshiped, to a great extent, on both banks of the river: the god Amon of Karnak was also the lord of the mortuary temples on the west bank and visited them regularly.

The sacred places on the east bank are grouped around two sites—the enormous conglomerate of the temple of Karnak and the temple of Luxor. Unfortunately, the prehistory of both sites is unknown, and therefore a full understanding of their significance is impossible. It is not known whether any cult centers existed in the region of Karnak as early as the Old Kingdom. But a temple of Amon existed here in the Eleventh Dynasty and in the Middle Kingdom (see p. 81). Apparently an antecedent of the Luxor temple existed also in the Middle Kingdom.

KARNAK AS A WHOLE

Three parts independent of each other form the Karnak conglomerate of today.

1. The complex of the temple of Amon, the "state temple," stands in the middle. It is bounded by an enclosure wall and is oriented simultaneously toward the east and the west. The enclosure contains, in addition, a number of other temples; of these, the temple of Khons especially strongly suggests the existence of predecessors.

2. Toward the north it is immediately joined by the sacred site of the nome god Monthu, which also contains several temples and is oriented toward the north (the expression "orientation" is here used for the direction toward which the temple opens up).

3. A few hundred yards south of the Amon conglomerate is the horseshoe-shaped Lake Asheru, which surrounds three sides of the temple of the vulture-goddess Mut. This temple consequently faces north, with the lake at its rear. The most important other sanctuary inside the enclosure wall of the temple of Amon is the temple of Khons. It is situated in the southwest corner of the site and faces south. According to occasional allusions in older inscriptions and certain topographical remarks in the temple's own inscriptions, it must be considered as a separate unit. The entire picture is confusing, especially because of the mutual cutting of temple axes, which are not related to each other. The situation becomes even more confusing if one considers that further temples existed toward the east of the Amon conglomerate, for example, the buildings of Amenhotep IV, which are submerged under cultivated land and have not been systematically excavated. We must approach the situation with the rather unsatisfactory explanation that the single sanctuaries are partly placed on older sacred sites of local significance, which determined the area and the direction. Later sites of worship with new cult needs were added, and in the end the (secondary) interrelation of the single sites found permanent expression in the construction of processional roads.

The orientation of the temple of Amon toward the west and the Nile is apparently most natural, for it was thus that the god left his house and crossed in his barque toward the west bank. The situation of the temple of Mut seems also to have been dictated by nature. It is connected with the temple of Amon by an

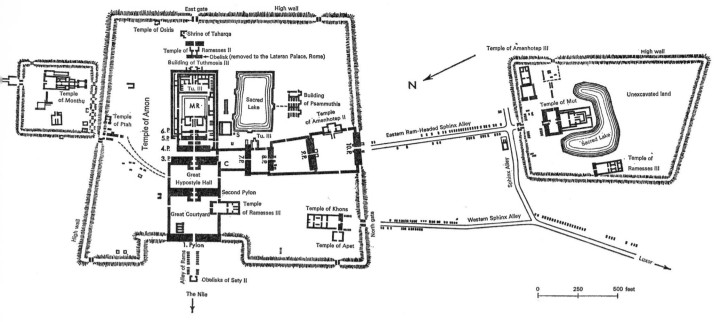

Figure 10. Temple at Karnak. General survey. After E. Brunner-Traut and V. Hell, 1962.

avenue of ram sphinxes and by the pylon road (the seventh to the tenth pylon). This road ended near the enclosure of the temple of Amon in front of the fourth pylon; in other words, until the middle of the Eighteenth Dynasty it ended on the square in front of the temple. This monumental road was begun under Tuthmosis III, and at that time the fourth pylon formed the boundary of the temple of Amon in a westerly direction. It must be assumed that the direction of the temple of Khons was fixed by earlier data. The present building dates only from the time of Ramesses III, while its decoration is even later. It has its own processional road which leads to the south and leaves the enclosure wall through the gate Bab el Amara of Ptolemy III (Euergetes I). The three deities Amon, Mut, and Khons stand in a cult relation with the temple of Luxor. This relation finds its architectural expression in the great sacred road connecting Karnak with Luxor. It ends in front of the Luxor temple, and in recent years several hundred yards of the road have been cleared by the Service des Antiquités. In Karnak the road begins in front of the fourth pylon and leads from here to the temple of Mut; from the front of this temple, following the enclosure wall, it turns westward, and after about 200 yards it is joined by an avenue of ram-headed sphinxes that comes from the north from the temple of Khons. Here it turns again southward and leads now—through the present village of Karnak—to the Luxor temple. In this way the temples are spatially connected with each other and with the temple of Luxor.

The temple of Monthu, north of the temple of Amon, remains completely apart. Inscriptions and architectural remains testify to its origin in the Eighteenth Dynasty. The temple has an enclosure wall of its own, and from its rear it was joined by a temple of Maat, "truth," which faced south. During the Twentieth Dynasty court sessions were held here. In the northwest corner of the site is a sacred lake; and a processional road leads from the temple northward through the Bab el Abd gate, which derives from the time of Ptolemy III (Euergetes I) and Ptolemy IV (Philopator), to a quay of its own; from here there was a connection with the Nile by means of a canal.

87

No attempt will be made to give an architectural history of the complex, which is, especially here at Karnak, extremely intricate and abounding in unsolved problems. A description of the existing buildings, however, seems to be necessary. In particular, it must be asked what this accumulation of monumental buildings signified in the religious life of Thebes. What kind of thoughts did they express concerning the nature and influence of the gods worshiped there? How was the life of the individual and the state connected with them?

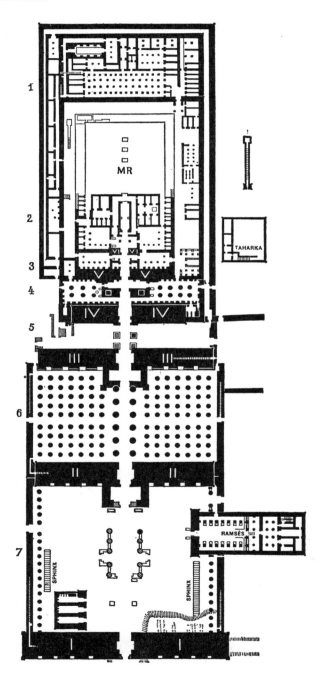

THE STATE TEMPLE

The nucleus of the enormous estate of the temple of Amon was formed by the sanctuary for the god's barque behind the sixth pylon, and it was Tuthmosis III who was mainly responsible for the design of this innermost part, although the actual sanctuary of the barque dates only from the reign of Philip Arrhidaeus. Here in the innermost part of the temple, to the left of the sanctuary, Tuthmosis recorded his military enterprises, the "annals of Tuthmosis," and also a report of the booty and the delivery of tribute. A visible expression of the link between kingship and godhead is found here in the conviction that it was Amon who gave the command. Historical inscriptions were part of the temple decoration until the time of the Ramessides, and occasionally even later. In the Late Period, when the sovereignty of the king and the god were dissociated, it was logical not to continue this tradition.

The function of the sanctuary raises some

Figure 11. The temple at Karnak. The temple site of the Middle Kingdom. 1: Festival temple of Tuthmosis III. 2: Chambers of Hatshepsut and second "hall of annals." 3: First "hall of annals" and courts of Tuthmosis III. 4: Obelisks of Hatshepsut and pillared court of Tuthmosis I and Tuthmosis III. 5: Obelisks of Tuthmosis I and Tuthmosis III. 6: Hypostyle hall. 7: Great front courtyard with the colonnade passage of Taharqa (middle) and the temple of Sety I (to the left in the foreground). The pylons are marked I–VI. After Henri Chevrier, 1936.

fundamental questions concerning the nature of the temple and the related cult. It is certain that the god's processional barque was kept permanently in the sanctuary. During festival processions there was carried in it a picture of the god standing in a shrine or hidden by a veil. It is not known for certain where this picture used to be kept as a rule; it may have been in a side room of the sanctuary of the barque. This helps one to recall some basic facts about the appearance and qualities of Egyptian cult images. We must not imagine them as monumental, possibly over life-size stone statues, at least not at this time. Certainly since the New Kingdom they must usually have been small portable effigies. In addition to the cult image, there were other representations of the god in the round and in relief. Inevitably the conclusion must be drawn that at least according to the orthodox theological doctrine the image was never the god himself but only a figure of him, a dwelling place which he might choose as his abode; and written evidence supports this idea.

The common people, on the other hand, who had no access to the temple proper, believed that the figures of the gods and even the representations in relief were real and approachable gods; for the belief in the life force of images was deeply rooted in the Egyptian way of thinking. This attitude differs markedly from the official doctrine, but we shall meet the phenomenon frequently on Theban soil.

A second important question for the understanding of the temple is also connected with the sanctuary. The extant sanctuary, as mentioned above, was built by Philip Arrhidaeus, and we know nothing of the earlier one which it replaced. It is even possible, although not very likely, that an earlier sanctuary had been destroyed by the Persians. In that case, a replacement would have been an obvious necessity. But the matter of the renovation of the sanctuary leads to an earlier and widespread phenomenon. We know that especially during the Eighteenth Dynasty sanctuaries and roadside chapels were renewed at short intervals. I should like, with all reservation, to advance a suggestion concerning this practice. According to the notions of the Egyptians, the rule of each new Pharaoh who was selected by Amon signified also in some way a new beginning of the world. It would be quite feasible to imagine that this new beginning obliged the king to create a new house for the god. This idea can be supported by parallel events. One could point, for instance, to the fact that several kings of the Fifth Dynasty founded sun temples for Ra in the region of Abusir and accordingly fulfilled an obligation to create a new sanctuary for the god. One could also mention the pertinent

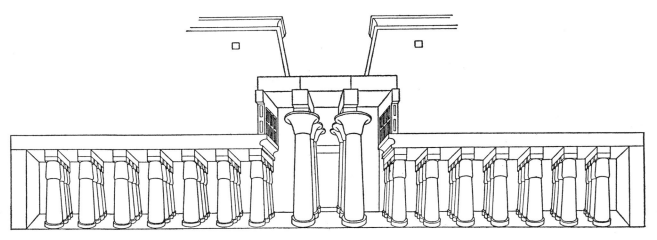

Figure 12. The temple at Karnak. Transverse section through the great hypostyle hall of Kings Sety I and Ramesses II at the top of the main passage from north to south, with a view toward the western exit. After K. Lange and M. Hirmer, 1955–61.

89

new building of a mortuary temple on the west bank of Thebes (see p. 105); for the temple was not the mortuary temple in the sense of the ancient period but a temple of the god Amon, in which there was also—but only as an appendix—room for the worship of the deceased king. Furthermore, I should like to refer, in this context, to the usurpation of buildings and monuments by later kings, that is, the process often noted whereby a king claimed for himself a monument of his predecessor by cutting out the name and replacing it with his own. I suggest that this is not only a token of insufficient productive power—which is obvious—but also a new consecration, a bringing up to date of the older monuments.

As a result of these enlargements and renovations, one architectural element was often hidden, although we are used to seeing it in a free-standing position in front of the temple pylons: I mean the obelisk. The obelisks of Hatshepsut were shut in between the fourth and the fifth pylon by Tuthmosis III. The pair of obelisks of Tuthmosis I—of which only the southern one is still standing—was confined between the third and the fourth pylon. During the Eighteenth Dynasty obelisks occur as a rule in pairs in front of the pylons, and they thus seem to serve only a decorative purpose. Originally, however, the obelisk was not an additional, decorative architectural element, but was itself a cult object, and for this reason it was raised inside the temple precincts. For reasons that are not perfectly clear, it was regarded as a symbol of the sun-god, and as such its origin was in the sun cult of Heliopolis. In the sun temples of the kings of the Fifth Dynasty at Abusir (between Giza and Saqqarah) a massively constructed obelisk formed the center of the temple precinct. Even in the Eighteenth Dynasty the obelisks were not merely beautifying objects: Tuthmosis III instituted special sacrifices for his obelisks, and the same king erected a single obelisk as a cult object for an exclusive little temple to the east of the state temple in Karnak. This obelisk was taken to Rome in A.D. 357 and was later on erected in front of the Lateran palace.

Amenhotep III began to enlarge the fore part of the temple in a westerly direction. He erected the third pylon, using several older buildings as filling material. The processional road from Luxor, beginning from the temple of Mut, no longer ran into the forecourt of the temple but behind the new pylon into the temple itself. This pylon is of special importance for us in connection with the earlier architectural history. For Amenhotep, in using as filling the stones of older buildings—those of Sesostris I, Amenhotep I, and Hatshepsut—did this so thoroughly that some of the buildings thus disassembled could be put together again in our time. The Ramessides constructed the great hypostyle hall and the second pylon, and in their era the urge for monumental building reached its purest expression. This forest of columns consisted, originally, of 134 columns on an area of five thousand square yards. The height of the middle row of columns was seventy-nine feet. Perhaps one should compare the monumental grandeur of this construction only with that of the pyramids of Giza; and yet, in view of their highly distinctive character, the two are incomparable. In its complete state, the pillared hall must have given the impression of infinity. It received light only in the middle passage from above, while the aisles were kept in increasing darkness. It is impossible today, it seems, to imagine the actual distribution of light and shade. One may ask whether a special ritual function was connected with this immense construction, apart from its being an expression of greatness and power. The growth of the temple in a frontal direction meant, primarily, an extension of the sacred road which the god had to pass inside the temple. In addition, the hall probably served as a sacrificial court, as a place, that is, where the presentation of offerings was prepared. In spite of its large area, it does not seem that it was serviceable for the ceremonies proper. But the columns and the walls offered space for a representation of

90

Colorplate X. The temple at Karnak. View across the sacred lake to the middle of the temple of Amon.

the gods of the land in symmetrical order, who could thus be present when the god appeared from the innermost part of the temple.

During the time of the Ramessides, an open courtyard was situated in front of the second pylon, with the little three-chapel sanctuary of Sety II and the Amon temple of Ramesses III opening up toward it from right and left. Later on, in the Bubastite Period, the court was narrowed in by pillared passages on both sides, and in the end it was closed by the first pylon of the Ptolemaic Period. The road across the courtyard between the second and first pylon was marked by Taharqa by a pillared passage; but only one column of this still stands.

This courtyard was the earliest place in which the god of the temple and the people could meet, except, of course, for the priests, who were admitted into the temple proper. We must imagine that in this court as well as in the courts that were formed by the seventh to the tenth pylon on the way toward the temple of Mut, statues of kings as well as of private persons were put up. Originally the king granted to favored persons the privilege of erecting a statue in the temple; this gave them the chance to be represented perpetually on holy ground in imperishable form and also to take part in the festivals and offerings of the god. It was probably here that the conversation took place between Herodotus (II, 143) and the priest of Amon concerning those statues—Herodotus' report mentions only wooden statues—in the course of which the difference between Greek and Egyptian genealogies was discussed. According to the statement of the priest, all these statues represented "human beings" who were sons of each other. Perhaps one need not take this last point literally. But we know of a great number of such priestly statues from the first centuries of the last millennium B.C., especially from Karnak, and from them we have gained long genealogies of priests. It is therefore pardonable if all the representations are attributed to one genealogy only, and the language difficulties between Herodotus and the priests may have something to do with it as well. After the time of Herodotus, a great number of the statues were removed and put into a pit in the courtyard to the north of the seventh pylon, where they were discovered in 1904. Besides other objects, no fewer than 770 statues were buried here.

It is hard to understand the eastern part of the temple of Amon. The sanctuary facing in opposite directions proves that it too was visited by Amon and was not merely a complex of rear or side rooms such as magazines and store chambers. An area now cleared shows traces of Middle Kingdom temples, but we do not know what had originally been present there and on what occasion the god came to visit it. Further eastward Tuthmosis III erected—at right angles to the axis of the temple—a festival temple, a building which served
21 for celebrations during the jubilee of his reign. Its purpose was therefore the same as that of the kiosk of Sesostris I. Perhaps one may assume that this row of temples was specially dedicated to the royal cult. Further
24,25 to the east are the rooms in which Tuthmosis III depicted the plants and animals that had been observed in Syria. The chambers to the south of the festival temple appear, according to the inscriptions, to have been dedicated to the cult of the deceased king. Could it be possible that royal statues had been put up here in order to receive sacrifices or to be carried around in procession at certain festivals?

Still further to the east follow ritual buildings of Tuthmosis III as well as of Ramesses II. They underline the twin aspect of the whole construction: they open eastward—though in not quite so monumental a form—in the same way as the temple stretches out in a westerly direction.

Colorplate XI. The temple at Karnak. View upward in the main passage of the hypostyle hall.

92

On the occasion of the jubilee of his reign, the *sed* festival, Amenhotep II erected outside the central temple a small, broad cult building opening up toward the processional road to the temple of Mut, a road which at that time was still in its beginnings and stretched from the seventh and eighth pylons. It may therefore be compared with the festival temple of Tuthmosis III in the east. Its form and arrangement of rooms is peculiar; it is also strange that apparently there was no sanctuary, for the building ended toward the east with a false door. In spite of their mediocre state of preservation, the reliefs are of exquisite beauty.

Our short review of the most important buildings should indicate clearly the extent to which the term "state temple"—which was not used in ancient Egypt—is applicable to the temple of Karnak. Almost all of the kings of the New Kingdom endeavored to enlarge the temple; it was repeatedly the site for the royal jubilee. Of the many historical documents published and immortalized in it, the following may be named:

23 The annals of Tuthmosis III: an adaptation of the war diaries of the king from his twenty-second to his forty-second year. They are recorded in the annals rooms to the north of the sanctuary.

The royal list of Karnak: on it Tuthmosis III is represented bringing offerings to his royal ancestors. Similar monuments are known at Abydos (p. 54). The list, now in the Louvre, comes from the first chamber to the left of the entrance to the festival temple of the kings.

The stelae of King Kamose: on two stelae a report concerning the beginning of the war against the Hyksos is related. Two fragments of one stela were found in 1932 and 1935 in the filling of the third pylon; the other was found in 1954 under the foundation of a colossal statue in front of the second pylon.

The treaty of Ramesses II in his twenty-first year (1278 B.C.) with the Hittite king Hattusilis. It is to be found on the western external wall of the courtyard to the north of the seventh pylon.

A chronicle of the early kings of Bubastis is inscribed in the passage beside the temple of Ramesses III in the first courtyard.

Great shares of booty from the military expedition were transmitted to the temple. It was also repeatedly the place where the king was chosen by Amon and where he was crowned, although it is not certain of how many Pharaohs of the New Kingdom this is true. A description of such an event was provided by Queen Hatshepsut. She tells how Amon, on his return from the festival at Luxor, met her near the palace, which may have been situated between the bank of the Nile and the temple of Karnak. He performed great miracles, led her to the coronation, bestowed the sovereignty upon her, and entrusted special tasks to her as queen: to increase the fertility of the country, to provide divine offerings and to keep the regulations of the temple, to issue excellent laws, in short to perform all works of peace. After the coronation, the queen presented herself to the people and pointed to the miracles that Amon had performed for her, as never before, and she swore that she would reign together with her god. It was a lucky chance that this document was recovered, because it shows impressively the close connection between god and sovereign; the idea of being commissioned by the god and of the consequent obligation is also clearly expressed.

At the same time, it illuminates the sanctity of the place where all this happened: Karnak is the place where god and king meet; the divine impulse revives its control over the land through the person of the Pharaoh. An inscription of Tuthmosis III suggests a similar encounter with the divine, but its details are much less lively than Hatshepsut's narrative.

94

All this, and especially the reflection of history in a monument, is related in particular to the temple of Amon. To the south of the temple is to be found a second sacred site, the Lake Asheru with the cult of the vulture-goddess Mut. When this goddess first gained a cult center in Thebes is quite uncertain. Only during the Eighteenth Dynasty can she be attested there by inscriptions and archaeological finds, whereas outside Thebes her name occurs earlier. It is possible that she—like Amon himself—found her home here only in a secondary function, as goddess of the king and of the crown. Then proximity in space of the two deities gave an opportunity of connecting the two cults in thought and ritual. A device often used to express such a relation was employed here: Mut is regarded as the wife of Amon. The original difference in form—Amon is mostly represented as a man, Mut as a female vulture—did not disturb the Egyptian, since it had long been accepted that the human form could be used by all gods, and anthropomorphic ideas pervaded generally the actions and the appearance of the deities. Mut could also be represented as a woman, who bore the skin of a vulture on her head like a cap, in memory of her original form. She had been equated, too, with the lion-goddess of Memphis, Sekhmet. A number of seated monumental figures represented her in that form (as a woman with the head of a lioness); some of these are still standing today in the grounds of the temple. It is a structure deriving from the time of Amenhotep III and is now in a very fragmentary state. The same is true of two other temple sites of the Ramesside period that lie within the precincts of Mut. One of them is to the left of the entrance at a right angle to the axis of the temple, and another, built by Ramesses III, is to the west of the sacred lake. The former of these could have special significance for the history of the cult, for the partly preserved reliefs show scenes that are related to the birth, circumcision, and childhood of the divine child. These scenes indicate a theme that in the Ptolemaic Period is treated in smaller temples standing as a rule in front of the main temple and also at right angles to it—but on the right-hand side—the birth houses. In conformity with the human custom that birth takes place outside the house in some kind of bower, a similar building is erected in stone for the mythical birth of the divine child. Although the later birth houses differ architecturally from this Ramesside temple at Karnak, their position and their reliefs hint possibly at a similar function. In the context of the Theban mythology this would mean that the divine child of Amon and Mut, most probably the god Khons, was born here.

The two temple sites of Amon and Mut were connected by the processional road, which has already been mentioned several times. A row of pylons, the seventh to the tenth, built by Tuthmosis III, Hatshepsut, and Horemheb leads from the temple of Amon through an avenue of ram-headed sphinxes to the temple of Mut. Flanking the road were a number of smaller temples. Of these, one of Amenhotep II, which is situated between the ninth and the tenth pylon—and was therefore at one time in front of the row of pylons—is especially remarkable for the charmingly beautiful reliefs on its pillars. There were also a number of station sanctuaries on this processional road and on the one which led to Luxor. Remains of two such sanctuaries are to be found at the point where the street turns westward before reaching the temple of Mut. From the time of Hatshepsut quite a number of similar sanctuaries are known by name and through representations. As a rule, with some variations, they are in the form of peripteral temples: a pillared cella stands on a pedestal and is open in front and to the rear. During the procession the god's barque was deposited in it and received offerings.

There is finally at Karnak an originally independent temple unit which was drawn within the enclosure wall
27 of the state temple: the temple of Khons and the smaller temple of Opet at its side, in the southwest corner
of the precincts. The place where the temple was situated bore its own name, Benenet, which is difficult to
translate. It is somehow connected with the Egyptian conception of the primeval hill and was therefore one
of those sacred sites equated with the first piece of land believed to have emerged out of the primeval ocean
when the world was created. Anthropomorphically the idea that corresponds to the creation of the world
is the birth of a god. The physical phenomenon of the emergence of the first dry piece of land is anthropomorphically the birth of a (young) god, and this idea is repeatedly expressed in the deities and legends of the
two temples. Both temples are certainly late and only enlighten us about notions that had often been modified
by the late era. The temple of Khons had a predecessor in the Middle Kingdom, but it has not been preserved.
The nucleus of the extant temple derives from the period of Tuthmosis III; only in the Ramesside period,
however, and the time of Herihor, did it receive its present form and decoration. Unfortunately, we know
practically nothing about the original significance of the god Khons. He is considered the son of Amon and
Mut and forms the third member of the Theban triad. During the festival procession his barque, together
with those of the two other deities, goes to Luxor and the western part of Thebes. He is also regarded as a
moon deity, and according to an ancient, perhaps incorrect, etymology, his name is interpreted as "he who
pervades." He possesses also the cognomen Neferhotep. This is really a personal name that occurs frequently
in the Middle Kingdom and afterward. It was therefore suspected that the complex figure of the god absorbed
a deified man of this name. Indeed, Khons seems to have absorbed also a number of popular gods in the
course of time. Divine titles known in Karnak include "Khons the schemer," "Khons the calculator of the
times," "Khons the marksman"; some of these have temples of their own. In the Late Period, moreover,
Khons pronounced oracles and worked miracles. It is told, for example, that the miracle-working picture of
"Khons the schemer" was once sent to the Middle East in order to heal the disease of a Princess Bentresh of
Bekhten (Bactria?). This allegedly happened under Ramesses II, but the text is in fact a later glorification of
the god. The popular beliefs of the Late Period apparently left a deep impression on the different Khons
deities and their activities.

In the temple of Opet, to the west of the temple of Khons, the idea of the birth of a god is expressed clearly.
It is also called the birthplace. The temple itself is very late (late Ptolemaic and Roman), and its theology
accordingly offers a complex syncretism that is difficult to unravel. Its central myth is as follows: a pregnant
goddess came here and asked Amon for permission to be confined here, whereupon she gave birth to the
divine child in this place. This narrative nucleus gets so entangled in mythological speculations that it is
difficult to define the mythic personality which was meant to find expression here. The divine child is called
at one and the same time Osiris, Horus, Amon, and so on. But the decisive feature is the theme of the legend,
not its theological interpretation.

It thus appears that the oldest sacred site of Karnak was situated in this district alongside the temple of
Mut, which was originally independent of it: it was the creative primeval hill where the first land emerged,
the birthplace of the first god. Theology took hold of this site and connected it, inevitably, with the cult
facts of the neighborhood and the city and also with later theological developments.

With this the number of temples here is by no means exhausted. The smaller temple of Ptah deserves above all to be mentioned. Erected by Tuthmosis III on the site of an older building, it lies to the north of the temple of Amon and quite near to the enclosure wall of the precinct of Monthu. It is understandable that the god of the ancient capital of Memphis should have a place of worship here as well. Later generations, until late into the Ptolemaic era, enlarged it by building gates in front.

It was only at a remarkably late stage that Osiris was admitted to Karnak. The reason for this may lie in the fact that he was expressly a god of the dead and as such somehow inferior before Amon's claim to total power. On the way to the temple of Ptah lies the small temple of "Osiris the lord of Life," with the cognomen, "He who gives answers to the unhappy," which was built in the Twenty-fifth Dynasty.

Naturally we shall not try to enumerate all the chapels found on this immense site. The countless names and forms which occur in Karnak in places of worship as well as in statues and pictures justify in this respect alone the name state temple. In fact, all the gods of the reign were present here in one form or another. And Thebes preserved this central position far beyond the time when it was the residence of the king.

EASTERN THEBES—THE PRESENT-DAY LUXOR

About one and a half miles south of Karnak lies the other great Theban temple of Amon-Mut-Khons, the temple of Luxor, which is connected with the temple of Karnak by a processional avenue. Here, too, the existence of a temple of the Middle Kingdom can only be guessed from remains, while its exact position remains unknown. Possibly it was situated in the present great courtyard which now contains the three-chapel sanctuary of Ramesses II, itself a renovated building deriving from the Eighteenth Dynasty. This would mean that the oldest temple faced the great temple, whose nucleus was built by Amenhotep III. This, again, strengthens the idea that there existed originally a closed cult center, which only secondarily and in gradual stages was absorbed by the cult of Amon. Ramesses II built the great courtyard and pylon and thus moved the axis of the building complex in the direction of Karnak. The original cult of the temples is unknown. The Egyptian name of the temple is usually translated "harim" (that is, the harim of Amon); but

Fig. 13

28,29

36, Fig. 14

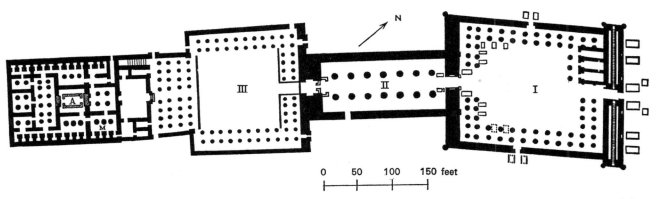

Figure 13. Eastern Thebes, Luxor. Temple of Amon-Mut-Khons. Ground plan. To the left (in the southwestern part of the temple site) the temple house and in it the sanctuary (A) and the birth hall (M). III: Great colonnaded forecourt of Amenhotep III. II: Colonnade of Amenhotep III. I: The great forecourt and adjacent to it in the northeast the great pylon of Ramesses II. After Daressy, from B. Porter and R. L. B. Moss, 1929.

the translation seems to be too narrow in reference, even if later on the name was understood as such by the Egyptians. The general meaning of the word is "that which is out of the way," "the closed"; even that tells little of its significance. Every year on the fifteenth day of the second month Amon came in a great procession to visit this place. He was worshiped here in his special form of Amenapet, that is, Amon of Luxor, a god of fertility. He was represented in human form and as ithyphallic; and in this form he was regarded as equivalent to the fertility-god Min of Coptos. Unfortunately, little is known about the special cult form of this temple or even about the meaning of the Luxor festival itself. In the center of the temple is again a sanctuary for the barque, which was dedicated by Alexander the Great. It is not quite certain how far this agrees with the original form of the temple. It may have been built to conform with the uniform plans for temple buildings which were fashionable at the time. In the room to the left of the antechamber are the well-known reliefs depicting the procreation and birth of Amenhotep III. A similar picture cycle was installed by Queen Hatshepsut at Deir el Bahari (see p. 110). According to the royal dogma of the period, the god Amon assumed the form of the king father and begot on the queen the successor to the throne. The myth of the divine creation of the king signified for the Egyptian a dogmatic crystallization of the doctrine of the Pharaoh's divine nature. But it is also one of the literary themes which exerted influence far beyond the frontiers of Egypt. Among the legends woven around the life of Alexander the Great is one that proclaims his mysterious procreation. In this legend mythical dogma is mixed with rationalistic propaganda: Nectanebo II, it is said, one of the last of the native Pharaohs, reached Macedonia during his flight from the Persians. There he took the form of Zeus Ammon, approached the wife of Philip II as the Olympian god, and by her procreated Alexander. While in ancient times the god had taken the form of the king, it was now the king who made use of the form of the god. The purpose of the tale is clear: it is meant to prove to the Egyptians the legitimacy of Alexander's rule.

The rooms behind the sanctuary of the barque, which are separated from it by a transverse hall, deserve some attention. Some of them may be stores for ritual utensils, but from its position one may assume that the middle room was something like a holy of holies. In it can be recognized a fairly high, table-like pediment. One is somehow forced to the conclusion that it was here that the original cult center of the sanctuary was located. Here, then, we should look for the evidence concerning the form of cult which was first enacted on this site.

The decoration of the Ramesside period (the courtyard of Ramesses II, the pylon, and the enclosure wall) brings again an abundance of historical inscriptions and representations. On the pylon we find representations of the battle of Qadesh and the words of the "Qadesh Poem." Recently the inner side of the eastern pylon tower, with its splendid representation of the festival of Min, has been made accessible. On the southwestern side of the court is a representation of the temple itself, and the walls of the pillared hall, beginning in the northern corner of the northwest wall, show the low reliefs of Tut-ankh-amon and Horemheb, with the representation of the whole procession moving toward Horemheb. Recently about a hundred yards of the processional road was cleared in front of the pylon. One of the obelisks which stood before it was taken to Paris in 1836 as a present from Mohammed Ali. It now stands in the Place de la Concorde.

The temple of Luxor, which functioned as a town center, seems to have survived Pharaonic Egypt longer than Karnak. A Christian church was established in the temple itself, and the rear wall of the room behind the pillared hall of Amenhotep III was changed into an apse, where even today the traces of ancient paintings

98

Figure 14. Eastern Thebes, Luxor. The great pylon of Ramesses II in the temple of Amon-Mut-Khons, with the two obelisk about A.D. 1800. After Denon, *Voyage dans la Basse et la Haute Égypte*, Paris, 1802.

on plaster are recognizable. Still later the mosque of Abu'l-Haggag (see p. 131) was erected on the east wall of the courtyard of Ramesses II, and it is still in use today. The high point of the religious life of Thebes was the Luxor (Apet) festival, the great procession of Amon, Mut, and Khons from Karnak to Luxor, which took place in the second month of the year. In more ancient times—under Tuthmosis III—it lasted for eleven days, and later—under Ramesses III—for twenty-seven days. There the splendor of the gods could unfold itself publicly. At the same time, the connection between king and god experienced an impressive demonstration. Very often the king himself took part in the procession, and several kings were elected during this occasion: among others Hatshepsut and Horemheb. The god revealed his will also in other public affairs such as a choice of priest or oracular decision. It was in this festival that Herihor was confirmed as leader of the divine state. It is difficult for us to judge these deeds of electing and commissioning by the god. The allusions in literature to "cunning priests" who manipulate the oracle are quite unfounded as far as the older period is concerned. During the Eighteenth Dynasty, however, the priesthood was undoubtedly unable to interfere in the question of the succession. A reference to the "half-sincere, half-feigned faith" (Eduard Meyer) of those who were chosen by oracle does not do justice to the faith of a very different age. If we want to understand these phenomena in the context of their own period, we must take them quite seriously. May it not be possible that a successor to the throne or a candidate for the office of high priest or a political leader like Herihor actually interpreted a movement of the barque or divine image as a real decision concerning his success? However well his claims were founded, it was the immediate presence of the god that gave the final blessing. If it can be believed that a divine power took possession of the image, there is no reason why it should not have used this medium to express its will. During the Late Period, as far as we know, the use of oracles increased, and questions concerning problems of daily life and decisions in litigations were put before the god. The already mentioned representation of the festival procession to the temple of Luxor has come down to us from the time of Tut-ankh-amon and Horemheb. At first an offering is brought by the king, in the sanctuary of Karnak, to the sacred barque with the closed shrine. Then it is carried on the shoulders of priests down to the Nile. And from there it makes its journey to Luxor, together with the barques of Mut and Khons. Choirs of temple singers, troops of soldiers, and a huge crowd of common people accompany it on the river bank. After their arrival in Luxor the barques are carried into the temple, and there they rest until their return journey. Although the pictures give a general idea of the festival's progress, they reveal very little about its meaning, as they are solely concerned with its official aspect. But what exactly took place in the temple of Luxor? The Egyptians remain silent. The attempted explanations of modern scholars may all be right in parts. It remains doubtful, however, whether any one of them has got to the bottom of the matter. Since we know very little about the real origin of the festival and the basic significance of the temple of Luxor, we must consider the possibility that the Egyptians themselves lost the true understanding of the festival in the course of time.

There is little reason to consider the journey as a symbol of the sun's course. It is not easy to see, either, why the festival should have been connected with the celebration of the new year. It is possible that Amon went to Luxor in order to consort... but with whom? It has also been suggested that it was a festive repetition of the first arrival of the god—a historical reminiscence, as it were. In fact, something of all of these explanations may be vitally present in the festival. Yet I should like to think that the Egyptians of the New Kingdom, too, surrounded the mysterious character of so great a festival with a multitude of possible interpretations.

100

Although the ritual buildings of the city of Thebes seem in themselves rich and impressive to us, we must not forget that we see only the sacred places—or rather the skeletons of them—of what was once the center of a populous city. Even if the expression "Thebes of a hundred gates" is minted in the image of a Greek *polis*, we can nevertheless judge from it the impression this town once made upon the whole world. There are no clues from which we could judge the extension of the town during, let us say, the Eighteenth or Nineteenth Dynasty, and the number of its inhabitants during its acme. But at one time or another it must have contained royal palaces, offices of the central government, military barracks, and living quarters for the rich and poor. Certainly all these buildings may have been made of sun-dried bricks only; nonetheless, they enclosed for centuries a way of life that expressed its religious needs in monumental buildings of stone.

WESTERN THEBES

Yet this was in the end only half of the whole. For the western bank, from Medinet Habu on the south to Dra' abu'l-Naga on the north, was not only a gigantic necropolis but also an inhabited town. During the Nineteenth Dynasty the kings whose residence proper was in the Delta possessed palaces near their mortuary temples, and during the Twentieth Dynasty the west-side town was ruled by its own mayor. Here, too, we are naturally much better informed about the sacred buildings and the religious life than about the everyday world. One should not forget, though, that the sacred buildings, too, belonged to a work-a-day life and can be understood only in connection with it. It was only in the time of the Roman emperors that they acquired the attraction of a museum for ancient tourism.

On the west side of Thebes there probably existed two ancient starting points for later cult centers. In the north the cult of a cow-goddess seems to have prevailed in the mountain gorge of Deir el Bahari. In the Eleventh Dynasty, in the time of Mentuhotep, she was already identified with Hathor of Denderah, who herself could appear in the form of a cow. The reason for the identification of a local deity with the famous goddess Hathor may be found in the desire of the king of an emerging dynasty to elevate the importance of a hitherto little-known cult center. Such assimilations of originally differing deities were not at all uncommon in ancient Egypt. Under the pressure of the surroundings the goddess Hathor, who was worshiped on the west bank of Thebes, accepted the character of a goddess of the necropolis; she was also called the "sovereign of Thebes." A cave sanctuary near the great terraced temple was established and dedicated to her in the Eighteenth Dynasty.

A second focal point in the south was the region of Medinet Habu, the sanctity of which attracted later temples. The oldest preserved temple here, the "small temple of Medinet Habu," dates only from the time of Hatshepsut-Tuthmosis III. But in a dedicatory inscription the king calls his building activity the "renovation of an older temple which was near collapse." The significance of the place is not apparent. In any case, unlike the other temples on the west side of Thebes, this is not a mortuary temple. Naturally, it too was dedicated to Amon. This name, however, could possibly cover up an originally different divinity. Perhaps it was a primeval god in the shape of a serpent who was worshiped here—the shape of a serpent is often used in Egypt for pre-existing primeval gods. The name of such a snake-god is known in a later period as "he who has finished his course of life" (Greek Κνηφ). He then appears as ancestor of the god who is buried here, a homonymous forefather of Amon of Karnak, who visits him regularly and brings him offerings.

The oldest preserved temple building on the west bank of Thebes is the temple of Mentuhotep, which we have briefly described above. Its association of pyramid, rock tomb, and terraced site presents an original idea never afterward repeated. To the south of it Sankhkare, the successor of Mentuhotep, began to build his tomb, but only the preparatory work for the path leading upward has been preserved. Private tombs from the time of the Eleventh Dynasty are partly situated half up the rocky heights of Deir el Bahari and partly on the plain of Asasif. At the end of the Middle Kingdom the kings were probably being buried again in Thebes. On a statue of this period a mortuary temple of a King Sebekhotep is mentioned. In the northern part of the west bank of Thebes only a few mortuary buildings of the predecessors of the Eighteenth Dynasty are preserved.

THE BUILDINGS OF AMENHOTEP I

It was in the Eighteenth Dynasty that the planned development of the western town of Thebes began. Then it was that the town received its monumental form. Very little is preserved of the buildings of the first king, Amenhotep I, but an innovation is due to him which had hitherto been unknown: the architectural division between the royal tomb and temple. The king's very modest tomb is situated on a lonely spot on the mountain over Dra' abu'l-Naga. Of his equally modest temple only the foundation walls are preserved today on the edge of the cultivation—from that time onward, this remained the situation of the royal temple—to the south of the present-day village of Dra' abu'l-Naga. Apparently he shared the tomb and temple with his mother, the queen Ahmes-Nefertari. What induced the king to this separation of tomb and temple is not easy to understand. The explanation that the tomb was hidden in the folds of the western mountains in order to protect it against spoliation is by no means satisfactory. Admittedly, the architect of the tomb of Tuthmosis I, Ineni, states that he accomplished the building of the tomb "as being the only one present, no one seeing, no one hearing." But if the desire for seclusion was in fact the moving reason, subsequent events did not prove it right. All the tombs, with the exception of that of Tut-ankh-amon, which was entered and then resealed, are known to have been pillaged in antiquity; we possess copious documents dealing with legal procedures against tomb robbers from the end of the Twentieth Dynasty. Nor would this offer an explanation for the fact that the royal temples were no longer mortuary temples in the ancient sense, as, for example, the temples of worship of the pyramids. They do not seem to have played a role during the king's burial, and their cult was not intended for the king, at least not primarily; but they were all temples of the god Amon, which contained, in addition, a cult of remembrance for the dead king. It seems to be almost certain that their first and general function began already during the lifetime of the king who built them. The reason for the division of tomb and temple is therefore to be found in a new idea of the divine nature of the (dead) god and in a new ritual task of the temple. It may even express, in spite of all the pathos, a diminution of the king's divinity: a place of worship is erected for the god of the state and the world, and in it his mortal son is also remembered and provided with offerings; but the king himself has descended to the underworld which lies behind the mountains.

THE ROYAL TOMBS

One can contemplate this gigantic city of temples as a kind of triangle whose base is formed by the line, as the crow flies, between Medinet Habu and the temple of Sety I at Qurneh, and its sides by the lines Medinet

Colorplate XII. Selqet, Queen Nefertari led by Isis, Khepre, Maat. From the tomb of Queen Nefertari, one of the wives of King Ramesses II (1290–1224 B.C.). Western Thebes, Valley of the Queens (Biban el Harim). Eastern wall of the antechamber and entrance to the southern side chamber.

Habu–Deir el Bahari and Deir el Bahari–Qurneh temple. But before we turn our attention to this, a word must be said about the royal tombs. In antiquity they were inaccessible and therefore did not play any outstanding part in everyday life or in festive activity. Yet the fact that one knew of their existence gave to the district a mysterious religious sanctity.

From the time of Tuthmosis I, the kings and the queen Hatshepsut were buried in the Valley of the Kings (Biban el Moluk), a group of mountain gorges behind Deir el Bahari. This is not the place to describe the tombs in detail one by one. Their distribution in the rocky gorges seems to be unplanned. Only the tomb of Queen Hatshepsut (no. 20) lies on the west slope of the mountain ridge, whose eastern side forms the background of her temple at Deir el Bahari. Its situation is therefore related to the site of the queen's temple. Such a relation is not to be found with the other tombs. As far as we know, there existed no places of worship near the tombs, a unique occurrence in Egyptian tradition. After the king's funeral the entrance to the tomb was blocked up with brickwork and closed with the seal of the necropolis police. We shall discuss later what kind of cult prevailed in the mortuary temples. Broadly speaking, we can say that the tombs represent an image of the other world, in which the dead person is present. They treat the theme of the 40,41 underworld in the light of a special dogma: it is concerned with the sun's journey through the twelve hours of the night, which are represented by twelve regions in the underworld. The sun-god enters the west in the form of a ram. He stands in his barque in a shrine which is enclosed and protected by the serpent of the underworld. Spirits draw the barque from one district to another. During his passage the sun-god brings to the dead of each district one hour of light and life. He arranges the distribution of offerings and receives worship. As soon as he leaves one district its inhabitants are submerged once more in darkness and sleep. In the morning, at the end of the twelfth hour, he reaches the eastern horizon, where he changes into the shape of the sun-beetle and travels through the horizon victoriously to rise again as the sun of the new day. In addition to this, the tombs occasionally contain different ritual representations concerned with the resuscitation of the dead. As far as I know, only the tomb of Ramesses III contains representations of themes taken from daily life, similar to the pictures of private tombs. But they are so extensively damaged that they can be consulted only from copies made in the last century.

The Valley of the Queens (Biban el Harim), situated behind the southern end of the necropolis of Deir el Medineh, contains some tombs of the Eighteenth Dynasty, but more especially tombs of queens and princes of the Nineteenth and Twentieth Dynasties. Their plans and decorations are much more modest than those XII of the tombs of the kings. A quite enchanting beauty characterizes the tomb of Nefertari, wife of Ramesses II; here the colored wall paintings display, in spite of their funerary themes, an openly sensuous quality.

One must imagine the valleys of the royal tombs generally as inaccessible and watched by a police force. They formed a world of their own without any direct ritual connection with the world of the living and without any need of it. In no other place in Egypt did the idea of a true kingdom of the dead find an expression so impressive and consistent.

The gangs of workmen who constructed and decorated the tombs lived on the eastern mountain slopes and reached their place of work under supervision. There are workers' settlements at Deir el Medineh where the small houses are closely crowded together. From there a narrow track led along the mountain slope on top of the necropolis and reached the Valley of the Kings through a pass between the mountain top, called 39 El Qurn, and Deir el Bahari. A control station was situated on the top and had to be passed by the companies

104

on their way out and back. Near it, on the mountain slope, a primitive chapel was erected, probably for Hathor, the mistress of the necropolis. Yet all the safety measures of the royal necropolis were in vain in the long run. Its heaped-up treasures offered too strong a temptation, especially in times of need, and this fact is clearly illustrated by the legal proceedings against tomb robbers at the end of the Twentieth Dynasty. At that time the royal tombs were pillaged by organized bands, whose work was made possible by the fact that the local authorities, including the mayor, were involved in it too. During the Twenty-first Dynasty the mummies of the kings were collected and buried anew after their tombs had apparently been completely pillaged; for example, Ramesses I was buried in the tomb of Amenhotep I. In the end, after several reburials, the mummies of nine kings were hidden in the tomb of Amenhotep II (no. 35 in the Valley of the Kings), and a larger number in the lonely rock-cut tomb of a Queen Inhapi (no. 320, to the south of Deir el Bahari). The priests who did the salvage work identified each mummy by means of a small tablet. During the seventies of the last century a family in Qurneh discovered the hiding place, and "single finds" appeared in the shops of the antique dealers. It was only in 1881 that the Egyptian government succeeded in taking measures to secure the safety of the mummies. The cache in the tomb of Amenhotep II was discovered in 1898. Today all the royal mummies are accommodated in a special room of the museum in Cairo.

THE MORTUARY TEMPLES

The development of the sites which faced the east took a different turn. We saw that from the time of Amenhotep I the kings used to build their temples there, and in so doing they followed a definite sequence: in the Eighteenth as well as in the Nineteenth to Twentieth Dynasties they began in the north and continued farther southward from generation to generation. Naturally, this rule was not always strictly adhered to. XIII, The terraced temple of Hatshepsut represents an exception in its position as well as in its construction. Of the other Eighteenth Dynasty temples only few remains have been preserved. Under Amenhotep III the southern end of the necropolis was built up, and here the sites included the palace town and a sacred lake (Birket Habu) and must have extended from the Memnon colossi to beyond Birket Habu. After the era of Amenhotep IV, the immediate successors—Tut-ankh-amon, Ay, and Horemheb—returned to Thebes. Their mortuary temple, used by the three kings one after the other, is situated immediately to the north of the later temple of Ramesses III at Medinet Habu. The first king of the Nineteenth Dynasty, Ramesses I, does not seem to have had a temple of his own. His son Sety I built again in the northern part; Ramesses II located his temple, the Ramesseum, farther to the south; and Ramesses III constructed his temple even farther to the south, at Medinet Habu.

It is obviously not my duty here to describe the preserved monuments in chronological order. Rather, we shall try, with the help of the intelligible remains, to give a picture of the typologically different sanctuaries that endowed the western town of Thebes with its distinctive face. First place must be given to the mortuary temples, with which the great temple of Deir el Bahari can be associated only after making certain reservations. The palace town of Amenhotep III possessed only ephemeral significance. And finally, the "little temple" of Medinet Habu must be mentioned, since it developed a cult theme of its own which is of great importance for the Amon theology.

Because of the cult forms preserved in them, the mortuary temples represent a complicated mixture of traditional elements and theological speculations. Above all, they are temples of the Theban god Amon; he owns the center of the site. This, at least, is the situation in the middle of the Eighteenth Dynasty. It is not quite certain in what form the god was present in the temple. He certainly visited it on the occasion of the valley festival (see p. 116). The god's barque crossed the Nile from Karnak and was carried to the temple, where it stopped for a while, receiving offerings and so on. Probably the route was extended to include all contemporary extant mortuary temples, which must have been visited by the barque. Naturally not all temples, multiplying as they did from generation to generation, could be regarded as contemporary. In some of them the cult had been extinguished soon after the death of its builder. As a result, the number of temples visited will always have been limited mainly to those of the ruling king and his immediate predecessors. The god was accompanied by his Theban associate gods, Mut and Khons, and their three barques formed the nucleus of the procession. The fairly well-preserved temple of Sety I at Qurneh shows the spatial requirements of this divine visit in its earliest and clearest form, as its center is formed by three oblong rooms for the divine barques and two parallel side rooms for the ritual requirements. The temples of the Eighteenth Dynasty are unfortunately badly preserved, and conclusions concerning them are drawn from analogies with the temples of the Nineteenth Dynasty. The triple division can be clearly recognized in the Ramesseum. Here, however, we do not find three rooms alongside each other; instead, the middle temple has three parallel areas. In the mortuary temple of Ramesses III at Medinet Habu the rooms for the barques of Mut and Khons are likewise situated to the right and left of the room for the barque of Amon; but this room is marked more forcefully than in the other temple as the center of the site.

A second constituent element of the temple's activity was the cult of the deceased royal ancestor, the immediate predecessor of the building's founder. As a rule, seen from the entrance, it is situated to the left of the areas reserved for the gods. In Deir el Bahari rooms for the commemorative cult of Tuthmosis I are situated to the left in the uppermost terrace. In the Sety temple are rooms for the cult of Ramesses I, in Medinet Habu for the cult of Ramesses II. A primeval cult element is also provided: a false door (but it is missing at Medinet Habu). This is a stylized monumental imitation of a door, which was a necessary part of the tombs of the Old Kingdom and also of the pyramid temples. It is a symbol in the true sense of the word. Through it leads the way into another world; offerings are put down before it and concomitant prayers are transformed, as it were, by its intervention. This architectural element also plays here the role of a mediator for the deceased king, whose body rests far away in the Valley of the Kings, and whose transcendent form abides in the world beyond. In addition—but it is not certain when this began and whether it was always so or not—the dead king himself possessed a processional barque, probably in order to carry one of his statues. It accompanied the barques of the gods during the procession of the valley festival.

A third cult element is a place of worship for the sun-god. As a rule this is situated to the right of the center. Its essential feature is an altar in an open courtyard, a natural place of worship for the god who is visible in the sky.

This trinity—Amon, king father, sun-god—of the mortuary temples is a somewhat schematical grouping, but relevant parts of the temple can be proved to have existed at Deir el Bahari, Qurneh, the Ramesseum, Medinet Habu, and the temple of Ay and Horemheb. If we knew more about the temples of the early Eighteenth Dynasty, about those of Amenhotep I, Tuthmosis I, and so on, it would be possible to show whether this cult program had existed from the beginning or whether changes took place in the course of

106

time. The architectural task of uniting the three cults in one temple building was solved in different ways. In some cases, for example, at Deir el Bahari (pp. 109–10), other cults were associated with them. It is fascinating to compare the different adjustments and to observe how new arrangements sometimes stand beside those that had been devised earlier. A judgment concerning the beauty or aptness or originality of a single building is possible only if one knows the tasks of the architect and the previous designs to which he could resort.

In addition to an understanding of the architectural evolution, an insight into the theological data is necessary, and indeed is equally important. What is the relation of the three deities who are worshiped one beside the other: the deified king father, the visiting Amon of Karnak, and the sun-god? The Egyptian theologian would have given an answer tending to maintain that all three are in the end only different forms of appearance of one and the same god, Amon-Ra, the king of the gods. The composite name Amon-Ra, which is testified from the Middle Kingdom, proves clearly that Amon and Ra were regarded as one and the same god. It implies that the old sun-god Ra can be approached under the cult form and name of Amon. Furthermore, the Thebes of the New Kingdom seems to have nurtured the idea that the deceased king is united with his divine father Amon, returning, as it were, to him from whom he had sprung. Concerning the death of Amenhotep I, it is accordingly said: "*After he had gone to heaven, he was united with the sun and joined with him from whom he had sprung.*" The sporadically mentioned "*Amon of the temple of Medinet Habu*" would thus mean that the special Amon of this temple is in fact only the deceased king of the temple, who has again become Amon.

The question as to the position of the royal builder of the temple still remains open. For up to now we have been concerned only with the royal ancestor. In fact, this question is a very difficult one, for it was a predominant part of the builder's plan that the temple should be used during his lifetime. Therefore, it was thought of, at first, as the place where the living king himself fulfilled ritual actions. We can deduct this from the fact that certain rooms show the ritual purification of the king, which preceded his enacting of the cult: his introduction to the company of the gods, and so on. In other representations, the king himself is shown enacting rites, for example, in front of his divine father, but also before Amon, the lord of the temple. Here, too, a certain canonical distribution of the rooms seems to have been the rule. The chambers that served for ritual preparations are as a rule situated in the right half of the temple and in front of the cult chambers proper, but naturally behind the forecourts.

In addition, other cult chambers could be prepared for the king with the purpose of serving his commemorative cult after his death. In Qurneh, for instance, two rooms to the left of the central hall—therefore opposite the royal purification chambers—are reserved for the cult of Sety I after his death. One may infer from the pictures that he possessed a cult barque of his own, which was carried with his image during the valley festival.

The variety of the cult actions is by no means exhausted by the above account. Apart from the three cults already named, which were essential for the nature of the mortuary temple, other cults were added, according to the size of the temple, especially for Hathor, the mistress of Thebes, and beside her now and then also for gods of the dead like Anubis. It is remarkable that the role of Osiris is of lesser importance, especially in earlier times. Only since the Nineteenth Dynasty, probably in consequence of the restoration after the Amarna period, can definite cults of this god be traced.

Finally, one other component of the temples is to be mentioned, the royal palace. Archaeologically it can be traced from the end of the Eighteenth Dynasty in connection with several temples, such as those of Tut-ankh-amon, Ay, and Horemheb. According to inscriptions of the Eighteenth Dynasty—from the time of Hatshepsut and Tuthmosis III—a royal palace must have existed on the west side of Thebes, although archaeologically nothing is known of its position. It is, of course, possible that it was situated somewhere in the cultivated land between the temple district and the river bank. But after the Amarna period the palace became part of the temple site itself. It also had a fixed place in the total plan, namely, to the left of the first courtyard, at right angles to the axis of the temple and opening up into the courtyard. At Medinet Habu the preserved remains permit an exact reconstruction. Apart from the doors it was connected with the temple courtyard by means of the window of appearance, a balcony-like decorated window in which the king appeared on certain occasions. In the tomb of Ramose, for example, a relief shows Ramose receiving rings of the "gold of honor" from Amenhotep IV at his window of appearance.

DEIR EL BAHARI

In essence the great terraced Eighteenth Dynasty temple of Hatshepsut and Tuthmosis III belongs also to the mortuary temples. It reveals an original design which crowned an architectonic task; it had special

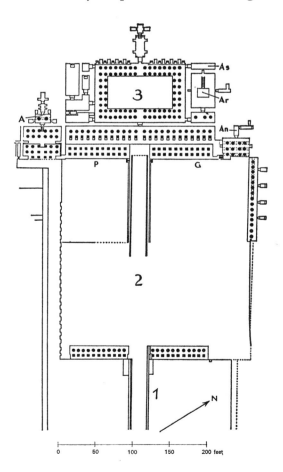

Figure 15. Ground plan of the temple of Queen Hatshepsut in western Thebes, Deir el Bahari. The ground plan cuts through several planes. The lowest plane is on a level with the temple courtyard (1). The next plane is on a level with the lower terrace (2) with the punt hall (P) and the birth hall (G), the sanctuary of Hathor (A), and the chapel of Anubis (An), with its vestibule hall. The uppermost plane corresponds with that of the upper terrace, on which were situated the hypostyle hall, the hall of the statues of Hatshepsut, the holiest sanctuary inside the rock (on the median), and the mortuary chapel of Hatshepsut (in the western corner). As: hall of Amon; Ar: altar dedicated to the sun-god. After H. Ricke, 1950.

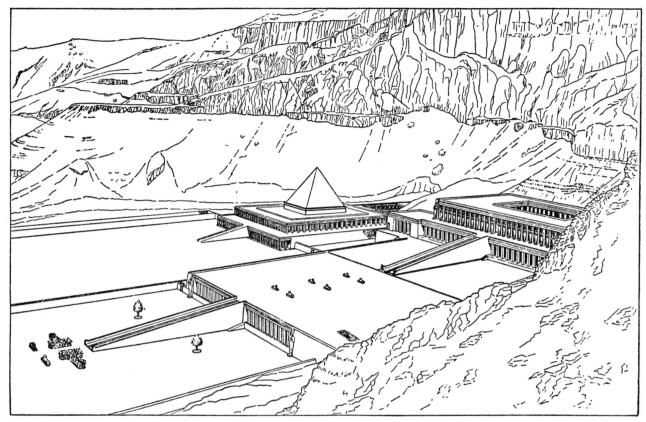

Figure 16. Western Thebes, Deir el Bahari. The temple of Queen Hatshepsut from the northeast. In the background is the mortuary temple of Mentuhotep II (Neb-hepet-ra). Reconstruction. After G. Steindorff and W. Wolf, 1936.

significance during the valley festival, and it fulfilled a function beyond Pharaonic times, outlasting most of the other temple buildings; all this justifies a brief study of the achievement involved.

When Hatshepsut planned her site, she had to pay heed to two monuments which were situated in the same place: the mortuary site of Mentuhotep in the southern corner of the valley gorge and a small sanctuary dedicated to Hathor immediately to the north of it. Private tombs of the Middle Kingdom, which were located on the slope and probably no longer received any funerary cult during her time, were built upon. The example of Mentuhotep's temple and the structure of the landscape in general made it imperative to build the temple in terraces. The special task was to construct a temple of Amon with consideration of the cult requirements of the west side of Thebes. Terraces here took the place of the forecourts of the other temples, which were used in connection with festival processions. The sanctuary was cut into the rock. In its outer room is a representation of the divine barque with the deified ancestors, Tuthmosis I, Queen Ahmes, and their daughter Bitnofret standing behind it: pictorial expression is here given to the nexus of the cult of the gods with ancestor worship. The uppermost terrace fulfilled the function of the central pillared hall of the other temples as a connecting link between the single cult chambers and a sacrificial hall. To the right is linked the open court with altar, the center of the sun worship, while to the left are chambers for the

109

memorial cult of Tuthmosis I. The focus of this cult, a false door of granite, is now in the Louvre. The middle terrace is isolated from the upper one by colonnades to the right and left of the connecting ramp. Here we have what might be termed the historical part of the temple, which in other temples is assigned to the pylons and to the outer walls. It is a kind of memorial, an account of her government, rendered by the queen to her father Amon. The left wing contains the representation of the great expedition to Punt, the land of incense on the Somali coast, while the right wing contains the legend of her divine procreation and birth. It is not by chance that the queen does not commemorate here any warlike feats. In conscious contrast to the male members of her family, she aimed politically at peace and inner reconstruction. This is attested by a great number of inscriptions of the queen and, last but not least, by the emphatic resumption of the policy of conquest by Tuthmosis III. Two external cult centers are situated on each side of the rear colonnades. They are, in fact, independent temple sites and are also approachable from the middle terrace: to the right is a sanctuary of Anubis, the god of the cemetery, whose cult here is quite appropriate, and to the left a sanctuary for Hathor, the mistress of Thebes.

In connection with the temple, one other detail is worth mentioning: Senmut, the queen's favorite and educator of her daughter, installed near the lower terrace a secret tomb of his own in such a way that the tomb entrance is situated outside the temple precincts, but the tomb chamber itself reaches under the enclosure wall into the temple site, so that, as a result, he was buried within the temple precinct. As far as I can see, this arrangement is unique for its period, and only a man in his position was able to afford it. For the time when tombs could be freely situated inside temple precincts was still far away.

THE BUILDINGS OF AMENHOTEP III

We have already briefly mentioned above that several kings of the Eighteenth Dynasty had palaces on the west bank of Thebes. It would be wrong, therefore, to imagine the region as only one vast town of the dead. Eventually Amenhotep III built a whole palace town to the south of Medinet Habu. Its preserved remains, unfortunately, are so small that even an approximate reconstruction is impossible. Probably the mortuary temple of the king, behind the colossi of Memnon, belonged to the total complex and most likely also the temple of the enlistment officer Amenhotep, son of Hapu (see p. 129). The king's building complex is introduced from the east by the two so-called colossi of Memnon; one could compare with them the colossi of Ramesses II in front of the temple of Luxor. The king's mortuary temple stood behind them. Other sites, among them the palace, were probably situated behind the Birket Habu. It is likely that there were also some temple sites here, among them a temple of Amon. It was here that the king celebrated the jubilee of his reign. To judge by the variety and significance of the buildings, one might gain the impression that we have here some forerunners of the Amarna period, when the break with the cult of Amon was completed by his son and successor Amenhotep IV, who finally decided to transfer his residence to Tell el Amarna.

In fact, we still know far too little about the history of the period, with all its tensions, in order to be able to express a final judgment. It is certainly not fortuitous that the divine name of Aten, which later on became so important, occurs here in one of the king's temple names as well as in one of the king's foundations in Nubia: *"The house of Nimurija* [that is, Amenhotep III]: [named] *it is Aten who shines."* In view of the fact that his son left Thebes and promulgated a new doctrine and to a certain extent persecuted the cult of Amon,

Colorplate XIII. Temple of Queen Hatshepsut (1490–1468 B.C.). 18th Dynasty, New Kingdom. Western Thebes, Deir el Bahari.
At the left side of the middle zone to the south of the temple lies the temple of Mentuhotep II (Neb-hepet-ra) of the 11th Dynasty.
View from the southeast.

the buildings of Amenhotep III were probably only short-lived. The colossi of Memnon certainly outlasted the age, and already at the time of the Roman emperors they were visited by travelers in search of knowledge, among them the emperors Hadrian and Septimius Severus.

For the development of religious cults in the western town of Thebes, the mortuary temple of Amenhotep, son of Hapu, was of greater importance. Today only its foundations, which were excavated in 1934 and 1935, are to be seen. That he was at all able to possess a temple of his own adjacent to and in the same form as the royal funerary temples is certainly a unique distinction for a private person of his period. We possess a copy of a decree from the Twenty-first Dynasty in which the cult privileges of this temple are asserted, that is, from a period when the buildings of Amenhotep III, his king, were probably no longer standing. This may be connected with the fact that for some unknown reason Amenhotep assumed a godlike role in the faith of his people. In the Late Period he was still worshiped with a religious fervor that was especially characteristic of Thebes. It kept the sanctity of the former residence alive and in the end transformed its belief and cult.

THE TEMPLE OF MEDINET HABU

Among the buildings of Medinet Habu one special complex first attracts our attention, for although it is not one of the greatest, it played a significant role in the development of the faith and theology of the god

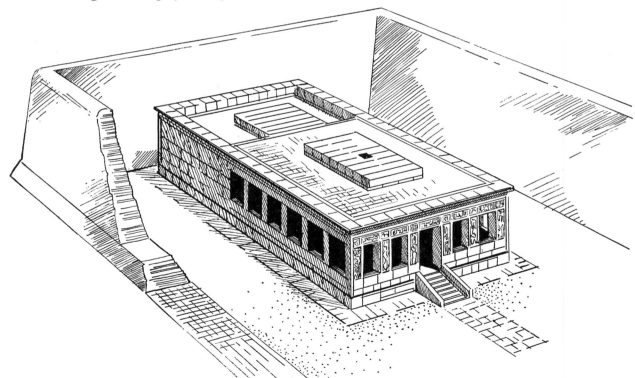

Figure 17. Medinet Habu. Small temple of the 18th Dynasty. The reconstruction shows the temple as it appeared in the 18th Dynasty. The pillared hall in front was accessible by a ramp and enclosed the room for the barque. The rear part was lower and contained six smaller rooms with groups of statues of Tuthmosis III and Amon. Apart from the room for the barque, the nucleus of the temple has been preserved almost unchanged. After U. Hölscher, 1933.

Figure 18. Medinet Habu. Roman forecourt and Ptolemaic pylon in front of the small temple of the 18th Dynasty. The old drawing shows the temple in a state typical of most Egyptian temples until the middle of the last century, namely, covered with sand up to the roof. It is thanks to this state of affairs, more than anything else, that the temples were preserved at all. The process of clearing them during the past hundred years has unhappily exposed them to new damage. After Norden, *Travels in Egypt and Nubia*, 1757.

Amon. It is usually termed the "small temple of Medinet Habu." When Ramesses III erected his enormous Fig.17 mortuary temple there, he included it in his over-all plan. The nucleus of the preserved site dates only from the Eighteenth Dynasty and the reigns of Hatshepsut and Tuthmosis III. But we have cause to believe that in fact we are dealing here with a primeval sacred site on which the edifice of the Tuthmosid replaced an older building belonging possibly to the Middle Kingdom (see p. 102). Naturally it is Amon again who is named here as the lord of the temple. But it is again another aspect of this many-sided god that is evoked here, and in contrast to the mortuary temples there is no mention of the valley festival. As suggested above, it is possible that the cult of this temple was originally dedicated to a serpent-god. For the Egyptians tended to ascribe a serpent form especially to those deities who were thought to derive from the chaotic state of the world before order was engendered by an act of creation. We have thus to do with a primeval god from the most ancient epoch of the world. At a time when the gods were endowed with human traits and in imitation of the human example belonged to divine families, and so on, such a primeval being is regarded as a divine ancestor, a venerable forefather of the gods who are now living and active. Following again the human example, they are obliged to offer to this deity some kind of funerary cult. Amon of Luxor, therefore, travels to Medinet Habu at the beginning of every decade to bring funerary offerings to his venerable ancestor at the "sacred primeval place." We shall have to speak later of the role that this temple played in the theology of Thebes (p. 123). Because of its religious significance, new building activities were again and again con-

113

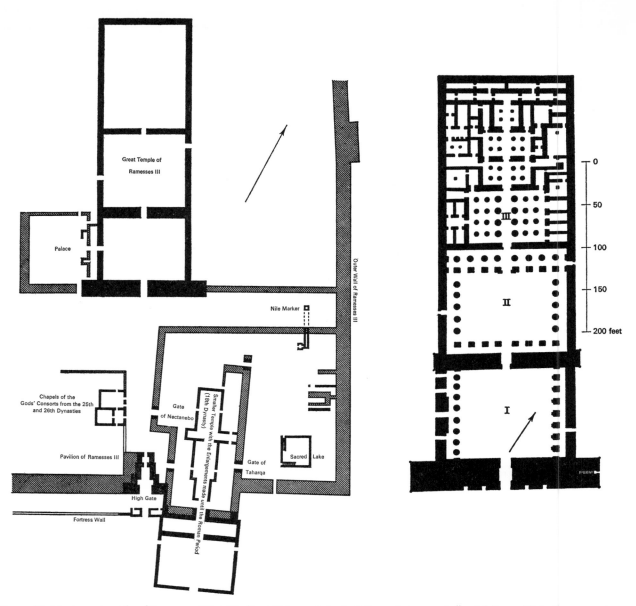

Figure 19. Mortuary temple of Ramesses III at Medinet Habu and the buildings that preceded and followed it in the same place. Plan of the whole. After E. Brunner-Traut and V. Hell, 1962.

Figure 20. Mortuary temple of Ramesses III at Medinet Habu. Ground plan. I, II, III: First, second, and third courts, respectively. After K. Lange and M. Hirmer, 1955–61.

cerned with this temple from the Eighteenth Dynasty onward. Until the Roman period it received enlarge-
Fig.18 ments by which new parts were added in a frontal direction, according to the usual mode of expansion in Egyptian temples. The temple proper was divided into two equal parts of differing ritual significance, and accordingly of different architectural shape. The rear part consists of six fairly small chambers, the largest of which was in the middle and contained a statue group of Amon and the king. The image received light

114

Figure 21. Mortuary temple of Ramesses III in western Thebes, Medinet Habu. South wall of court I. Schematic design of the arrangement of the wall. On the sides are passages leading to the royal palace behind, and near these the king is represented as stepping out or driving in a chariot. The middle part protrudes a little and contains the window of appearance. It was here that the king appeared at festivals and in order to receive homage. From here, too, he distributed the "gold of honor" to deserving noblemen. The window ledge is decorated with heads of enemies molded in the round in such a way that they seem to carry the parapet on their necks. To the right and left of the window the king is shown slaying a group of enemies. The group of three bound enemies on the right is shown on plate 45. After U. Hölscher, 1933.

through an opening in the ceiling; it must have been visible even at the entrance, in effective contrast to the semidarkness of its surroundings. The part in front of it has the shape of a peripteral temple, with a cella divided in two for the barque of Amon.

Near this small temple, located within his enclosure wall, Ramesses III erected his enormous mortuary temple. It is the most grand and monumental of all the preserved mortuary temples at Thebes. The nucleus Figs.19,20 is formed by the mortuary temple proper, with its ritual chambers for the divine barque of the sun-god and for the royal funerary cult. There are also some remains of the royal palace. It opens up toward the first courtyard with passages and a well-preserved window of appearance. In addition—and unlike all the other Fig.21 mortuary temples—it is surrounded by a mighty fortress wall, of which the high gate was part. This gate 42 structure in the east apparently imitates the design of contemporary fortress buildings. The space between the wall and the temple was filled with military barracks, stables, office buildings, and dwelling places.

Figure 22. Mortuary temple of Ramesses III in western Thebes, Medinet Habu. From the north wall in the second court. Procession during the festival of the fertility-god Min. The register in relief contains individual scenes from the festival of Min. The carrying of the image of the god Min on the right and the king in his sedan chair on the left are reproduced on plates 47 and 46. The middle scene shows the god standing under a canopy; in front of him the king brings incense on the instrument called the censing arm. The cycle is continued to the right. One recognizes the king again with the red crown, and before him the white bull, which is also led in the procession. After Denon, *Voyage en Égypte*, 1802.

115

Inscriptions and reliefs adorn the temple, and they are of the greatest importance for our understanding of the significance of mortuary temples, for it is possible to infer from them almost with certainty what the ritual function of each part was. Furthermore, the temple contains detailed representations of the celebrations 46-48, Fig.22 at the festivals of the Memphite god Sokar and the god of fertility, Min. The outer and inner walls carry representations with historical content, for example, concerning the wars against the Libyans and the Sea 43-45 People; they also have generously composed hunting scenes in relief.

It speaks for the historical self-esteem of this king that he copied part of his reliefs from the temple of Ramesses II, the Ramesseum, which is situated somewhat to the north of Medinet Habu. Although its structure is essentially different from the temple of Ramesses III, its decoration can be partly restored with the aid of the copies made by Ramesses III.

THE NECROPOLIS OF WESTERN THEBES

While glancing at the great and more or less official sacred sites on the west side of Thebes, one must not forget the necropolis, which is one of the biggest and most revealing—as far as its decoration is concerned—of all the necropolises in Egypt. One cannot overrate the knowledge of Egyptian art and cultural history that was obtained here. Possibly in the time of the Pharaohs this cemetery did not appear as monotonously yellow and desert-like as it does today, since the façades of the tombs were intact and in addition the frequent visits of relatives on the occasion of funerary festivals had an enlivening effect. Nevertheless, the contrast 50 between the monotonous surface and the colorful gladness of the world of the tomb pictures is astonishing. For all the importance of Thebes as a sacred place, the necropolis had only local significance. During the most brilliant days of the city the highest officials of the state and the priesthood of the temples were buried here. But nobody from Memphis or from the Delta would aim at possessing any kind of tomb here. Thebes was not *the* sacred town of the dead of Egypt in the same way as Abydos.

The official record today includes almost 450 tombs which extend from the period of the Old Kingdom (that is, about 2200 B.C.) to the time of the Ptolemies. Naturally the funerary cult was not perpetually continued in all the tombs from the day when they were first finished, but the dead are remembered for a longer or shorter period and provided with offering gifts according to their position and the resources of their descendants. Some tombs were also re-used, after a lapse of time, by later generations. The daily life of western Thebes went on, as a rule, in that part of the town which was situated between the Nile and the temples. However, once a year in the tenth month, the great necropolis woke up in colorful life on the occasion of the "beautiful festival of the desert valley," an event that is attested from the Twelfth Dynasty. Then Amon in his barque crossed over from Karnak and visited Deir el Bahari, that is, the "desert valley." Priestly watchmen were posted above the temples in order to announce and observe the approaching procession. In the Eighteenth Dynasty Amon was accompanied by his associated gods, Mut and Khons. He visited not only Deir el Bahari but also at least some of the mortuary temples that were still in use. Moreover, the common people, too, took part in this festival and celebrated together with their dead in their tombs with songs,

Colorplate XIV. Tuthmosis III before Amon-Ra. Rear wall of the Hathor chapel of the temple of Queen Hatshepsut in western Thebes, Deir el Bahari. Cairo Museum.

banquets, and carousals. The tomb became the "house of the heart's rejoicing," and by giving offerings the relatives allowed the dead to take part as well.

As the necropolis was in use for a long time, certain changes in the beliefs concerning the next world can be noticed. To put it broadly, the tombs of the Eighteenth Dynasty contain scenes that are like picture-book accounts of daily life, although they keep to a certain tradition and are limited to special themes. Their meaning may be explained as the recording in pictures of a life that is closed and passed; or simply as expressing pleasure in artistic creations; or again as the magical projection of the represented person into another world; or—as is possible in this relatively late period—something of all three intentions is present. Yet the objects represented belong mainly to this life here and now. It does not matter here that certain themes are on principle taboo and that the individual traits of the life represented are given little scope. But all this changed during the Nineteenth and Twentieth Dynasties. Admittedly, in the freshness of their colors and in the delicacy of their design the scenes are fully equal to the products of the previous periods—especially at Deir el Medineh, where the artists and artisans themselves were buried; but the themes are now turned toward the afterworld. Judgment of the dead, demons, scenes in the other world—even where the cultivation of the land is concerned—form now the decorations of the tombs. The change may possibly be connected with the effect of the shock after the collapse of the Amarna period. Confessions of guilt and thoughts on atonement appear in the prayers of this time; and in the same spirit, apparently, it did not seem fitting to perpetuate the colorful joy of this world in the tombs.

In the Late Period, from the Twenty-fifth or the Twenty-sixth Dynasty onward, the western town of Thebes was again renovated. The splendor of the capital city had long faded. Since the Twenty-first Dynasty the kings were no longer buried in Thebes; the focal point of world politics had finally been transferred to Lower Egypt, so that Thebes, it seems, was well on the way to accepting a provincial status. The town itself began to dissolve into a number of villages and settlements. It is significant that Herodotus, who paid an admittedly short visit to the town about 430 B.C., had almost nothing to say about it. On the west side of Thebes the religious life—and probably also the actual settlements—crystallized around three points: Deir el Bahari, Deir el Medineh, and Medinet Habu. The growth of the last-named temple has been sketched above; it may be that the mysterious cult of the primeval gods reached its highest point at this period. The fortification walls of the great temple of Ramesses III were destroyed, and perhaps it had already become the dwelling place of the population (see p. 131). Some new cult centers appeared, however, in the forecourt of the temple: the mortuary chapels of the Ethiopian divine consorts Shepenwepet I, Amenirdis, Shepenwepet II, and Ankhnes-neferibre (see p. 85), of which the first and the last are almost completely destroyed. The reasons for siting them here in the temple district are not quite clear. Perhaps they were attracted by the sanctity of the place. The temple of the primeval gods, which had been considerably enlarged by the Ethiopian king Taharqa, was in their immediate vicinity. One must remember, too, that the kings of the Twenty-second and Twenty-third Dynasties were buried in the temple precincts at Tanis. The choice of place (on the part of the Ethiopian consorts of Amon) may also have been influenced by the increasing insecurity of the vast extent of the town of the dead, which had been left to its fate. The architectural shape of the chapel of Amenirdis is interesting. It probably follows Nubian patterns. A simple cella is closely surrounded by a roofed outer building, the distance from the inner to the outer wall being three and one third feet. The tombs themselves are immediately under the chapels.

118

Colorplate XV. Sen-Nedjem and his wife in the fields of Iaru. From the tomb of Sen-Nedjem. Western Thebes, Deir el Medineh, tomb 1. 20th Dynasty, New Kingdom (1186–1070 B.C.).

At the same time enormous tomb buildings were raised in the north (at El Asasif, below Deir el Bahari) for the tombs of Mentuemhet (no. 34), Pedi-ameuapet (Peduamenap, no. 33), Ibi (no. 36), Harwa (no. 37), and others. Very little remains of their upper buildings, which consisted of sun-dried bricks; but the remains suggest big courtyards with pylons in the form of temples. The subterranean structures are very impressive, especially in point of size, which often surpasses that of the royal tombs. Furthermore, their surveying technique is astonishing, for although they were located within a comparatively narrow space, these enormous tombs were planned in such a way that the subterranean passages did not touch each other. We cannot tell as yet whether these extended subterranean sites are part of a planned homogeneous system, with a certain admitted degree of variation. A complete publication with exact measurements is still lacking. Possibly the burial places themselves are imitations of tombs of Osiris. This may be inferred from the fact that the coffin chamber of some of them (for instance, of the tomb of Pedi-ameuapet) is a sort of raised island in a sub-terranean hall.

To the north, at Deir el Bahari, there are buildings from the era of the Ptolemies; witness the colonnade before the sanctuary of the uppermost terrace. The cult of Amon was scarcely continued, but contemporary deities, especially deified human beings like Amenhotep, son of Hapu and Imhotep, as well as Hygieia, had taken possession of the place. Here must be mentioned also the enlargements at Medinet Habu and the small temple of Qasr el Aguz. To the Ptolemaic era belongs also the temple of Deir el Medineh, which was itself no longer dedicated to Amon but to the deities of the dead and of the necropolis.

III. THEBES AS A SACRED CITY

Our survey of the history of Thebes and its cult edifices had naturally to be selective, and only the most important places and events could be included. If one considers Thebes as a sacred site, it appears beyond doubt that it received this position because of its close connection with the rulers of the New Kingdom. This is the city from which the successful reunification of the country was twice completed. It was the center of the Empire as long as this lasted; and it remained even afterward for centuries the repository of great memories. All this was enhanced by an added distinction, the fact that the city's importance in the history of the world was matched by its spiritual achievement. Such an achievement was not the result of independent evolution; rather, it was instrumental in conferring on the singular and transient historical events a religious and spiritual form that grew essentially out of the religion of Egypt. As is usual in ancient Egypt, the names and personalities of the priests who achieved this remain unknown to us. So we can only state that the priesthood succeeded in creating from the extant local data a theological system that could match the possibilities and needs of a capital city in which the king resided. This system is possibly the most comprehensive and deep-searching ever produced in Egypt and fully expressed one aspect of the Egyptian religion. It could not be something completely new and was not intended as a panacea to meet the immediate need of each period, but it had to encompass the whole religious past. For the Egyptian demands that any new and con-temporary idea must also enclose the sum total of past experience.

When Thebes started its historical mission in the Eleventh Dynasty, a new god, Amon (see p. 80), appeared. After the period of unrest and collapse between the Old and the Middle Kingdom, it would hardly have been

120

possible to connect renascent religious thought with one of the ancient deities like Ptah of Memphis or Ra of Heliopolis, in whose name the Old Kingdom had flourished and perished. It might have been natural to choose the falcon-god Monthu of Hermonthis as the protective deity of the new town and the new dynasty, especially as his hawk shape agreeably approached that of the falcon-god Horus. But apparently the religious demands of this skeptical age, with its search for new ways, could be satisfied only by the invisible god Amon. And throughout centuries of priestly speculation and historical change, he always retained something of this mysterious, shapeless invisibility.

He was certainly at once burdened with the demands of a ritual that had taken centuries to develop: faith and thought may be quick-moving and changeable, but the forms of worship through which they are represented and confirmed remain conservative and rigid. The faith of the common people gets hold of him, too; the simple man feels the need of a god who is comprehensible and visible. These three components, priestly speculation, ritual tradition, and general human need, determine the development of the god in his city.

AMON: THE GOD OF THE KINGS AND THE KING OF THE GODS

From the very beginning this new god was thought of as a royal god, that is, on the one hand as father, protector, and representative of the dynasty, but on the other as king of the gods and the world. This idea is thus expressed in his name, "Amon-Ra, king of the gods, lord of the thrones of the two lands." In this function as a royal god, Amon also accepts the name of the sun-god Ra. Since the height of the Old Kingdom, this god, whose name probably means simply "the sun," had been regarded as the real ruler of the world, and the kings were considered to be the sons of Ra. He himself certainly had also a predecessor, the falcon-shaped sky-god Horus, and already during the earliest dynasties the Pharaoh was considered as his earthly form of appearance. A connection between the two older royal gods is expressed in the compound name Ra-Harakhti, that is, "Ra and Horus of the horizon." When Amon or Amon-Ra became the royal god, he certainly accepted the position and function of his predecessors, but he did not simply replace them; for all the later kings, too, were still incarnations of Horus and all of them carried the title "son of Ra."

Although the new royal god Amon-Ra can be clearly recognized only in the kingship of the Eighteenth Dynasty, he must have already existed in a similar form during the Middle Kingdom. Evidence for this is found in the kings called Amenemhat, in the special building activities of the period, and in the fact that Sesostris I erected here in Karnak a building to celebrate the jubilee of his reign. Our sources of information from the Middle Kingdom are sparse as far as Thebes is concerned, and we have to content ourselves with these few sporadic but indubitable facts. The changes in the god-king relationship are most incisively expressed in the changed situation between Amon and the king. The dogma of special vocation under Tuthmosis III and Hatshepsut gave a new form to the ancient idea of divine rule. We find here a much stronger personal element in the connection between Amon and the king. Amenhotep III, through his love of gigantic monuments and of splendor, prepared the way for the prophet-like role of the king, which was convincingly assumed by his son Amenhotep IV. How different was the relation in the time of Ramesses II! Admittedly the edifices of his period—the pillared hall at Karnak and the Ramesseum—show a predilection for the great and powerful. But there is also a completely new feeling of dependence, which expresses itself in the pathetic outcry of the king during the battle of Qadesh, when he sees himself cut off from his troops: *"What is it then, my father Amon? Hath a father indeed forgotten his son?... I call to thee, my father Amon. I am in the midst of foes whom I know not.... My soldiers have forsaken me and not one of my chariotry hath looked round for me...."* [Erman-Blackman].

Finally, the Theban temples can teach us something also of that period of the divine state when the earthly rulers were depreciated in favor of the divine king Amon and become mere representatives and administrators. It is also in Thebes that one can best understand the somewhat bigoted piety of the Ethiopian kings, who allowed Egyptian forms to be permeated with African sentiments.

AMON AS A LOCAL DEITY

The moment the first temple was built for the god Amon at Karnak he became a local deity, that is, a god who is at home on a certain place and must therefore adopt some kind of attitude toward the gods who live around him. This happened at Karnak in two ways which were by no means original. On the one hand he formed a triad together with the vulture-goddess Mut of Asheru and the god Khons, the three of them forming a family of father, mother, and son. It is significant that his female equivalent proper, the goddess Amaunet, does not enter into this. Such triads play an important part in the composition of the Egyptian pantheon. It is founded on the primeval concept—which is by no means limited to Egypt—that the sacred number three is fundamentally a unit, though containing three components. This expedient to unite gods is preferably used on local ground. From a circle of local gods a triad is chosen which represents all the gods of a place and in fact is a divine whole. It is only a secondary feature that they are in some instances interpreted as a family, the urge being to represent the theological idea in familiar human form. Amon, Mut, and Khons constitute, then, the divine circle of Karnak. They possess temples near to each other and appear together in the great festivals. It was the local function of the triad that was the reason for excluding Amaunet, who belongs conceptually to Amon, but did not find a cult and a home at Karnak.

The ennead of Karnak was another creation of theological speculation. It is a product of theological thought in relation to numbers. Nine as the second power of three signifies "all," a sum total of gods which is composed of "very many." Here, too, the fundamental idea is a group conceived as a unit, which is composed of several single members ($9 = 3 \times 3 =$ plural of plurals). The idea of an ennead, too, is much older. We know, for example, of the ennead of gods of Heliopolis, and the ennead of nations, which are not named in detail but must be understood as the sum total of all the nations living on earth. It even happens that this "very great number" does not contain exactly nine members, but a few more or less. Thus the ennead of Thebes contains all the nine gods of Heliopolis; they were absorbed merely for the sake of completeness— and in addition, we find Horus, Hathor, Sukhos, and other gods of the Theban nome. If one ventures to count these gods, which should not be done, according to the Egyptian way of thinking, one finds no fewer than fifteen gods. The meaning of this combination is that "all" the gods are represented in the temple and somehow belong to it. This certainly increases the significance of the temple beyond the local borders and gives it the appearance of a sacred place with many roads leading to it.

AMON AS FERTILITY-GOD

Furthermore, the god Amon expands his nature mainly in two directions that are potentially already extant in him and are also encouraged by the wider cult environs. There is at first his relation to Luxor (see pp. 97–98). He becomes a god of fertility, which is quite consistent with his nature as a pre-existent primeval god. For the cosmos and all that exists, gods, men, and animals, somehow emerged or were created, it was thought, from the primeval state of the world. Therefore, it is quite appropriate for the primeval god to incorporate in himself a special potency of fertility, claiming to be the procreator of all. In this quality—taking the old and expressing it in new forms—Amon merges with Min, the ancient fertility-god of Coptos and Akhmim, whose ithyphallic shape he accepts. This side of his nature is expressed in the double name Amon-Min. Often "the bull of his mother" is added as a special epithet, which means that in a mysterious way the special procreative power that continues to create itself again and again is joined in him. Quite possibly this title preserves a prehistoric conception of the ruler according to which the mature son, upon receiving sovereignty, assumes power also over the wives of his aged father. But that is a different question.

This conception forms a bridge to his identification with a neighboring deity. As we have mentioned above, the holy bull Monthu was worshiped in Medamud, Tod, and Hermonthis. Now bulls are forms of appearance particularly preferred by fertility-gods. Consequently, Amon becomes also the god of this sacred animal, and as Thebes is added to the cult centers (in Medamud, Tod, and Hermonthis), he becomes one "in whom the four male beings are united in the form of a bull." This identification doubtless met the demands of the common people, for whom, as always, the god's visible animal form of appearance was more important than a theological speculation. In this way, again, the tie with Min is strengthened; for since ancient times, probably before his Theban period, a white bull was led along during his festival. This, then, was a visible proof that the equation was correct.

AMON AS PRIMEVAL GOD

The links between Amon and the place of worship at Medinet Habu are of a quite different kind. Most probably this sacred place included the cult site of a serpent-shaped primeval deity who possibly boasted the title "he who has fulfilled his span of life" ($Kv\eta\varphi$). The anthropomorphic way of thinking may have transformed the idea of an animal that lives inside the earth into that of a tomb possessed by a primeval being. This again agrees with an aspect of Amon that belongs to his original nature. The king of the gods from Karnak encounters here, as it were, his own primeval image. It has been mentioned above that he visited this ancestor every ten days. We do not know the form of this ancestor worship, but we may assume that it was formed somewhat after the pattern of the human funerary cult. This primeval Amon who rests in Medinet Habu again attracts to himself two older theological creations who are associated with him on account of their primeval nature. There is, on the one hand, the Memphite Ptah-Tatenen. He represents a union of Ptah, the principal god of Memphis, with Tatenen, who was also worshiped at Memphis. Literally his name means "the raised land," a personification of the first land to rise out of the primeval flood. It is essentially, therefore, a pictorial expression for the first primeval period of the earth. On the other hand, the cult of the eight primeval gods is added here. These are four deities who denote the forces of chaos: darkness, pathlessness, infinity, and invisibility. They obviously come from Hermopolis, and Amon himself was originally one of them. It is almost impossible for us to understand with rational means the multiple nature and depth of this divine being. He is at one and the same time father and son, human being and animal, and the invisible one who reveals himself in countless forms.

AMON AND OSIRIS

All these developments naturally did not happen at once; they were the outcome of a long evolution, which enabled Amon to become at last "the lord of the sky, the earth, the waters, the mountain lands, and the underworld." The last-named epithet, implying rule over the underworld, made him in a sense the rival of Osiris. As a matter of fact, this god played only a subordinate role at Thebes. He certainly possessed several temples even at Karnak and as a matter of course he is found with some regularity in the tombs as lord of the judgment of the dead. But taken as a whole, this immense and most noble necropolis was unable to accept the real god of the dead as its proper lord. Thus it is intelligible that here too the polymorphous Amon could become the lord of the underworld, the more so as he was already the lord of the mortuary temples. That this sovereignty was understood literally is proved, among other examples, by a papyrus of the Persian epoch. In it Amon publishes a formal decree by which he deifies Osiris in the underworld and arranges his cult on earth, installs Horus as heir, and takes care of Isis. In other words, the whole of the Osiris religion is subordinated to the protection of Amon.

In the light of the Theban data this development seems natural and inevitable. Yet, in fact, it is only a local variation of a dispute that can be traced through the whole of Egyptian religion: the antagonism between the god of the sky and the sun on the one side and the chthonic god of the dead on the other. Naturally we are unable to follow up this point in detail. It occurs as early as the Pyramid Texts of the Old Kingdom; there we find a passage where it is expressly stated that the dead king rises up to heaven and is not left in the power of the gods of the dead. The religion of Amarna is only an episode in this dispute, proferring as it does an extreme and one-sided emphasis on the cult of the sun. Noticeably increasing support for the cult of Osiris comes afterward as a natural reaction. It is less evident, however, in Thebes, although here too we find special sanctuaries of Osiris; but in Abydos it is conspicuous.

AMON AS SPIRIT

It is hard to think of any god whose inherent potentialities were as richly developed as those of Amon. Through favorable circumstances his theology and cult became for centuries the most perfect expression of Egyptian thought. In the attempt to fathom the real nature of this polymorphous and difficult god the priesthood attained an explanation that was consistent at once with his name and with his acknowledged omnipotence. The name Amon was explained as "the enduring one"; this is linguistically possible, but it is naturally only an artificial interpretation. The meaning of this explanation was given as follows: it is he who remains in all things and all beings, the invisible, ever-present, all-quickening element of life in all forms of appearance of the cosmos. Thus a final spiritualization is achieved which transcends all forms of appearance, representations, and particular qualities. The nature of the divine is here understood as a spirituality almost

124

devoid of matter, which approaches the Greco-Christian, Πνεῦμα, but at the same time does not exclude the "immanence" of the god in reliefs and images.

For there is a reverse side to all priestly speculations and refinements: these depictions were in fact indispensable for a god who was not only the vehicle of reflections on the nature of the divine and the world, but also the object of the faith and prayers of all those who needed him in their everyday life.

Up to now we have been mainly concerned with theology, with official cults and festivals. It is well to ask at this point, How did things appear in the eyes of the common people? How far did they take part in it all? For although this was a priestly religion, it manifested a faith that was accepted and formed by many.

FOLK RELIGION

The uninitiated laymen apparently took only a limited part in the official cult. The daily temple service, for example, which took place in the innermost chambers of the temple, was completely out of their reach. Usually only priests were allowed to enter the innermost rooms of a temple. The Opet festival and the valley festival were two of the official feasts which allowed a direct encounter between the god who was carried in the procession and the common folk. Even then the distance between them was still great, and it was hardly possible to approach the god directly for the sake of prayer or invocation.

The distant official cult could not satisfy the requirements of the faith of the people. They had to correct this and create forms that answered their need; and thus they influenced the development of Egyptian religion considerably. This phenomenon was, of course, not limited to Thebes itself; but because of the number of well-authenticated sources, it is here that we can trace it best. First of all, there were the different animal forms of appearance of the god Amon. We cannot be sure, in every single case, how he obtained them. It is a primeval phenomenon of Egyptian religion that gods can manifest themselves also in these forms and that animals may be regarded as bearers of divine powers. During the New Kingdom—the period which is relevant for us here—theology had already treated and decided the problem as to whether the animal was really identical with the god. The answers tend to assert that it is possible for the deity to appear in animal form, but that, nevertheless, the god and his form of appearance are not identical. Seen from the theological point of view, the worship of animals is a striking expression of the idea that the divine can be met everywhere and in all beings. Seen by the eyes of popular belief, it meant that the divine can be enclosed in intimate and familiar forms. We do not know, however, how the sacred animals of Amon were worshiped. Perhaps—like other sacred animals—an example of the species was kept in a certain place. The bull (see p. 130), which was taken over from the god Monthu, the Nile goose, and the ram were all sacred forms of Amon.

But folk religion created still other gods for the use of the people, and the immediate cause of this was their exclusion from the temple. In the New Kingdom the gates of the temple, the pylons, and the walls are covered with depictions of partly historical and partly religious character, such as representations of festivals and ritual actions of the kings before the gods. These representations are available for everybody to see. A statue in the forecourt, holy trees, and so on may also be approached. In a letter of the Ramesside period, the following are invoked in support of the recipient's welfare: "Amon, Mut, Khons, 'useful is he,' the [sacred] cedar tree beloved by Thebes, near the ram street [therefore a sphinx avenue], Amenhotep [probably Amenhotep I] from the forecourt, Amenhotep the beloved, Hathor of the persea tree, Amon of Luxor,

Figures 23 and 24. The image of the deified Amenhotep pronouncing oracles during a procession. From the tomb of Amenmose the high priest of the temple of Amenhotep I. Western Thebes, Dra' abu'l-Naga, tomb 19. 19th Dynasty, New Kingdom (1306–1186 B.C.).

To the far right in Figure 24 the pylon of the temple of the deified king (known as the "Temple of King Amenhotep of the Forecourt") is represented. Next to it on the left the image of the king is carried in a litter by four priests and is accompanied by fan bearers. The inscription reads: "The good god, son of Amon, protector of him who is found in Thebes [i.e., Amon], the splendid scion, the sacred egg, whom the king of the gods begot, king of Upper and Lower Egypt, lord of the two lands, lord of the rite of Djeser-Ka-Ra, son of Ra, Amenhotep, gifted with eternal life." Moving toward the group is the first prophet of the god-king, Amenmose, carrying a censor in his left hand. He receives the answer of the god—that is, he interprets the movement of the picture as answer. The text above him elucidates: "Speech of the first prophet of King Amenhotep, Amenmose; he says: 'My Lord!' The god answers: 'The servant Ramose-nakht is in the right; Heka-nakht is in the wrong!' Then the god reiterated: 'In the right is the servant Ramose-nakht!'" Thus, what is being dealt with is an altercation between the two named parties, which the god decides; but the cause of the argument is not stated. Next follows the almost destroyed figure of one of the litigants, Ramose-nakht, who is uttering a paean of praise to the god, which is also almost entirely destroyed. At the far left we see the family group of Amenmose, in whose tomb the picture is situated (cf. Plate 51).

the eight baboons who are in the forecourt, Hathor in Thebes, the great gate of Beki [a gate built by the high priest Bekenkhons under Ramesses II to the east of the temple of Karnak], all gods and goddesses of Thebes." This enumeration shows clearly that besides the great gods there were other divine emanations which played a great part. Among these are a statue of Tuthmosis III, which had been erected by this king in Karnak. Statues of kings and gods often have a cognomen; and this one had an epithet frequently used for statues, "He who listens to prayers," which convincingly suggests the role of "sacred objects" of this kind.

Before we speak in detail of the cult of statues, some more examples of the veneration or invocation of divinities on temple walls should be mentioned. During the Twenty-first and Twenty-second Dynasties a

wall built by Sesostris I must still have been standing at Karnak. On it Amon and Thoth were represented. A prayer is preserved that was directed to the two deities in the relief; it must have been inscribed beside them or under them during the Twenty-first Dynasty; it was copied by a scribe during the period of King Takelot (of the Twenty-second Dynasty) on a papyrus and has thus come down to us. In Medinet Habu a "Ptah of the great gate" is mentioned (on the first pylon), who is also known from invocations on stelae. Inside the second pylon of the same temple is a representation of the king offering in front of Amon-Ra. Later on a special epithet was added to this picture of Amon: "Amon-Ra in the breadth of the passage"; apparently it, too, was worshiped as a special form of the god.

In the west also we know of statues of gods (e.g., "Amon who listens to prayers") and of kings. Amenhotep I especially and his mother Ahmes-Nefertari assumed for centuries the function of divine patrons of the necropolis. He had his own festival, "the departure of Amenhotep," which was celebrated shortly after the ^{Figs.23,24} valley festival. The name hints at a procession of statues, and we know that he also pronounced oracles. ⁵¹ The reasons for their divine roles are not known to us; in particular, we do not know why the king mother was included in the veneration. Little is known of their historical significance. Possibly they received their divine function as the first planners of the western town of Thebes. Both are frequently invoked on stelae. Amenhotep possessed among others a statue called "Amenhotep of the town" or "lord of the town." The "town" mentioned is probably the settlement of workers and artists at Deir el Medineh. The role of Ahmes-Nefertari was even more important. According to the evidence of representations of the Ramesside period, her barque was carried in the procession of the valley festival, and in addition, she frequently appears on official cult reliefs of this time as a kind of mediator between king and god. Her ascent is typical of the course ⁵²

taken by the process of deification in Egypt. Those who get into its stream, whatever the reason for it may be, become divine, can bear divine epithets, and are invoked as gods even when the knowledge of their temporal and historical existence remains correct and exact. We shall find still more examples of this here at Thebes. In certain cases it can be proved indubitably that such gods owe their existence to folk religion. This again is part and parcel of the discrepancy between temple religion and folk religion. Of necessity, the simple and faithful folk must search for near and familiar figures; and in the end the intensity of their faith forces the official theology to recognize these gods as well.

The existence of other gods in the necropolis is due to the life-giving imagination of the people who lived and worked there. To this context belongs the "western mountain top," a personification of the pyramid-shaped summit that rises domineeringly over the necropolis. Today it is called El Qurn, "the horn." Another such being is the snake-goddess Merseger, "she loves the silence," who was specially worshiped by the inhabitants of Deir el Medineh. She possessed a cult recess on the mountain over the path to the Valley of the Kings; this she shared with Ptah, the god of the artisans. Some known deities were identified with this goddess, for example, the snake-goddess Renenutet, who provides nourishment and fertility, or even the royal uraeus serpent. It was the snake form common to all the deities involved that made these connections possible. One may note, by the way, that it is remarkable how precisely the faith and thought of the Egyptians differentiate between male and female snake-deities. For instance, this snake-goddess has no relations whatsoever with the neighboring snake-god Kem-Atef of Medinet Habu.

In matters such as the worship of single images and statues of deified human beings and the veneration of impressive natural phenomena, we are touching the timeless substratum of Egyptian religion. It must have existed in the beginning, and we meet it again in the last phases of religious development in Egypt.

We must not imagine, however, that the movements and creations of folk religion were somehow suppressed by the official theology and the temple cults during the "classic" periods of the Pharaohs. In each era one force was fed by the other; and the sources of the Late Period allow us to recognize the individual power of folk religion more clearly than has been possible for the other periods. This development, which is traceable in Thebes because of the abundance of its sources, can be supposed to have existed also in other places of which we know fewer details, but of course with other gods and in different forms. A special expression of popular belief was found in the way the gods were used to pronounce oracles. It is quite certain that the election of kings and priests by Amon (see p. 98) is to be placed on the same level as the questions pertaining to ordinary life that are put before the gods and decided by them. The one may have developed out of the other; it may also have been the prerequisite at first only for those special and elevated cases. We are unable to decide this on the basis of our source material. It is a fact, however, that since the Twentieth Dynasty oracular decisions in ordinary everyday matters are more and more frequently attested. Some reports describe the pertinent situations in detail, for example, when an agreed payment has not been made, or when the modest furniture of a working man at Deir el Medineh has been seized by members of his family. Then the god is called upon to give a decision. Another group of sources is to be found in the ostraca (pottery sherds), on which a precise question has been put down; they are laid before the god, who announces his "yes" or "no" by certain movements. The questions are concerned with varying circumstances of life, such as: "Will they select Sety to be a priest?" or: "Is it he who has stolen a coat?" or: "Shall I go away to the north and continue to press on with the introduction [into the priestly office]?" These examples indicate that it was not only Amon who was consulted but also lesser gods; one can, of course, infer that the small man was more intimately linked with such deities. They also show that one cannot really speak of special "oracle-gods" who originally possessed this gift; but the nature of the Egyptian gods was so vague with reference to their activities that, if asked for it, they were able to fulfill this requirement too. Some of them became favorite oracle-deities because human intelligence found them more effective as a result of trial and error.

DEIFIED HUMAN BEINGS AND GODS OF HEALING

Another phenomenon of the later religious life, which also was not limited to Thebes alone, was the worship of deified human beings as gods of healing and deliverers in need. Semitic and later Greek influences may have been at work here, the latter rather in ritual practices than in questions of ideology. But this is still a matter of conjecture. In western Thebes, we are able to pinpoint this phase in two places: in the small temple of Qasr el Aguz, a little to the south of Medinet Habu, and at Deir el Bahari.

The temple of Qasr el Aguz, which was built by Ptolemy VIII (Euergetes II), is dedicated to two deities each called Thoth. They possess some of the epithets peculiar to this god, but their cognomens hint at quite different beings. One of them holds the name written *setem* in Egyptian. This may be a late spelling for the word "he who listens," that is, he who answers a prayer; in that case, he would be one of those special deities who listen to prayers, such as we have described above with reference to the sacred statues; or else it stands for the priestly title that is usually written *sem*. In that case we would certainly have to do with a deified priest of this order whose secular name has not been handed down. The other Thoth is called Theos, the Ibis. He certainly represents a deified man, for Theos is a personal name often used in the Late Period, and his name Ibis points to a form of appearance of the god Thoth. Alongside these two principal gods we find above all Amenhotep, the son of Hapu, and Imhotep, therefore two deified "wise men" (see p. 110), who lived under Amenhotep III and Zoser (of the Third Dynasty). It appears as if a number of helpful deities near to the people had been gathered together, although it is difficult to say anything precise about this cult. The plan of the temple certainly differs considerably from that of other temples. The temple may have served as a place for incubation (temple sleep), during which the faithful found means of help and healing by way of dreams. This suggestion is supported by the fact that the custom of incubation can be traced here at western Thebes as early as the Twentieth Dynasty.

Deir el Bahari likewise experienced late a period of prosperity for the same purpose until about A.D. 200. The cult of Amenhotep son of Hapu was transplanted here, too, and he was worshiped together with Imhotep as a healing deity. Ptolemy VIII (Euergetes II), the king who erected the temple of Qasr el Aguz, built a chamber in front of the sanctuary and also the colonnade that is still standing today. From that time onward this place became a regular "sanatorium." According to the testimony of inscriptions, it was mainly visited by Greco-Egyptians in search of health, and Egyptian physicians were active here. If we remember the gods who grant healing here and their history, we have in this cult a good example of the Greco-Egyptian fusions typical of the era. On the other hand, as far as the Egyptian partner in this divine association is concerned, it offers an instructive and not at all unique example of how the attitude to the gods was changed to meet the needs of the faithful. After the eighth century, even in the official religion, an inclination can be noticed to use a personal relation to the gods in order to ask them for personal favors. Even centuries earlier this tendency can be traced in the folk religion. The gift of health, protection from disease, and cure take more and more a central position in the prayers. This, by the way, is a development that is not limited to Egypt alone but is noticeable—with certain differences in time—in the whole of the ancient world. It would be worthwhile to write a history of the conception of disease and healing as part of a history of religion. The gods become healing deities (θεοὶ σωτῆρες), with little regard to their original mythological and theological roles. This is especially true of the "sanatorium-gods" of Deir el Bahari. Amenhotep the son of Hapu has already been mentioned several times in this connection. We know, and the Egyptians naturally knew, that he had been a recruiting officer under Amenhotep III. We do not know, however, what qualities and achievements of his were the cause of his deification. Because his father's name Hapu sounded like the Egyptian name of the Apis bull of Memphis, he is often also called son of Apis, which would prove his divine descent. That is no reason for supposing that his human descent had been forgotten or intentionally suppressed. The Egyptians may have regarded the relation between the divine and the earthly father in the manner of the king, in whose case the religious fatherhood of Amon was associated with the equally important legitimate descent from the royal family. The position of Imhotep (the Greek Imuthes) is similar, and it can be proved that the Egyptians of the later era knew of him as a historical personality. He had been the architect of King Zoser (about 2700 B.C.) and was probably the builder of the step pyramid at Saqqarah, perhaps also of the unfinished pyramid of King Sekhem-khet, Zoser's successor. In the course of time he too joined the circle of human beings who received divine honors, and at Memphis he even had priests of his own, and his festivals were celebrated at Medinet Habu as well. He also receives a divine father, namely, Ptah, the patron god of artists and artisans, but equally in his case the knowledge of his human father is not forgotten. An inscription from the period of Darius names, quite correctly, his human father and mother. During the Ptolemaic period his veneration as a healing deity was so widespread in Egypt that he was identified with the Greek god Asclepius. The Greek goddess Hygieia, the goddess of health, joins Amenhotep and Imhotep-Asclepius as the third deity in a triad. In spite of the great Greek influence that is apparent in this association of gods, it cannot have been merely a matter of chance that the Egyptian formative scheme of a divine trinity was effective here once more.

IV. THE AFTERMATH

It is a far cry from the funerary temple of a queen of the Eighteenth Dynasty and the cult of Amon of the valley festival to the sanatorium in the Greek style. But it impressively teaches us the potentialities of development and change of which Egyptian cult centers, under certain conditions, were capable. At the same time, it should be a warning not to draw far-reaching conclusions from transient facts as to the development and prehistory of sacred places.

At about the time of the birth of Christ, this is the picture of the once powerful Thebes: the town as such has disintegrated into a number of villages partly grouped around the ancient temples. In Luxor, the Roman forum lies beside the ancient Pharaonic temple. Karnak, Qasr el Aguz, and Deir el Bahari are visited by sick and unhappy people in search of healing. At the same time, the sites are visited by travelers from Greece and Rome who come as tourists in search of knowledge. But this, too, ceases after the second century. The repeated invasions by nomadic tribes—Blemmyes and Nobades—made life in Upper Egypt poor and insecure.

Even so, life in Thebes was not yet extinguished. With a rare longevity it survived for several more centuries. I do not mean that people continued to live there during the Middle Ages and in modern times, but that the history of the sacred sites at Thebes can be traced even beyond the Roman period.

During the second and third centuries the Christian faith spread across the region. For more than a century heathens and Christians live side by side; after that we have to deal with a mainly Christian population, to which the name Copts is given. If the people turned to the monastic life—and the number of monks and nuns is astonishingly large at times—two possible ways of life were open to them: communal life in monasteries or the secluded life of the hermit. Graffiti which are not always attractive in form have been found in numerous tombs, revealing that the tombs were used by hermits as cave dwellings. Place names formed with "Deir" (Arabic for "monastery") show the former existence there of a monastery: for example, Deir el Bahari, Deir el Medinet, and Deir el Bakhit. The multitude of monasteries stems not only from the special piety of the Egyptian Christians, but also from a desire to escape into the relative security of the monastic community. At Deir el Bahari, to the right of the temple, brick walls of the monastery are still partly preserved. Very often Coptic churches are found in ancient Egyptian temples—for example, in Qurneh, Medinet Habu, Deir el Medineh, and Luxor. The reason for the continued sanctity of the place under Christian auspices must be understood not only as a survival of a sacred site, although it happens very often in the world that Christian sanctuaries are founded on sacred pagan sites. A more practical idea must be given consideration: the massive stone walls of the temple had already survived for centuries and offered a solid support for later enclosed buildings. If the Copts had been attracted solely by the sacredness of the place, they would surely have destroyed the heathen site and would have built a church on top of it. But in fact the existing rooms were used together with their heathen decoration. The roofs were supported by columns or pillars, apses and new gates were worked into the wall, and extant reliefs were covered with plaster (as at Luxor). At Medinet Habu the traces of Coptic enclosed buildings can be clearly recognized; a church was sited in the second courtyard. The rest of the building and the space between the temple and enclosure wall served, as it were, as the skeleton of the Coptic town. Holes were cut into the walls to hold the beams for several floors; capitals of columns were hollowed out to serve as water basins for the upper rooms. The whole complex must at times have been as thickly populated as a beehive. This we know not only from excavations but also from documents, as when such a "house" is divided room by room among the heirs and the common use of the stair and passages—a quite timeless human custom—is documentally safeguarded for all the inhabitants.

These enclosed buildings of sun-dried bricks certainly also helped to preserve the temple, since the dry and not very durable material, together with the incoming sand, filled the rooms and supported columns and walls. In this way the buildings were somehow preserved and protected against destruction by human hand as well as by erosion, sandstorm, and winds. The cleaning of the buildings since the last century has involved opening them up again and exposing them, at the same time, to all these dangers.

A continued preservation of the sanctity of the place may perhaps be assumed at Luxor. Here, too, a Christian church existed within the walls of the temple. And once more the place attracted an additional sanctuary, the tomb of Jusuf Abu'l-Haggag. It is said that he died A.H. 642 (that is, A.D. 1244) and was buried together with his three sons and his wife Tharzah in the place where the mosque is now situated on the wall of the temple. According to tradition, he died in Armant, or else he was there when he felt death to be near. But then angels came, lifted him up on their wings, and deposited the dead body between the columns of the temple at Luxor. Several accounts of his life are given. One of these will be mentioned here because it offers an example of the traditional motif that appears in such stories. A Christian king reigned (according to Legrain) over Egypt and was in danger of losing his country to the Syrians in the north and the barbarians in the south. He had a daughter Tharzah, who since her birth had been dedicated as a bride of Christ. Then Abu'l-Haggag, a warrior from the Hedshas, offered his help together with three fellow warriors, asking as his reward as much earth as one can encompass with the skin of a camel. Abu'l-Haggag defeated the enemies of the kingdom and returned to the king, who fulfilled his promise. Then Abu'l-Haggag asked for the skin of a camel, cut it into long thin strips, and surrounded with them the region of the town of Luxor, which he now possessed and ruled. But Tharzah had seen the young hero and fallen in love with him. Abu'l-Haggag refused, however, to marry a Christian, and Tharzah was then converted to Islam. After her the king too and the whole of his people turned to the new religion, and when he died Abu'l-Haggag became king.

Just as in the story he had accepted the king's heritage, so did his cult accept the heritage of Amon. His festival had a procession as its most conspicuous element, and in this the barque of the saint was carried through the streets of Luxor.

It is a long way that leads from the first modest cave tombs over the monumental buildings of the era of the world empire to the Coptic monasteries and the mosque of Abu'l-Haggag. Having traversed it, one may rightly put the question, How far can Thebes be considered to be a sacred site? For it is not enough that we, ike generations before us, stand in awe before the stone witnesses of a great exotic past which is not our own. The venerable appearance of age and the flight of centuries may recall bygone ages and teach reverence and self-knowledge; but in itself it is nothing sacred.

We must try to look at things through the eyes of the Egyptian. For him the divine spirit of the ordered world was revealed in the actions of the Pharaoh and in the totality of his empire. The coincidence of divine and wordly rule sanctified the site of the human ruler and turned it into a place where divine action is revealed in this world. Only thus does Thebes with its temples and tombs become the lasting memorial of unity between the divine and the human. The town can be understood only in the light of its history.

In addition, there is something else: The eras when Thebes was the center of the Egyptian world were—apart from the age of the pyramids—historical eras rich in decisions and tensions. Accordingly, the life that developed in them constituted a high point in the historical as well as in the spiritual existence of the country; this was the center where the new formation of the kingdom occurred after the collapse during the First Intermediate Period, and also its new foundation after the Hyksos period together with the entry into a situation of high importance for world politics. The religious reforms initiated in response to this historical situation, though they themselves are only a part of history, have therefore special significance for the Egyptian nation. For in these reforms the nation expressed itself effectively. And the enduring visible remains of all this are the buildings and pictures in the ruins of the city of Thebes.

NOTES TO THE COLORPLATES

Colorplate IX

KING MENTUHOTEP II (NEB-HEPET-RA) (2060–2010 B.C.). Sandstone, painted. Complete height 6 feet. 11th Dynasty, Middle Kingdom. Exh. 287, Cairo Museum.

The seated statue was found wrapped in linen bandages in a subterranean recess in front of the king's pyramid at Deir el Bahari. It represents the king with the red crown and wrapped in the *sed*-festival robe. Apparently such an image of the king was buried on the occasion of the *sed* festival, that is, the jubilee festival, and the death of the ruler was thus symbolized. On the day after the burial the festival celebrated the start of a new rule.

Colorplates X and XI

THE TEMPLE AT KARNAK

Colorplate X. VIEW ACROSS THE SACRED LAKE TO THE MIDDLE OF THE TEMPLE OF AMON. To the left the seventh pylon is visible. It belongs to the processional avenue between the temple of Amon and the temple of Mut. To the right is the first pylon. Before it, in the middle of the picture, the hypostyle hall stands out clearly. In front of it are the remains of the third pylon to which the processional road led from the temple of Mut. To the right are the obelisks still standing of Tuthmosis I and Queen Hatshepsut. The mountains of western Thebes can be seen in the background on the other side of the river.

Colorplate XI. VIEW UPWARD THROUGH THE HYPOSTYLE HALL, WHOSE MIDDLE PASSAGE IS FORMED BY TWO ROWS OF COLUMNS WITH OPEN FLOWER CAPITALS. The columns of the lateral aisles have closed capitals. Flanking the middle passage were windows, which were the only source of light in the hall. They were enclosed with stone rails. The columns are decorated all around with reliefs and inscriptions, which were originally colored.

Colorplate XII

SELQET, QUEEN NEFERTARI LED BY ISIS, KHEPRE, MAAT. From the tomb of Queen Nefertari, one of the wives of King Ramesses II (1290–1224 B.C.). Western Thebes, Valley of the Queens (Biban el Harim), tomb 66. Eastern wall of the antechamber and entrance to the southern side chamber.

On the front wall of the niche to the left stands the goddess Selqet with the scorpion on her head, while Maat stands on the extreme left in the picture, at the entrance to the southern side chamber. The rear wall of the niche shows the queen dressed in a long pleated coat and led by Isis, who holds her hand, to the beetle-faced Khepre, a form of the sun-god, embodying his ceaseless reappearance.

Colorplate XIII

TEMPLE OF QUEEN HATSHEPSUT (1490–1468 B.C.). 18th Dynasty, New Kingdom. Western Thebes, Deir el Bahari.

The view is from the southeast, across the Asasif, a part of the Theban necropolis, to the mountain slopes of Deir el Bahari. The entrances of the tombs are now situated in depressions of the valley. One can clearly recognize the composition of the terraces of the 18th Dynasty temple. The temple of Mentuhotep II (Neb-hepet-ra) is situated to the left. Seen from this viewpoint the platform on which the pyramid of the king once rose is quite prominent. In the rock fissure on the extreme left of the picture is the tomb in which the royal mummies were discovered in 1875 and secured by the authorities in 1881.

Colorplate XIV

TUTHMOSIS III BEFORE AMON-RA. Rear wall of the Hathor chapel of the temple of Queen Hatshepsut' in western Thebes, Deir el Bahari. Exh. 445–446 (inv. 11549), Cairo Museum.

This chapel of the 18th Dynasty temple is covered with a flat barrel vault. In its rear Tuthmosis III is shown in his ritual costume with a short kilt and a long ritual tail, offering in front of "Amon-Ra, the lord of the sky, the lord of the thrones of the two lands."

Colorplate XV

SEN-NEDJEM AND HIS WIFE IN THE FIELDS OF IARU. From the tomb of Sen-Nedjem. Western Thebes, Deir el Medineh, tomb 1. 20th Dynasty, New Kingdom (1186–1070 B.C.).

The barque of Ra is represented in the vaulted register. He is being worshiped by two baboons. The wall painting beneath is divided into five registers. In the uppermost row is shown the dead in adoration before Ra, Osiris, Ptah, and two unnamed gods. Beside him in a barque is his son Ramose and a second son named Khonsu completing the ceremony of the opening of the mouth. The rest of the registers represent the fields of Iaru, a kind of country of the blessed, pervaded by water streams and possessing the two kinds of palms, the date palm and the dom palm, also sycamores and all sorts of shrubs. The deceased and his wife are seen performing agricultural work. Harvesting and work in the fields are frequently depicted in the tombs of the 18th Dynasty. But those are pictures of life on earth. Here the same task is transferred to a transcendent other world. The work is not performed by servants and slaves but by the owner of the tomb and his wife, both of whom are wearing festival dresses and artistic wigs.

NOTES TO THE BLACK-AND-WHITE PLATES

Plates 21 to 27
THE TEMPLE AT KARNAK

Plate 21
SANCTUARY ERECTED BY KING SESOSTRIS I (1971–1928 B.C.) on the occasion of his *sed* festival, the jubilee of the ruler's reign.

The reliefs on pillars suggest that the building was dedicated to Amon-Min, that is, the principal god Amon identified with the ithyphallic god of fertility, Min.

Plate 22
OBELISKS OF TUTHMOSIS I AND QUEEN HATSHEPSUT. Originally there were two obelisks of King Tuthmosis I (1516–1494 B.C.) in front of the fourth pylon and two of Queen Hatshepsut (1490–1468 B.C.) in front of the fifth pylon (on the left in the picture). Of these one of each pair is still standing. In front of the obelisk of Queen Hatshepsut the northern wing of the fourth pylon of Tuthmosis I is still visible.

Both obelisks are made of Aswan granite. The height of the obelisk of Tuthmosis I is 71 feet and the diameter of the base is 6 feet. The height of Hatshepsut's obelisk is 97 feet and the diameter of its base is 5 feet. Their weight has been calculated as 275 and 325 tons, respectively. On the obelisk of Tuthmosis I is a dedicatory inscription by this king and additional vertical lines concerning Ramesses IV and Ramesses VI. On the obelisk of Hatshepsut there is one line of inscription on each face, and in the upper part, in addition, a representation of Hatshepsut, Tuthmosis I, and Tuthmosis III before Amon.

Plate 23
FROM THE SECOND "RECORD HALL" OF KING TUTHMOSIS III (1490–1436 B.C.). 18th Dynasty, New Kingdom.

To the north of the sanctuary of the temple at Karnak lies the second "record hall" of King Tuthmosis III. In it the king reports on his Syrian campaigns, the towns conquered and the tributes delivered each year, basing his account on current war diaries and thus perpetuating in the temple his foreign political successes. The part pictured here contains the lists of tributes from the year 42 of the king's reign; the end of the text reports his order to commemorate in the chapel all his victories from his 23rd to his 42nd year. The statues of Amon (on the right) and Amaunet (not seen in the picture) were dedicated by Tut-ankh-amon.

Plates 24 and 25
THE SO-CALLED BOTANICAL GARDEN, WITH FIGURES OF PLANTS AND ANIMALS WHICH TUTHMOSIS III (1490–1436 B.C.) BROUGHT BACK FROM HIS CAMPAIGNS.

Plate 24. REPRESENTATIONS OF ANIMALS AND PLANTS ON THE WEST WALL. The animals and plants of the Syro-Palestinian landscape are depicted with much love and exactness. The inscription—here not visible—calls them "all herbs which grow, all the beautiful flowers which are in the land of the god [that is, in the east]. The power of his Majesty brought them when his Majesty went to Upper Retenu [Syria] to defeat the northern foreign countries." The king wanted them to be depicted "so that they may be in front of his father Amon in his palace Akh-Menu [the festival temple] forever and ever." Of the plants depicted in the upper part only a vine stem in the right half of the picture can be identified with certainty. But the birds in the upper register can all be identified; they are: serpent neck, rock pigeon, turtle dove, frigate bird, rock partridge, spurred lapwing; and in the lowest row stands a heron. The series is continued below. The plants and fruit depicted here mostly defy identification. On the right, however, is the *Nymphaea caerulea* (the blue water lily), and on the left is the *Mandragora*. Among the birds a standing crane can be recognized; in front is perhaps a jackdaw.

Plate 25. VIEW ACROSS THE WHOLE OF THE "BOTANICAL GARDEN." The chamber behind the festival temple of Tuthmosis III rests on four papyrus plant-bundle columns. Here the king has represented plants and animals that he found during his campaigns in Syria; some of these he brought back to Egypt. The picture shows the columns standing in their full original height, while the walls of the room contain the reliefs of plants and animals, which are partly represented on Plate 24; some of the walls have been cleared down to the lowest level.

Plate 26
TEMPLE OF KING AMENHOTEP II (1438–1412 B.C.). 18th Dynasty, New Kingdom. Part of the southwest wing of the temple.

A temple of Amenhotep II is situated on the processional avenue which leads to the temple of Mut, the second member of the Theban triad, between the ninth and the tenth pylon. It is much damaged. The king built it for his first *sed* festival, which celebrated the jubilee of his reign. Like the festival temple of Tuthmosis III, it is exceptionally broad. Apparently it does not contain a sanctuary, but its rear wall is closed by a false door. The reliefs from the pillars which are reproduced here illustrate the beauty of its decoration. They show the king with differing crowns; on the pillar in front he appears with the red crown, on the pillar behind with the double crown; here he is in the process of entering the temple and being received by Amon.

Plate 27
THE TEMPLE OF KHONS. 18th to 21st Dynasties, New Kingdom.

The temple of the god Khons, who was the third member

of the Theban triad, was begun in the 18th Dynasty. Some temples raised to this god in the Middle Kingdom have not been preserved. The present building was continued mainly by Ramesses III and was finished during the 21st Dynasty. The heavy massive columns are reminiscent of the temple of Ramesses III in the forecourt of the great temple at Karnak. The view is from the pylon through the forecourt, with its double columns in the direction of the inner part of the temple.

Plates 28 to 37
EASTERN THEBES, LUXOR, AMON-MUT-KHONS TEMPLE: THE SO-CALLED TEMPLE OF LUXOR.

Plate 28 VIEW OF THE TEMPLE FROM THE SOUTH. From the roof of the New Winter Palace Hotel. In the foreground is the temple building. The still-roofed rear part of the temple can be discerned, the "temple house," with the sanctuary and the birth room, the hypostyle hall, the forecourt of Amenhotep III, the colonnade of Amenhotep III, and finally the forecourt with the great pylon, both from the period of Ramesses II. The change in the temple's axis can be clearly noticed. In front of the right (that is, the eastern) tower of the great pylon, the mosque of Abu'l-Haggag, which is built on top of the wall, is visible.

Plate 29
COLONNADE OF KING AMENHOTEP III. View from the great forecourt to the colonnade of Amenhotep III; in front of it, near the southwest wall of the great forecourt, are two colossal statues of Ramesses II. To the left is the rear wall of the mosque of Abu'l-Haggag.

Plates 30 to 32
FROM THE BIRTH ROOM IN THE TEMPLE HOUSE. Time of Amenhotep III (1402–1364 B.C.). Scenes from the cycle of the birth of Amenhotep in Luxor. Since the 18th Dynasty several cycles of reliefs with texts have been transmitted that refer to the procreation of the divine king by the god Amon, his subsequent birth, and accession to the sovereignty.

Plate 30. QUEEN MUTEMUYA, THE CONSORT OF KING TUTHMOSIS IV, CONCEIVES HER SON AMENHOTEP III FROM AMON. The representation shows the bridal couple: to the right the god Amon, to the left the future king mother Mutemuya, both on a couch. The protective goddesses Selqet and Neith support the couch, which is formed like the symbol for heaven.

Plate 31. KHNUM FORMS THE TWO BOYS, AMENHOTEP III AND HIS *KA*. After the procreation of the child—to the right in the picture—his divine father Amon commissions the ram-headed creator-god Khnum to form the body of the child. How this is done is shown on the left: Khnum is seated in front of a potter's wheel, on which he forms the body of the child and of his *ka*, a spiritual being who

is like him, as if they were clay figures. He is supported by the goddess Hathor, who is sitting face to face with him.

Plate 32. MUTEMUYA GIVES BIRTH TO AMENHOTEP III, SUPPORTED BY THE DIVINE ACCOUCHEURS. In the upper row the queen is seated on a cubic seat; her arms are held by two midwives; on the left more women are ready to give assistance. On the right a kneeling woman passes the figure of a child to a woman who kneels behind her. According to the inscription, this is not the royal child himself but his *ka*. The birth scene is meant only as a symbolic representation. In reality the Egyptian women gave birth in a kneeling position on the "brick of confinement." In the lower register numerous protective deities, some with human heads and some with animal heads, are shown in a kneeling position. Each of them holds the symbol of life in his hands.

Plates 33 to 35
FROM THE NEW YEAR'S PROCESSION

Plate 33
THE GREAT PYLON FROM THE TIME OF RAMESSES II. Representation in relief from the time of Ramesses II on the southwest wall of the great court built by Ramesses II. It gives a view of the great pylon of Luxor and of the final destination of the procession from Karnak to Luxor on New Year's day. A comparison with Plate 36 and Figure 14 shows that externally the great pylon of the Luxor temple has remained more or less the same until today. The pylon had four flagpoles and originally two obelisks (cf. Figure 14). The gateway was flanked by six colossal figures of Ramesses II, one sitting and two standing on each side. Following the Egyptian convention, these figures are shown in profile, as if they were standing at right angles to the entrance. In reality they were, of course, looking forward.

Plates 34 and 35
THE FESTIVAL PROCESSION FROM KARNAK TO LUXOR DURING THE LUXOR FESTIVAL. Relief from the time of King Tut-ankh-amon (1347–1338 B.C.) and Horemheb (1334–1306 B.C.) on the walls of the great colonnade of Amenhotep III. The sequence of the scenes begins in the northeast corner of the northwestern wall.

Only examples of the sequence are given here. They convey a lively impression of the reality of the Egyptian festival. The procession moves along the river Nile, as is shown by the lines representing water on Plate 35.

Plate 34. ACROBATIC DANCING GIRLS of the kind that appear also in other festivals. Behind them stands a group of girls playing the sistrum.

Plate 35. SOLDIERS, STANDARD BEARERS, MUSICIANS, AND LIBYAN MERCENARIES. Above are soldiers with maces and spears, between them are standard bearers.

Below are soldiers, standard bearers, and Egyptian musicians with lutes. Then come Libyan mercenaries with rattles and singers clapping their hands. The two scenes are consecutive.

Plate 36
THE GREAT PYLON FROM THE TIME OF RAMESSES II (1290–1224 B.C.). View from the northeast.

Comparatively little change has taken place since the time of Ramesses II, as is shown in this picture as well as in the relief in Plate 33 and Figure 14. Four long slots in the masonry show where the great flagpoles were reared against the face of the pylon. The seated statues of the king and the standing statue on the right have been re-erected. Of the two obelisks the right one is missing and now stands (since 1836) in the Place de la Concorde in Paris.

Plate 37
THE BATTLE OF QADESH. Main part of the relief on the left (eastern) tower of the great pylon.

The scene shows Ramesses II in his war chariot surrounded by a hostile chariot brigade. The great battle reliefs as well as the hunting scenes of the New Kingdom form a distinctive pictorial tradition of their own. Certain rules found in mural scenes, such as the division into zones, and rules concerning the intersection of lines are ignored in favor of a gigantic unit with numerous single figures and daring movements. The retreating foe, horses rearing and collapsing, soldiers dead and falling, fill the picture with a complex of details which are dominated by the over-life-size figure of the king. In agreement with the literary reports of the battle, the inscriptions affirm that Ramesses II faced the enemy "while nobody else is with him." Beneath the scenes in vertical lines are the reports of the battle.

The impressions in the wall to the right and left near the border of the picture are the recesses for flagpoles. At their upper ends the relief overlaps.

Plate 38
RELIEF IN THE AMARNA STYLE FROM THE TOMB OF THE VIZIER RAMOSE. Western Thebes, Abd el Qurneh, tomb 55. Late 18th Dynasty, New Kingdom (1360–1347 B.C.).

While the famous earlier parts of the reliefs of this tomb are executed in a style characteristic of the time of Amenhotep III (1402–1364 B.C.), the later unfinished reliefs tend toward the artistic mode of the Amarna period (1364–1347 B.C.). The examples shown here are part of an impressive representation of the king on the palace balcony throwing gold rings down to his vizier Ramose as a reward. The two pictures shown here follow each other (top right connects with bottom left). The picture above shows some of the courtiers in an attitude of servile courtesy typical of the period. The connected picture below shows a deputation of Nubians and Asiatics who hail the king.

136

Plate 39
MOUNTAIN PASS BETWEEN DEIR EL MEDINEH AND THE VALLEY OF THE KINGS.

A path still in use today led from the workers' settlement at Deir el Medineh over a mountain pass to the Valley of the Kings. This was the way which the artisans took to reach their place of work and to return from it. On the height of the pass are remains of a police control station comprising tiny stone houses, and near them a shrine of field stones for a mountain deity. While passing this station the working groups were counted to see if their number was complete.

Plate 40
THE NIGHT JOURNEY OF THE SUN THROUGH THE UNDERWORLD. From the tomb of King Amenhotep II (1438–1412 B.C.). Western Thebes, Valley of the Kings (Biban el Moluk), tomb 35. 18th Dynasty, New Kingdom.

This wall of the burial chamber contains scenes from the book of "What Is in the Underworld" (Amduat). The first hour (left) and the second hour (right) concern the night journey through the underworld. In the upper and lower registers of the first hour are the gods and demons who are the rulers of this hour and this district; they are figured and named. The sun barque is absent in this reproduction of the book. The barque on the left is that of the sun-beetle Khepre, which accompanies the sun-god, in order to be ready in the morning. The second hour (enlarged representation below) also shows in the upper and lower registers the beings who live there. The middle register shows five barques, of which that of the sun-god with its crew of rowers follows the other four. It carries the enshrined god and his followers.

Plate 41
FROM THE TOMB OF KING SETY I (1304–1290 B.C.). Western Thebes, Valley of the Kings (Biban el Moluk), tomb 17. Early 19th Dynasty, New Kingdom. Part of the tenth hall.

Two representations of the ram-headed sun-god, who passes through the underworld in his barque. The manning and decoration of the barque changes in the twelve districts.

Above: The journey of the sun barque after the representation in the Book of Gates. The shrine is protected by the encircling serpent. At the bow can be seen the line by which it is towed.

Below: The journey of the sun barque after the representation in the book "What Is in the Underworld." The accompanying followers are numerous; at the stern is the falcon-headed ferryman.

Plates 42 to 48
THE MORTUARY TEMPLE OF KING RAMESSES III (1170–1138 B.C.) IN MEDINET HABU. Western Thebes.

Plate 42
THE HIGH GATE. The southern wing as seen from the east. The entrance to the temple and palace district of Ramesses III is a fortress building inserted into the enclosure wall.

The towers up to the level of the first floor consist of massive stonework; the rooms in the upper part can be reached by means of outside stairways. On the side facing the passage of the left (southwestern) tower the king is represented below leading prisoners to Amon; above he is shown offering before Amon-Ra and Maat.

Plate 43
FROM THE FRONT OF THE SOUTHWEST TOWER OF THE GREAT PYLON. Ramesses III slays his enemy prisoners. The king strikes with his mace a bundle of enemies who are characterized by physiognomy and costume as Asiatics, Libyans, and Nubians. Below this representation is a list of conquered towns and countries. The names are written in rings, which are characterized as enclosure walls and personified by the upper part of a human body with bound arms which is projecting out of each ring.

Plate 44
FROM THE SOUTHWEST WALL OF THE SECOND COURTYARD. PRESENTATION OF PRISONERS. Prisoners from the war against the Sea People and Libyans are led before the king. Egyptian soldiers lead groups of two or three bound enemies. Basically only a few types of figures are used to represent the soldiers and the prisoners, but in detail they are variegated in such a way that one figure is hardly ever completely like another.

Plate 45
RELIEF NEAR THE WINDOW OF APPEARANCE ON THE SOUTHWEST WALL OF THE SECOND COURTYARD. BOUND PRISONERS ARE SLAIN. A group of three bound enemies is slain by the king. By their hair style and facial traits they are characterized as Nubian, Libyan, and Asiatic.

Plates 46 to 48
FROM THE NORTHEAST WALL IN THE SECOND COURTYARD. PART OF THE PROCESSION IN THE FESTIVAL OF THE FERTILITY-GOD MIN.

Plate 46. KING RAMESSES III MOVES IN HIS SEDAN CHAIR OUT OF HIS PALACE TO THE FESTIVAL. The sedan chair is carried by nobles decorated with feathers and accompanied by fan bearers; in front of the king walk priests with their faces turned backward; they are offering incense. In front of the lower priest walks the lector priest chanting from a papyrus roll the pertinent festival songs (cf. Figure 22). Below the king is seen bringing offering before the barque of Amon, whose bow is visible to the left (cf. Plate 48).

Plate 47. THE STATUE OF THE GOD MIN WITH RAISED ARM AND HIGH FEATHER CROWN IS CARRIED ON A PORTABLE FRAME. The carriers and the frame are covered by a cape decorated with star patterns. Lettuce, the sacred plant of the god, is carried behind him

in a flower box; on top of it is some kind of shrine or screen made of plaited work (cf. Figure 22).

Plate 48. THE PROCESSIONAL BARQUE OF THE GOD AMON. From the procession of the three barques of the divine triad Amon-Mut-Khons. The portable barque stands on a stone pedestal which is decorated with pictures of the king. Bow and stern end in richly decorated ram heads with sun disks. At the bow, near the ram's head, is seen a divine eye, an apotropaic symbol. In the middle of the barque stands the shrine, decorated with protective symbols and figures of gods. In it the image of the god is hidden. Apart from that the barque also carries little figures of gods, the followers of Amon, and flower decoration. Below the rear part of the portable frame stand divine staffs that accompany the procession of the god, much as standards accompany the king. In the lower row of Plate 46 King Ramesses II is shown offering in front of the barque.

Plate 49
THE BARQUE OF SOKAR. FROM THE TEMPLE AT DEIR EL MEDINEH IN WESTERN THEBES. The temple was begun under Ptolemy IV (Philopator; 221–204 B.C.) and was finished under Ptolemy VII (Euergetes; 145–116 B.C.). The southern sanctuary.

The originally Memphite god of agriculture and sowing had long since become a form of the god Osiris, and hence he is called here, as well as elsewhere, Sokar-Osiris. The barque rests on a base decorated with figures of the king. Its bow ends in a bull's head and the head of a gazelle turned backward. On top of the barque stands the cupola-shaped shrine of the god decorated with the head of a falcon with a sun disk. Below on a portable frame stands the symbol of the god Nefertum, a lotus blossom with high feathers. In front and at the back of the barque standards of gods are seen; foremost is that of "Horus who is on the papyrus," then those of Wepwawet of Upper and Lower Egypt, then again a standard of Horus and also standards of Thoth and Khons.

Plate 50
PURIFICATION OF THE DEAD. FROM THE TOMB OF SENNOFER, THE MAYOR OF THEBES. Time of King Amenhotep II (1438–1412 B.C.). Western Thebes, Abd el Qurneh, tomb 86. 18th Dynasty, New Kingdom.

The picture shows the purification of Sennofer and his wife Merit at the ceremony of the opening of the mouth, a means of resuscitation that was practiced on statues as well as on mummies. The two deceased are represented as if they were alive in festive dress with flowers and bouquets. The woman, who had been employed as a singer of Amon, carries in her right hand a *menit*, in her left hand a sistrum; both are rattles that were employed in the cult. In front of them stands the priest in a leopard skin pouring the water of purification over them. The ceiling of this room as well as that of other rooms is decorated with grapevines; hence the tomb is often called the tomb of the grapevines.

137

Plate 51
FROM THE TOMB OF AMENMOSE, THE HIGH
PRIEST OF THE TEMPLE OF AMENHOTEP I. Western
Thebes, Dra' abu'l-Naga, tomb 19. 19th Dynasty, New
Kingdom (1306–1186 B.C.).

From the procession visiting the image of the deified
Amenhotep I to receive the answer to an oracular inquiry:
relatives of the tomb owner Amenmose form the end of the
processional scene. Compare this with the representation of
the whole in Figures 23 and 24.

Plate 52
QUEEN AHMES-NEFERTARI AS MEDIATOR. Relief
dedicated by King Ramesses III for the hypostyle hall behind
the fifth pylon at Karnak.

The relief shows King Ramesses III offering to the god
Amon the figure of Maat, that is, the order or concord of the
world. Between the two, on the base of the divine throne,
stands Queen Ahmes-Nefertari, the mother of King Amenhotep I, who had died almost four hundred years before the
lifetime of King Ramesses III. She is shown naked with a
long wig, holding in her hands a sistrum and a necklace. This
representation is exactly the same as that of the ladies of the harim in the tower room at Medinet Habu. Thus the deified queen
appears in the relief from Karnak as a lady of the harim of
the god Amon and is called his beloved in order to make him
well disposed toward the king by means of her appearance
and by the sound of her rattles.

PLATES

The illustrative material has been rounded out by photographs from the following sources: Gaddis, Luxor, 30, 31, 32; Eberhard Otto, 39, 52.

Plate 21. Temple at Karnak. Sanctuary erected by King Sesostris I (1971–1928 B.C.) on the occasion of his *sed* festival, the jubilee of the ruler's reign.

Plate 22. Temple at Karnak. The obelisk erected in front of the fourth pylon of King Tuthmosis I (in the foreground to the right) and in front of the fifth pylon of Queen Hatshepsut (in the background on the left). In front of the latter obelisk the northern wing of the fourth pylon can be seen.

Plate 23. Temple at Karnak. From the second "record hall" of King Tuthmosis III (1490–1436 B.C.). 18th Dynasty, New Kingdom.

Plate 24. Temple at Karnak. The so-called botanical garden, with figures of plants and animals which Tuthmosis III (1490–1436 B.C.) brought back from his campaigns.

Plate 25. Temple at Karnak. View across the whole of the "botanical garden" from the time of Tuthmosis III (1490–1436 B.C.).

Plate 26. Temple at Karnak. Temple of King Amenhotep II (1438–1412 B.C.). 18th Dynasty, New Kingdom.
Part of the southwest wing of the temple.

Plate 27. Temple at Karnak. Temple of Khons. 18th to 21st Dynasties, New Kingdom.

Plate 28. Eastern Thebes, Luxor. Amon-Mut-Khons temple: the so-called temple of Luxor.
View of the temple from the south as seen from the roof of the New Winter Palace Hotel. In the foreground is the temple building.

Plate 29. Eastern Thebes, Luxor. Amon-Mut-Khons temple. Colonnade of King Amenhotep III (1402–1364 B.C.).
View from the great forecourt.

Left: Plate 30. Eastern Thebes, Luxor. Amon-Mut-Khons temple. From the birth room in the temple house.
From the time of Amenhotep III (1402–1364 B.C.).
Queen Mutemuya, the consort of King Tuthmosis IV, conceives her son Amenhotep III from Amon.
The bridal couple, Amon and the future king's mother Mutemuya. The protective goddesses Selqet and Neith support their bed.

Plate 31. Eastern Thebes, Luxor. Amon-Mut-Khons temple. From the birth room in the temple house.
Khnum forms the two boys, Amenhotep III and his *Ka*.

Plate 32. Eastern Thebes, Luxor. Amon-Mut-Khons temple. From the birth room in the temple house.
Mutemuya gives birth to Amenhotep III, supported by the divine accoucheurs.

Plate 33. Eastern Thebes, Luxor. Amon-Mut-Khons temple. Representation in relief from the southwest wall of the great court
built by Ramesses II (1290–1224 B.C.): the great pylon,
which was the destination of the procession from Karnak to Luxor on New Year's day.

Plate 34. Eastern Thebes, Luxor. Amon-Mut-Khons temple. From the great colonnade of King Amenhotep III (1402–1364 B.C.).
Acrobatic dancing girls and musicians playing the sistrum at the Luxor festival.

Plate 35. Eastern Thebes, Luxor. Amon-Mut-Khons temple. From the great colonnade of King Amenhotep III (1402–1364 B.C.). Soldiers, standard bearers, musicians, and Libyan mercenaries.

Plate 36. Eastern Thebes, Luxor. Amon-Mut-Khons temple. *Upper register:* The great pylon from the time of Ramesses II (1290–1224 B.C.).
View from the northeast. *Lower register:* The sphinx avenue, which leads from the great pylon to Karnak.
It is just in the process of being excavated.

Plate 37. Eastern Thebes, Luxor. Amon-Mut-Khons temple. Battle of Qadesh.
Main part of the relief on the left (eastern) tower of the great pylon.

Plate 38. From the tomb of the vizier Ramose in western Thebes, Abd el Qurneh. Late 18th Dynasty, New Kingdom (1360–1347 B.C.). Relief in the Amarna style. *Above:* Courtiers. *Below:* Deputation of Nubians and Asiatics.

Plate 39. Western Thebes. Mountain pass between Deir el Medineh and the Valley of the Kings (Biban el Moluk).

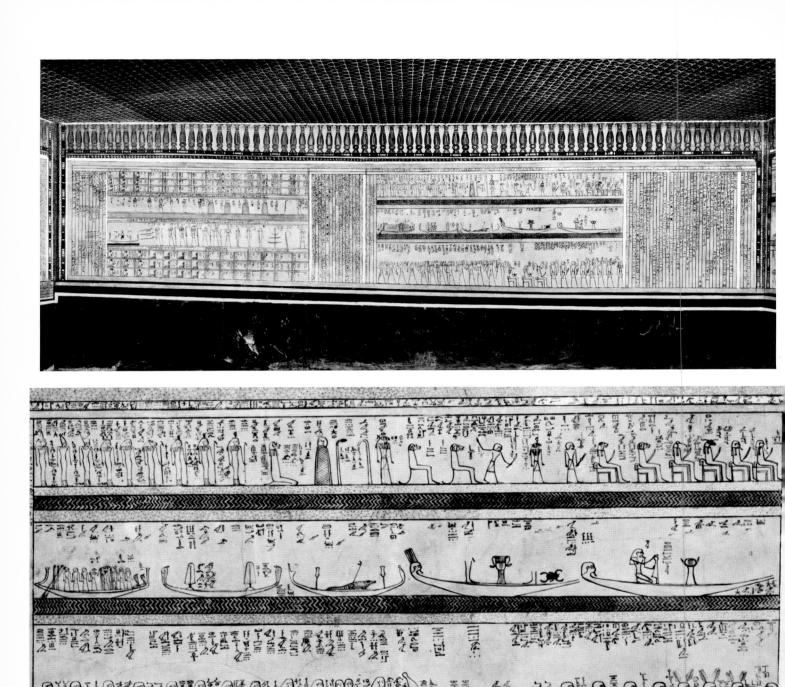

Plate 40. The night journey of the sun through the underworld. From the coffin chamber in the tomb of King Amenhotep II (1438–1412 B.C.). Western Thebes, Valley of the Kings (Biban el Moluk). 18th Dynasty, New Kingdom.

Plate 41. The journey of the sun-god through the underworld. From the tomb of King Sety I (1304–1290 B.C.).
Western Thebes, Valley of the Kings (Biban el Moluk). Early 19th Dynasty, New Kingdom

Plate 42. Mortuary temple of King Ramesses III (1170–1138 B.C.) in Medinet Habu (western Thebes). The high gate. The southern wing as seen from the east.

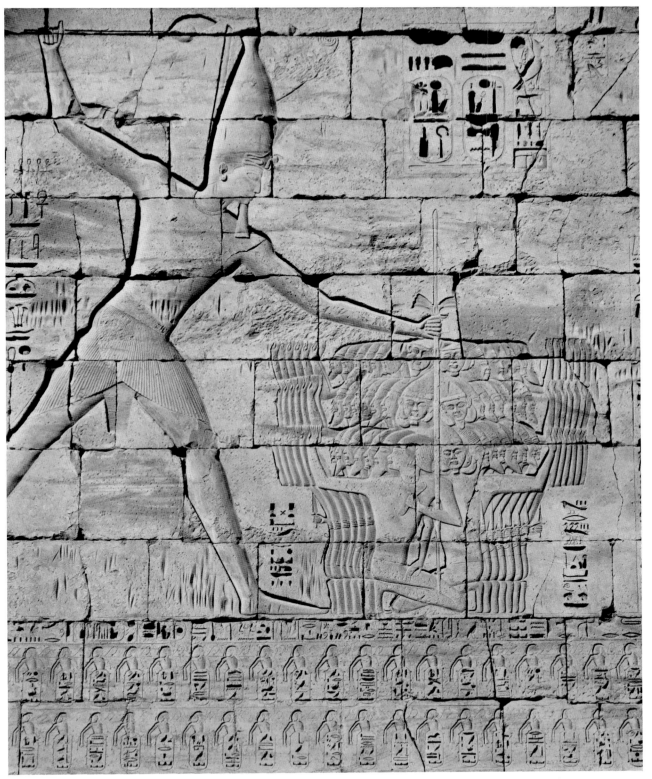

Plate 43. Mortuary temple of King Ramesses III (1170–1138 B.C.) in Medinet Habu (western Thebes).
From the front of the southwest tower of the great pylon. Ramesses III slays enemy prisoners.

Plate 44. Mortuary temple of King Ramesses III (1170–1138 B.C.) in Medinet Habu (western Thebes). From the southwest wall of the second courtyard. Presentation of prisoners.

Plate 45. Mortuary temple of King Ramesses III (1170–1138 B.C.) in Medinet Habu (western Thebes).
Relief near the window of appearance on the southwest wall of the second courtyard. Bound prisoners are slain.

Plate 46. Mortuary temple of King Ramesses III (1170–1138 B.C.) in Medinet Habu (western Thebes).
From the northeast wall in the second courtyard. Part of the procession in the festival of the fertility-god Min.
King Ramesses III moves in his sedan chair out of his palace to the festival.

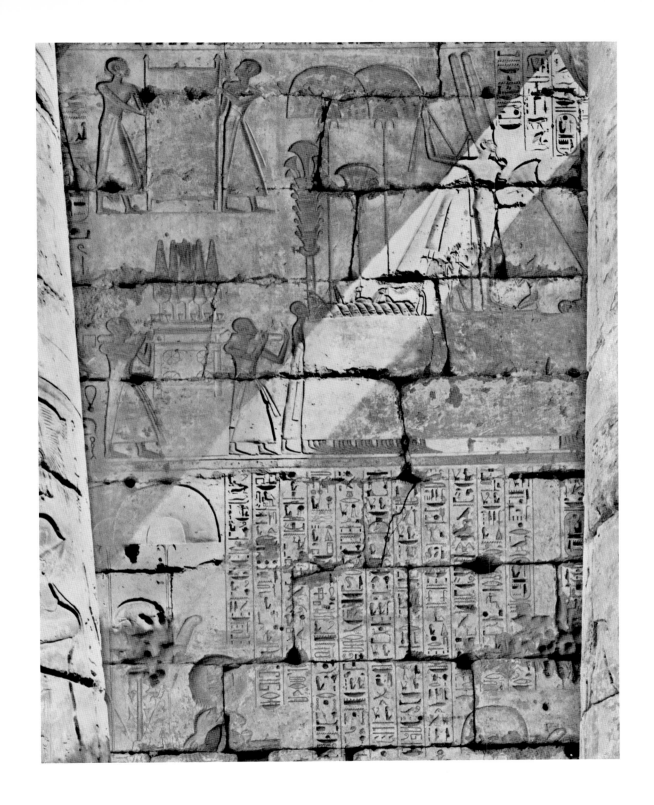

Plate 47. Mortuary temple of King Ramesses III (1170–1138 B.C.) in Medinet Habu (western Thebes).
From the northeast wall in the second courtyard. Part of the procession in the festival of the fertility-god Min. The statue of the god Min.

Plate 48. Mortuary temple of King Ramesses III (1170–1138 B.C.) in Medinet Habu (western Thebes).
From the northeast wall in the second courtyard. Part of the procession in the festival of the fertility-god Min.
The processional barque of the god Amon; from the procession of the three barques of the divine triad Amon-Mut-Khons.

Plate 49. The barque of Sokar. From the temple at Deir el Medineh in western Thebes.

Plate 50. Purification of the deceased Sennofer and his wife Merit. From the tomb of Sennofer, the mayor of Thebes. Time of King Amenhotep II (1438–1412 B.C.). Western Thebes, Abd el Qurneh. 18th Dynasty, New Kingdom.

Plate 51. From the procession visiting the image of the deified Amenhotep I.
From the tomb of Amenmose, the high priest of the temple of Amenhotep I.
Western Thebes, Dra' abu'l-Naga. 19th Dynasty, New Kingdom (1306–1186 B.C.).

Plate 52. Queen Ahmes-Nefertari as mediator between Amon and King Ramesses III.
Relief dedicated by Ramesses III for the hypostyle hall behind the fifth pylon at Karnak.

CHRONOLOGICAL TABLE

KINGS BEFORE DYNASTY 1

That is, they ruled over the whole of Egypt before the "union of Upper and Lower Egypt," as the monuments make clear: Ka-Sekhen, "Scorpion," Narmer.

EARLY DYNASTIC PERIOD

Dynasty 1: c. 3000 B.C. "Union of the two lands" (foundation of the historical state) through King Horus Aha (Menes); he was succeeded by the kings Zer, Zet ("Serpent"), Den (Dewen), the queen Merit-Neith, Anadj-ib, Semerkhet, Qay-a; like the kings before the First Dynasty, they were buried in Abydos.

Dynasty 2: with eight kings. The two last kings, Peribsen and Khasekhemuwy, were buried in Abydos.

OLD KINGDOM

Dynasty 3: c. 2700 B.C. King Zoser, builder of the step pyramid of Saqqarah, and four or five successors, among them Sekhem-khet, builder of the unfinished pyramid to the south of Zoser's pyramid.

Dynasty 4: c. 2600–2480 B.C. Great Pyramid Age: Sneferu (pyramids in Medum and Dahshur), Cheops (pyramid in Giza), Zedefre, Chephren (pyramid in Giza), Mycerinus (pyramid in Giza), Shepseskaf.

Dynasty 5: c. 2480–2350 B.C. Nine kings, with pyramids near Abusir and Saqqarah. Near Abusir two sun temples of King Sahura and Ne-user-ra have also been excavated.

Dynasty 6: c. 2350–2190 B.C. Tety, Pepy I, Mernera I, Pepy II, Mernera II. Dissolution of the centralized state; family ties of the dynasty with local rulers of Abydos.

FIRST INTERMEDIATE PERIOD

Dissolution of the state. Successors of the kings of the Sixth Dynasty were still ruling at Memphis as the "Seventh" and "Eighth" Dynasties. Then the Ninth and Tenth Dynasties ruled at Heracleopolis with several kings, among them Khety and Merikara, c. 2170–2050 B.C. Their tombs are not known.

MIDDLE KINGDOM

After c. 2130 B.C. the family of the nomarchs of Hermonthis in Upper Egypt ruled independently of the dynasty of Heracleopolis. Their members have the names Intef and Mentuhotep.

Dynasty 11: About 2050 B.C. Mentuhotep II (Neb-hepetra) reunited the state from his new residence at Thebes. Beginning of the Middle Kingdom. The older mortuary temple at Deir el Bahari belongs to this king. He had two successors, Mentuhotep III (Se-ankh-kara) and Mentuhotep IV (Neb-tawy-ra).

Dynasty 12: 1991–1786 B.C. Its founder was Amenemhat I (1991–1962 B.C.). The succeeding kings bore the names Amenemhat and Sesostris. The most important of them were Sesostris I (1971–1928), Sesostris III (1878–1843),

and Amenemhat III (1842–1797). Later, the Twelfth Dynasty was considered by the Egyptians as the classical period. In later tradition the name Sesostris was ascribed to a royal figure who united in himself characteristics of different rulers.

Dynasties 13–14: c. 1785–1680 B.C. A long line of short-lived rulers, among them Neferhotep. Apparently some of the kings ruled over a part of the country only.

SECOND INTERMEDIATE PERIOD (Hyksos Period)

Dynasties 15–16: c. 1730–1552 B.C. The Asiatic Hyksos, a collective name which includes rulers of Hurrian descent, ruled over Egypt from Avaris in the northern Delta. Most probably their rule was some kind of overlordship, with local nomarchs ruling under them.

NEW KINGDOM

Dynasty 17: 1680–1552 B.C. Theban kings, the last of whom were named Sekenenra and Kamose, fought against the Hyksos. Their tombs lie to the north of the Theban necropolis near Dra' abu'l-Naga.

Dynasty 18: 1552–1306 B.C. Ahmose (1552–1527), the brother of Kamose. Amenhotep I (1527–1506), continuing the fight against the Hyksos, crossed the frontiers between Egypt and southern Palestine. In Thebes he was the first king to separate the tomb and the mortuary temple; he was deified later on. Tuthmosis I (1506–1494). During his military campaigns he reached the third cataract in the south, and in the north he was the first Egyptian king to reach the river Euphrates. Tuthmosis II (1494–1490). Hatshepsut (1490–1468) deliberately rejected the expansionist policy of the dynasty. The terraced temple of Deir el Bahari. Tuthmosis III (1490–1436) added the years of Hatshepsut's reign to his own; for a time Egypt achieved its greatest expansion under his rule, from the fourth cataract in Nubia to the Euphrates. His monumental annals in Karnak record his campaigns and his endowments. Amenhotep II (1438–1412). Tuthmosis IV (1412–1402). Amenhotep III (1402–1364). Amenhotep IV (Akhenaten; 1364–1347) made a break with the traditional worship of gods, especially with that of Amon, and during the fifth year of his rule transferred his residence to Tell el Amarna. Semenkhkara (1351–1348), son-in-law and co-regent of Amenhotep IV. Tut-ankhamon (1347–1338) transferred his residence back to Thebes. Ay (1338–1334). Horemheb (1334–1306); like Ay, he was not of royal descent and not related to the royal dynastic family.

Dynasty 19: 1306–1186 B.C. Founded by Ramesses I (1306–1304), a descendant of an officer's family of Lower Egypt. He and his successors resided in Lower Egypt. Sety I (1304–1290), builder of the great temple of Osiris at Abydos. Ramesses II (1290–1224) fought against the

Hittites and made a compromising peace treaty (1278 B.C.). Merenptah (1224–1204) and four more kings.

Dynasty 20: 1186–1070 B.C. Ramesses III, builder of the temple of Medinet Habu. He kept the Sea People and the Libyans away from Egypt. Ramesses IV to Ramesses XI.

LATE PERIOD

Dynasty 21: 1090–950 B.C. Herihor and his successors rule in Thebes as administrators of the divine state of Amon. Lower Egypt possesses a dynasty of its own of unknown descent, which rules from Tanis.

Dynasties 22–23: 950–730 B.C. Kings of Libyan descent rule in Lower Egypt; the Bubastite Period takes its name from the town of Bubastis in Lower Egypt.

Dynasty 24: 730–715 B.C. Two kings reigned in Lower Egypt.

Dynasty 25: 715–656 B.C. Ethiopian rulers in Napata. Their King Piankhy conquered Egypt. Taharqa enlarged Karnak. Fights against the Assyrians who in 671 sacked Thebes.

Dynasty 26: 663–525 B.C. The Saite Period, named after their capital in Sais in Lower Egypt. Psamtik I, Necho, Psamtik II, Amasis, Apries, Psamtik III. The last-named lost the battle of Pelusium to Cambyses in 525. Egypt fell under Persian rule.

Dynasties 27–30: 525–332 B.C. Egypt under Persian rule; occasional successful revolts under Egyptian dynasties, which were mostly of Libyan descent.

332 B.C.: Alexander the Great conquered Egypt; establishment of Alexandria as new capital.

PTOLEMAIC PERIOD

323 B.C.: After the death of Alexander the rule was taken over by his general and former personal bodyguard (σωματοφυλαξ) Ptolemaeus, the son of the Macedonian Lagos from Eordeia and his wife Arsinoe. He first ruled for Philip Arrhidaeus, the half brother of Alexander, and then for Alexander's son Alexander IV. After Alexander IV was assassinated by Cassander, the Macedonian administrator of the state in 310–309, Ptolemaeus himself accepted the royal title in 305 B.C. as Ptolemy I (Soter).

305–30 B.C.: Rule of Ptolemy I (Soter) and his descendants until the time of Cleopatra VII, in Alexandria.

30 B.C.–A.D. 395: Egypt was now an imperial Roman Province and was administered by a prefect.

A.D. 395: Partition of the Roman Empire. Egypt became a province of the eastern Roman Empire, ruled from Byzantium.

A.D. 640: Conquest of Egypt by Amr ibn el-As, the general of Caliph Omar.

BIBLIOGRAPHY

GENERAL

Breasted, James Henry, *Ancient Records of Egypt*, I–V, Chicago, 1927.

Drioton, Étienne, and Vandier, Jacques, *L'Égypte*, 4th ed., "Clio," Introduction aux études historiques, II, Paris, 1962.

Kees, Hermann, *Das alte Ägypten, eine kleine Landeskunde*, 2nd ed., Berlin, 1955. English edition ed. T. G. H. James, *Ancient Egypt, a Cultural Topography*, London, 1961.

———, *Der Götterglaube im alten Ägypten*, 2nd ed., Berlin, 1956.

Lange, Kurt, and Hirmer, Max, *Egypt*, 3rd ed., London, 1961.

Morenz, Siegfried, *Ägyptische Religion, Die Religionen der Menschheit*, Vol. 8, Stuttgart, 1960.

Otto, Eberhard, *Ägypten, der Weg des Pharaonenreiches*, 3rd ed., Stuttgart, 1953.

Porter, Rosalin, and Moss, Berta, *Topographical Bibliography of Ancient Egyptian Hieroglyphical Texts, Reliefs, and Paintings*, I, Theban Necropolis, Oxford, 1960; II, Theban Temples, Oxford, 1929; V, Upper Egypt, Oxford, 1937, pp. 39ff; VI, Upper Egypt, Chief Temples, Oxford, 1939.

Pritchard, James, *Ancient Near Eastern Pictures Relating to the Old Testament*, Princeton, N.J., 1954.

———, *Ancient Near Eastern Texts Relating to the Old Testament*, Princeton, N.J., 1955.

Wolf, Walther, *Die Welt der Ägypter*, Stuttgart, 1955.

OSIRIS

Calverley, A. M., Broome, M. F., and Gardiner, A. H., *The Temple of King Sethos I at Abydos*, London, 1933.

Frankfort, Henri, *The Cenotaph of Seti I at Abydos*, The Egypt Exploration Society, London, 1933.

Helck, Wolfgang, "Geschichte der Stadt Abydos" (unpublished).

Kees, Hermann, *Totenglauben und Jenseitsvorstellungen der alten Ägypter*, 2nd ed., Berlin, 1956.

Naville, Édouard, *The Cemeteries of Abydos*, I–III, The Egypt Exploration Fund, London, 1913–14.

Petrie, Flinders, *The Royal Tombs of the First Dynasty*, I–II, The Egypt Exploration Society, London, 1900–1901.

———, *Abydos*, I–III, The Egypt Exploration Fund, London, 1902–4.

Winlock, Herbert, *Bas-Reliefs from the Temple of Ramesses I at Abydos; The Temple of Ramesses I at Abydos*, Metropolitan Museum Papers I and V, New York, 1921.

AMON

Blackman, Aylward M., *Luxor and Its Temples*, London, 1923.

Barguet, Paul, *Le Temple d'Amon-Re à Karnak*, Publications de l'Institut Français d'Archéologie Orientale du Caire, Cairo, 1962.

Davies, Nina M., *Ancient Egyptian Paintings*, I–II, Chicago, 1936.

Legrain, Georges, *Louqsor sans les Pharaons*, Brussels, Paris, 1914.

———, *Les Temples de Karnak*, Brussels, 1929.

Nims, Charles, *Thebes of the Pharaohs*, London, 1966.

Otto, Eberhard, *Topographie des thebanischen Gaues*, Berlin, Leipzig, 1952.

Pillet, Maurice, *Thèbes*, Paris, 1930.

Schott, Siegfried, *Das schöne Fest vom Wüstentale*, Mainz, 1952.

Steindorff, Georg, and Wolf, Walther, *Die thebanische Gräberwelt*, Glückstadt, 1936.

Wolf, Walther, *Das schöne Fest von Opet*, Veröff. Ernst-von-Sieglin-Exped. No. 5, Leipzig, 1931.

PLACE NAMES

MODERN PLACE NAMES

Akhmim, capital of the 9th Upper Egyptian nome; Greek: *Khemmis* or *Panopolis*.

El Arabat el Madfuuna ("the buried Araba"), town in the 8th Upper Egyptian nome; Greek: *Abydos*.

Armant, capital of the 4th Upper Egyptian nome; Greek: *Hermonthis*.

El Asasif, northern part of the Theban necropolis.

Ashmunen, capital of the 15th Upper Egyptian nome; Greek: *Hermopolis*.

Aussim, capital of the 2nd Upper Egyptian nome; Greek: *Letopolis*.

Badrashen, south of Cairo; Greek: *Memphis*.

Benha, capital of the 10th Upper Egyptian nome; Greek: *Athribis*.

Biban el Harim, Valley of the Tombs of the Queens.

Biban el Moluk, Valley of the Tombs of the Kings.

Deir el Bahari ("northern monastery"), mountain slope in the northwestern part of the Theban necropolis.

Deir el Medineh ("monastery of the town"), settlement and temple in the southern part of the Theban necropolis.

Denderah, place and temple in the 6th Upper Egyptian nome; Greek: *Tentyra*.

Dra' abu'l-Naga, village in the northern part of the Theban necropolis.

Edfu, capital of the 2nd Upper Egyptian nome; Greek: *Apollonopolis Magna*.

Ehnas el Medineh, capital of the 20th Upper Egyptian nome; Greek: *Heracleopolis*.

Esna, town in the 3rd Upper Egyptian nome; Greek: *Latopolis*.

Gebelein ("the two hills"), place and hill to the south of Luxor, near the Greek *Pathyris* ("house of Hathor").

El Kab, town in the 3rd Upper Egyptian nome; Greek: *Eileithyiaspolis*.

Karnak, village and temple to the north of Luxor, part of the Greek Thebes.

El Kharga, oasis to the south of the Western Oases; Greek: *Oasis Magna*.

El Khokha, village in the Theban necropolis.

El Kom el Ahmar ("the red mound"), town in the 3rd Upper Egyptian nome; Greek: *Hierakonpolis*; ancient Egyptian: *Nekhen*.

Lisht, village to the south of Cairo.

Luxor, town and temple, part of the Greek Thebes.

El Matariya, place to the north of Cairo; Greek: *Heliopolis*; ancient Egyptian: *On*.

Medamud, village to the northeast of Karnak.

Medinet Habu, temple in the southern part of the Theban necropolis; ancient Egyptian: *Djeme*.

Naqada, village in the 5th Upper Egyptian nome; Greek: *Ombos*.

Quft, capital of the 5th Upper Egyptian nome; Greek: *Coptos*.

El Qurn ("the horn"), pyramidal mountain dominating the Theban necropolis.

Qurneh, village in the northern part of the Theban necropolis.

Sa el Hagar, capital of the 5th Lower Egyptian nome; Greek: *Sais*.

San, town in the northeastern Delta; Greek: *Tanis*.

Saqqarah, necropolis with pyramids to the south of Cairo.

Shunet-ez-Zebib, brick building to the north of the temple of Sety at Abydos.

El Tod, place to the south of Luxor; Greek: *Typhium*.

Tell el Amarna, village in the 15th Upper Egyptian nome, capital of Egypt under Amenhotep IV.

Tell el Fera'in, capital of the 6th Lower Egyptian nome; Greek: *Buto*.

Umm el Gaab ("mother of the sherds"), name given to the wadi at Abydos in which the royal tombs of the first dynasty are situated.

Wadi Hammamat, valley through the eastern desert from Quft to El Quseir.

GREEK PLACE NAMES AND THEIR MODERN EQUIVALENTS

Abydos, El Arabat el Madfuuna.
Apollonopolis Magna, Edfu.
Athribis, Benha.
Busiris, Abusir (middle of the Delta near Mahalla el Qubra).

Buto, Tell el Fera'in.
Coptos, Quft.
Eileithyiaspolis, El Kab.
Heliopolis, El Matariya.

Heracleopolis, Ehnas el Medineh.
Hermonthis, Armant.
Hermopolis, Ashmunen.
Hierakonpolis, El Kom el Ahmar.
Khemmis, Akhmim.
Latopolis, Esna.
Letopolis, Aussim.
Memphis, Badrashen.
Oasis Magna, El Kharga.
Ombos, near Naqada.
Pathyris, near Gebelein.

Sais, Sa el Hagar.
Tanis, San.
Tentyra, Denderah.
Thebes (also *Diospolis Magna*) encloses on the eastern river bank the present-day Luxor and Karnak, and on the western bank the district of Qasr el Aguz in the south to Dra' abu'l-Naga in the north.
This (*Thinis*), unlocated place in the 8th Upper Egyptian nome, in the vicinity of El Arabat el Madfuuna.
Typhium, El Tod.

ANCIENT EGYPTIAN PLACE NAMES

Anedjt, expanse of water in the nome of Busiris.
Djeme, today Medinet Habu.
Herewer, unlocated cult center of Khnum of Hermopolis.
Heseret, unlocated cult center of Thoth in or near Hermopolis.

Isheru, lake near the temple of Mut in Karnak.
Nekhen, Greek Hierakonpolis, near present-day El Kom el Ahmar.
On, Greek Heliopolis, today El Matariya.

ACKNOWLEDGMENTS

The photographs for this book were taken in the beginning of 1965. My sincere thanks are due to the representatives of the Egyptian Antiquity Service, who gave me all support and help in the same spirit of friendship as was shown to me in 1954 and 1955 on the occasion of a similar excursion. I want to thank especially Dr. Mohamed Mahdi Ibrahim, Director General of the Department of Antiquities of the El Antikhana Museum at Cairo; Dr. Abd-el-Hafiz Abd-el-Aal, chief inspector for Upper Egypt; Dr. Yacoub Farah, formerly inspector of ancient monuments at Luxor and Karnak; Dr. Ramadan Saad, inspector of ancient monuments at Luxor and Karnak, and formerly inspector of the necropolis at Thebes; and last but not least, my friend Dr. Labib Habachi, who again favored me with his invaluable help, as he did in 1954 and 1955.

The photographs were taken in close collaboration with my son Albert Hirmer and my daughter Irmgard Hirmer, who is active as photographer in the photographic department of our publishing firm. Both deserve my gratitude for their valuable collaboration and their ever-willing readiness to assist. I also want to thank Mrs. Angelika Bauer-Asen for her careful preparation of the prints for reproduction.

MAX HIRMER

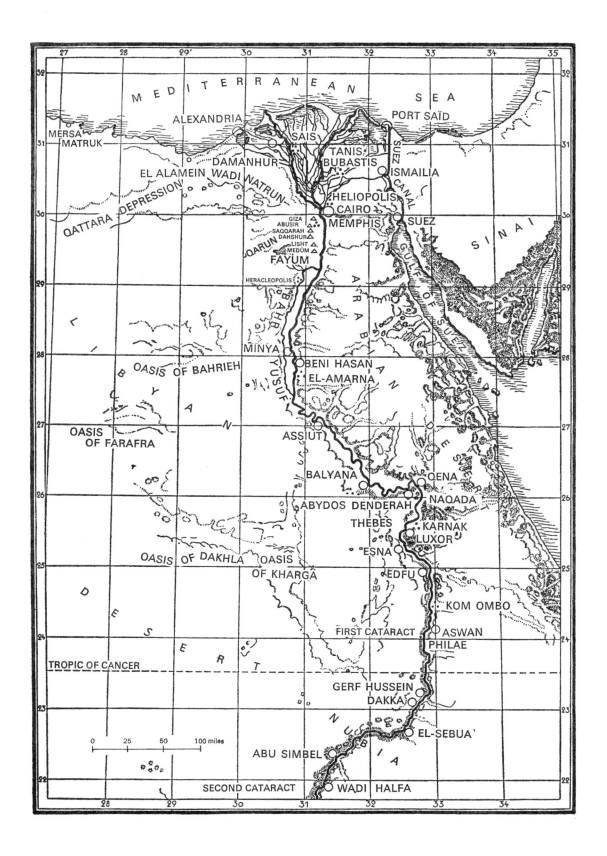